The 100 Best
Internet Stocks to Own

The 100 Best Internet Stocks to Own

Greg A. Kyle

McGraw-Hill

New York   San Francisco   Washington, D.C.   Auckland   Bogotá
Caracas   Lisbon   London   Madrid   Mexico City   Milan
Montreal   New Delhi   San Juan   Singapore
Sydney   Tokyo   Toronto

McGraw-Hill

A Division of The **McGraw·Hill** Companies

1 2 3 4 5 6 7 8 9 0 DOC/DOC 0 9 8 7 6 5 4 3 2 1 0

ISBN 0-07-135725-4

Printed and bound by R.R. Donnelley & Sons Company.

McGraw-Hill books are available at special quantity discounts to use as premiums and sales promotions, or for use in corporate training programs. For more information, please write to the Director of Special Sales, Professional Publishing, McGraw-Hill, Two Penn Plaza, New York, NY 10121-2298. Or contact your local bookstore.

 This book is printed on recycled, acid-free paper containing a minimum of 50% recycled, de-inked fiber.

Contents

Preface

I still remember my early online experiences with a certain nostalgia. When I first started using an online service back in 1983, it was an adventure. Navigating the Internet required learning various menu commands and a little bit of skill mixed with luck. In actuality, there was little to do except check hourly news summaries, search and download software and send e-mails using a complicated 10-digit address. Still, it was an exciting time.

Fast-forward to today. After being involved with the Internet and other online services on two continents both as a passionate user and as an analyst, I still find the development exciting. From the early days of CompuServe and the sometimes puzzling menu structure and arcane email system, to the birth of the Web and an easy-to-use browser, to the early attempts of Switzerland's proprietary online service – Videotext, and wireless Internet access through information appliances – first the Apple Newton and today Palm PDAs, the journey has been exciting and enrichening.

Today, people are swapping e-mails more often than phone numbers, TV viewership is declining as people prefer surfing the Web to watching television, computers are being used in the workplace as radios and at home as stereo systems, and companies are finding that the Internet allows them to conduct business faster, cheaper and better.

This book is designed to be the first of its kind, providing a guide to Internet stocks in order to help the individual investor understand the key issues driving the Internet sector.

1

The Internet Economy

Introduction

Nothing has created the opportunities nor the controversy that the Internet has. Often hailed as the Industrial Revolution in the Information Age, the Internet impacts every facet of our lives, empowering individuals and organizations on a scale – and a speed –that was not previously possible. On a personal level, the Internet allows people to communicate with each other in new and innovative ways: School children in Mexico can communicate with children in Argentina, Chile or even Singapore using Web cameras that sit atop a computer. Teenagers (and office workers!) are now spending hours chatting over the Internet rather than on the phone. Shopping is as easy as touring a virtual catalog or store, clicking on the item to order and having it delivered the same day – all in a matter of minutes. Banking and bill paying can be done from home in a fraction of the time it used to take, and investing in stocks and mutual funds is available easily to everyone over the Internet.

For businesses, sending emails is becoming a daily part of their communications with their customers and their partners. In fact, people are often handing out their email addresses more often than phone numbers. Vendors have instant access to inventory levels while out in the field. Collaborating on projects is being done from around the world, cutting project development times by as much as two-thirds. Businesses can collect much more customer data than previously possible, enabling them to better target their marketing campaigns at a fraction of the cost. Consider the difference. If Sears wanted to track customer shopping habits – which aisles they visited most often, how long they browsed in a particular area, which items they purchased most often – it would be impossible without hiring someone to follow the customer throughout the store and take notes. On the Internet, this is done automatically and instantaneously.

> ### A Few Points to Ponder
> - 35% of US households are surfing the Web
> - E-mail outnumbers snail mail by 10-to-1
> - 8 million investors trade over the Internet
> - E-commerce is a $50 billion industry
> - More people are on the Net than the population of Japan
> - **All this in five years!**

How far-reaching and pervasive the Internet is in our lives can be seen by the following facts: E-mail messages outnumber regular mail by a factor of 10-to-1, with 2.5 billion email messages being sent every day versus 290 million pieces of first-class mail. Eight million people are now trading stocks over the Internet. 35% of US households are online, up from 5% just three years ago. One in five Americans have shopped on the Web. More people are on the Internet than the entire population of Japan. What makes these facts even more impressive is that all this has happened within the last five years! In 1994 when people first started noticing the Internet, only 13 million people were using online services. Today, 10 times that number are surfing the Web.

What will the next five years bring? Soon, more people will be surfing the Web than the entire population of North America. Consumers will spend $150 billion shopping online. Total US e-commerce revenue will rival the gross domestic output of England. Over 60% of individual investors will trade stocks and bonds over the Web. Internet access will no longer be tied to a computer but will be available anywhere, anytime, using cell phones, hand-held computers and other Internet-capable devices. The Internet will become a central part of corporate strategy, allowing businesses to slash costs, improve cycle times and further strengthen customer relationships. And most important of all, we will still be discovering how connectivity is changing our lives.

There are several major factors that are shaping the emerging Internet economy. First is the demographic factor. People are embracing the Net at a pace not seen with any other medium. Second is the global factor. It is called the World Wide Web for a reason – the Internet is a global issue, not just an American issue, and to reach that global audience takes milliseconds. Third is the connectivity factor as more computers – and other devices – are connecting to the Web. Finally, there is the ecommerce factor. As the Internet moves beyond its childhood, businesses are finding new ways to reach and interact with consumers and other businesses.

The Demographic Factor – It's a People Issue

Although the Internet has been in existence since 1969, it wasn't until the birth of the graphical browser in 1993 that it began to develop as a mass medium for communication and electronic commerce. Prior to 1993, the Internet was used mostly by universities and government agencies to communicate and transfer text-based documents. At that time, Internet users numbered less than 9 million. Today, more than 184 million people are logging on to the Internet to do everything from sending e-mail and chatting with friends and relatives to reading and watching the news, shopping for books, music, computers and airline tickets as well as paying bills and conducting banking activities. Within four years, more than 430 million people will be surfing the Web.

When I first started using online services back in the mid-1980's there really wasn't that much I could do except send email to a couple friends and check hourly news summaries from Reuters. CompuServe had a limited offering in terms of information at that time, and navigation was a text-based menu that required memorizing various commands to get around. Although I enjoyed the service, it wasn't exactly known as user-friendly. Sending e-mail required knowing a person's ten digit ID number.

Over the years, things got a little easier – the amount of information increased and navigation improved – but it still wasn't a tool for the masses. Then, two things happened to change all of this. First, the World Wide Web was developed by a scientist at CERN in Switzerland in 1991 using hypertext[1] documents. Second, Marc Andreesen, prior to founding Netscape, released the first graphical browser for the World Wide Web in 1993. This revolutionized the way people viewed the Internet. Suddenly, the Web went from some esoteric medium to something people could visualize and interact with.

Since then, Internet usage has exploded. Although it took 20 years for Internet or online users to grow to 12 million people in 1993, that number doubled over the next eighteen months. By the end of 1999, there were an estimated 85 million Web users in the U.S, and 184 million worldwide. This translates to a 45% compound annual growth rate since 1993. Over the next four years, the number of new

Worldwide Internet User Growth
(in millions)

Figure 1-1 Worldwide Internet Users in Millions
Source: Pegasus Research Intl

	1994	1995	1996	1997	1998	1999	2000	2001	2002	2003
US Population	260.6	263.0	265.4	267.9	270.3	272.6	274.9	277.1	279.4	281.6
US Households	95.9	97.4	98.8	99.4	100.5	101.6	102.7	103.8	104.9	106.0
PC Penetration	24.1%	27.7%	31.8%	36.6%	42.1%	48.4%	54.2%	59.1%	62.6%	65.0%
Online Penetration	7.5%	9.9%	15.3%	22.1%	27.6%	31.6%	37.8%	45.1%	53.7%	59.1%

Source: US Census Bureau, IDC, Computer Industry Almanac, Pegasus Research Intl

---

[1] If anyone remembers the early days of Apple, this was similar to the hypercards where a user could click on a word on a particular file card, and they would be taken to that subject

Internet Growth is Faster Outside the U.S.
(in millions)

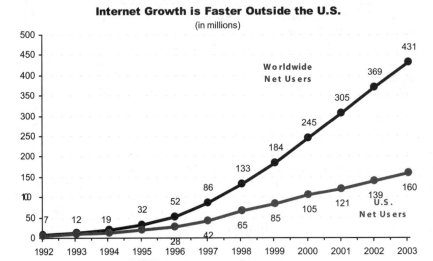

Figure 1-2   Internet Growth is Faster Outside the US
Source: Pegasus Research Intl

Net users will grow to an estimated 430 million worldwide or more than the entire population of North America and England combined. Heading into the new millennium, one million people will be logging on to the Internet for the first time every week. Very few industries can boast of even half this growth rate.

Another way to look at Internet growth is to compare household penetration rates for various forms of media and the computer. In 1998, there were approximately 101 million households in the US. Of these 101 million homes, 42% owned a PC and approximately 33% were connected to the Internet[2]. In 1999, rapidly falling PC prices helped push computer penetration in the US past the 50% mark for the first time in history. This is 22 years after the introduction of the first PCs by Apple, Commodore and Tandy in 1977. By 2001, eight years after the birth of the Web browser, more than 50% of US households will have access to the Internet.

It took radio nearly 38 years to reach 50 million listeners, television took 13 years to attract 50 million viewers, cable did it in 10 years, and the Web is expected to reach 50 million US users in only 5 years.

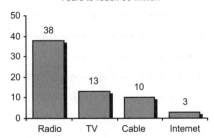

Rapid Net Penetration
Years to reach 50 million

Figure 1-3   Rapid Net Penetration
Source: Pegasus Research Intl, Morgan Stanley

---

[2] NTIA/US Census Bureau, Falling through the Digital Divide

The Global Factor – Sprechen Sie Internet?

The Internet may have started in the US, but it is by no means restricted to the United States. A few short years ago, the Internet was virtually unheard of outside of North America, with over 90% of Web users residing in the US. Today, that picture is considerably different. In 1999, just 51% of Web users are living in the United States, and in four more years, less than 41% of Netizens will call the US home.

Having lived in Europe for a number of years and having followed the Internet sector both as an avid "techno-geek" and as an analyst, it has been interesting to watch the global Web development. Back in the early 1990's, the only exposure Europeans had to online services was Minitel in France, T-Online in Germany, and Videotext in Switzerland. All of these systems were early proprietary online experiments from the government-owned PTT's (postal and telephone companies which were, incidentally, state monopolies).

Videotext in Switzerland was actually ahead of its time when it was first introduced. With the proprietary unit (reminiscent of a scaled-down Commodore Pet 2001) that I leased from the PTT, I could go online and pay bills through the local bank, check train schedules and telephone numbers and even shop online from some of the major retailers in Switzerland. Unfortunately, it was a system that never really caught on. Connection speeds were terribly slow, and in a country where you pay for phone access by the minute, telephone bills were rather expensive.

Now, most of these government-run online experiments are going the way of the slide rule, and the Internet is beginning to take off in Europe. However, it has been off to a slow start, hampered by low PC penetration and high telecommunication costs. Up until just two years ago, 20 hours of Internet usage would cost the average cybersurfer more than $80 per month in Germany: $30 for Internet access and $50 for local pay-by-the-minute phone charges.

With telecom deregulation driving down local phone charges and free Net access taking Europe by storm, Internet usage is quickly ramping up. By 2003, roughly 130 million people in Europe will be surfing the Web, up from less than 50 million in 1999. Europeans will also account for 30% of the worldwide Net population in 2003.

Latin America has been the fastest growing region, with new Internet users coming on to the Net at a compound annual rate of over 40% each year. From an estimated 6.2 million users in 1999, the number of Internet users will grow five-fold over the next few years to 21 million surfers (*cybernautas*) in 2003. However, with the large income disparities and low telephone penetration rates in most Latin American countries, the Internet will be largely a "rich man's" media. As in Europe, Internet users in Latin America also pay by the minute for local phone charges, which are in addition to monthly Internet access fees that ISPs charge.

However, free Internet access has just been introduced to Latin America, and this could speed Internet penetration. As this book went to press in early 2000, Latin American Internet portal, StarMedia, several banks and a number of startups in the region began offering free Web access. One of these companies gained over 400,000 subscribers in a matter of weeks.

In Asia, the Internet is currently a Japanese phenomenon, home to more than half of the Net users in the region. Japanese also happens to be the second most common language spoken by Web users. However, the landscape is shifting. Japanese Net growth will start to slow down in a few years just as other countries in the region start to pick up speed. In China, there could be over 21 million Net users within five years. India, despite crossing the one billion population threshold in 1999, has less than one million Net users.

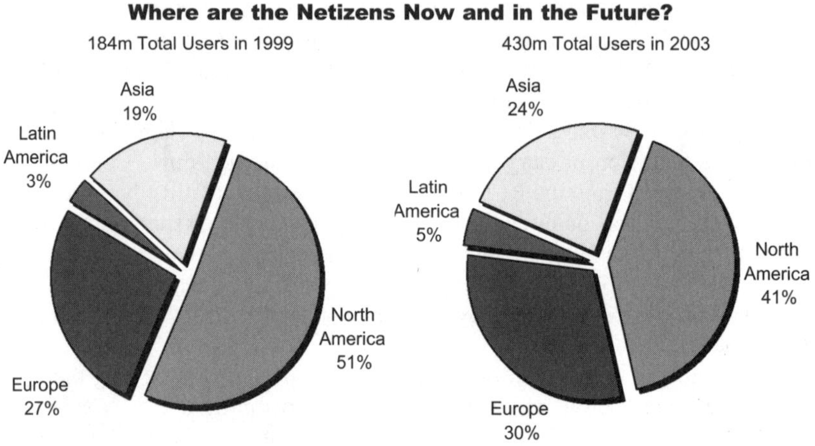

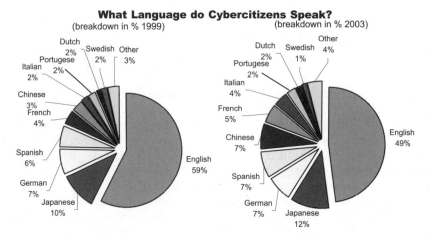

Figure 1-4   Where are the Netizens?
Source: Pegasus Research Intl

Figure 1-5   The Language of the Web
Source: Pegasus Research Intl

Worldwide Internet User Penetration Rates

	------ 1999 ------		------ 2003 ------			---------- Density Rates[3] ----------			
	Internet users[1]	% of pop	Internet users[1]	% of pop	GDP/ Capita[2]	Tele- phone	PC	Cable	Daily News
Total	183.9		430.6						
North America	**93.8**	**30.9%**	**177.1**	**56.5%**	**29,269**	**63.85**	**39.28**	**24.75**	**20.91**
US	84.6	31.0%	159.7	56.7%	30,375	64.26	40.67	24.59	21.50
Canada	9.2	29.7%	17.4	54.2%	19,522	60.23	27.06	26.14	15.70
Europe	**49.5**	**12.8%**	**129.8**	**33.3%**	**22,674**	**51.32**	**20.37**	**10.52**	**22.37**
Austria	1.1	13.3%	2.9	35.6%	26,085	48.41	21.07	13.20	29.60
Belgium	1.3	13.0%	4.0	39.1%	24,198	46.81	23.53	36.18	16.00
Denmark	1.3	25.0%	2.9	54.9%	33,050	63.30	36.02	23.86	30.90
Finland	1.9	36.2%	3.2	62.5%	24,446	55.68	31.07	17.00	45.50
France	4.7	8.0%	16.8	28.7%	24,354	57.42	17.44	2.77	21.80
Germany	10.6	12.9%	23.5	28.1%	26,097	54.98	25.55	21.05	31.10
Greece	0.4	3.6%	1.3	12.1%	11,286	50.87	4.48	--	15.30
Iceland	0.1	34.6%	0.2	61.8%	30,362	61.69	35.63	--	--
Ireland	0.5	12.9%	1.4	37.2%	22,439	41.10	24.13	14.74	15.00
Italy	4.3	7.5%	17.2	30.2%	20,450	44.02	11.30	--	10.40
Netherlands	3.0	18.8%	8.8	53.9%	24,316	54.04	28.03	37.18	17.70
Norway	1.6	36.2%	2.8	62.7%	32,999	52.79	36.08	16.02	58.80
Portugal	0.6	5.7%	2.1	21.4%	10,744	38.40	7.44	3.85	0.75
Spain	2.9	7.4%	10.1	25.7%	14,105	40.32	12.21	1.08	0.99
Sweden	2.9	32.0%	5.2	57.2%	25,242	67.93	35.03	21.81	44.60
Switzerland	1.6	22.4%	4.0	53.9%	36,412	64.21	39.49	34.60	33.00
United Kingdom	10.8	18.3%	23.3	38.7%	23,019	52.23	24.24	4.02	33.20
Latin America	**6.2**	**1.3%**	**20.7**	**4.1%**	**4,188**	**10.55**	**2.78**	**2.65**	**2.68**
Argentina	0.464	1.3%	3.178	8.2%	9,496	18.90	3.92	15.63	12.30
Belize	0.002	0.9%	0.006	2.3%	2,821	13.69	--	--	--
Bolivia	0.015	0.2%	0.033	0.4%	1,094	6.88	--	0.34	0.55
Brazil	3.294	1.9%	7.977	4.5%	4,583	9.57	2.63	1.63	0.40
Chile	0.462	3.1%	1.214	7.8%	5,276	15.59	5.41	4.28	0.99
Columbia	0.248	0.6%	1.263	3.0%	2,361	14.80	3.34	0.55	0.46
Costa Rica	0.041	1.1%	0.107	2.7%	2,844	16.86	--	1.44	0.94
Ecuador	0.017	0.1%	0.058	0.4%	1,602	7.53	1.30	1.18	0.70
El Salvador	0.011	0.2%	0.038	0.6%	2,112	5.61	--	0.44	0.48
Guatemala	0.014	0.1%	0.039	0.3%	1,606	4.08	0.30	2.85	0.33
Honduras	0.007	0.1%	0.019	0.3%	806	3.68	--	0.76	0.55
Mexico	1.094	1.1%	4.937	4.6%	3,990	9.61	3.73	1.52	0.97
Nicaragua	0.009	0.2%	0.028	0.5%	430	2.94	--	4.02	0.30
Panama	0.010	0.4%	0.032	1.1%	3,369	12.16	--	1.14	0.62
Paraguay	0.010	0.2%	0.029	0.5%	1,620	3.56	--	0.72	0.43
Peru	0.210	0.8%	0.689	2.4%	2,456	6.75	1.23	1.38	0.84
Uruguay	0.026	0.8%	0.139	4.1%	6,135	23.07	2.19	2.19	29.30
Venezuela	0.221	1.0%	0.963	3.9%	4,638	12.08	3.66	1.72	20.60
Asia	**34.5**	**1.4%**	**103.0**	**3.9%**	**2,622**	**8.11**	**2.28**	**3.59**	**4.02**
Australia	4.830	25.7%	8.748	45.4%	19,569	51.37	36.22	3.81	29.70
China	3.018	0.2%	21.030	1.7%	777	5.57	0.60	3.97	--
Hong Kong	1.102	16.1%	2.836	39.9%	24,833	56.08	23.08	6.15	--
India	0.852	0.1%	5.519	0.5%	390	1.86	0.21	1.88	--
Japan	18.703	14.8%	47.411	37.4%	30,041	48.80	20.24	11.48	57.80
Malaysia	0.679	3.2%	2.383	10.5%	3,406	19.55	4.61	0.52	15.80
New Zealand	0.946	25.8%	2.243	59.6%	14,922	48.57	26.39	--	22.30
Singapore	0.806	22.8%	1.796	49.4%	24,477	44.77	39.95	1.73	36.00
South Korea	1.935	4.1%	6.038	12.6%	6,418	44.40	15.07	16.24	39.30
Taiwan	1.299	5.9%	3.654	16.1%	14,059	50.10	14.65	--	--
Thailand	0.375	0.6%	1.291	2.1%	2,563	7.95	1.98	0.35	0.63

Source: Pegasus Research Intl, International Telecommunications Union (ITU), various

Notes
1. Internet users in millions
2. 1998 GDP in US$
3. main telephone lines, personal computers, cable subscribers and daily newspapers per 100 people

The Connection Factor – Computers on the Net

In 1969 when ARPANET (Advanced Research Program Agency Network) was first established to network computers together in case of a nuclear attack, there were four computers connected together at four universities, three in California and one in Utah. In 1973, the first two international connections were made, and by 1981, 200 computers or hosts were connected to what would soon be called the Internet. The Internet grew slowly at first. When I first started going online, there were only 560 hosts connected to the Internet. By 1987, that number had climbed to 28,000 but it wasn't until four years later that the number of hosts broke the one million barrier. Three years after that, ten million hosts were connected to the Internet, and today, after another three years have gone by, more than 74 million computers are connected to the Net.

This explosion in hosts connected to the Internet and the evolution of Web sites from simple brochureware for companies to complex, information-rich portals and shopping sites has meant that the number of Web pages has also grown exponentially. In 1993, with the graphical browser just being released, the Internet was devoid of any Web pages. In early 1999, an estimated 800 million Web pages were out there in cyberspace[3]. Just how many pages is 800 million? Imagine a stack of papers the height of 208 Empire State Buildings, or 800 million sheets lined up one next to the other. It would be enough to circle the earth five and a half times. By early 2000, that amount could double to 1.5 billion Web pages.

How people are connecting to the Internet is also changing. Up until recently, the only way for most people to connect to the Web was with slow dial-up modems. It wasn't that long ago that a 9,600 Baud modem capable of transmitting 10

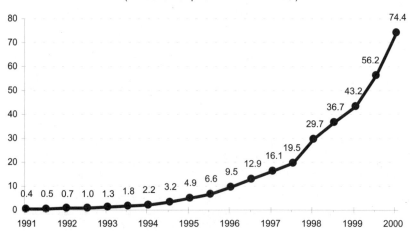

How Big is the Internet?
(Number of Computers or Hosts in millions)

Figure 1-6   How Big is the Internet?
Source: Network Wizards, Pegasus Research Intl

---

[3] NEC Research Institute

pages of text in 30 seconds was considered fast. Now, most people are using a modem that can transmit those 100 pages of text in 30 seconds. However, as Web sites become more complex and media-rich, higher bandwidth and faster modems will be needed. Broadband access, which is essentially a fatter pipe, promises to be the answer to bandwidth limitations. To highlight the difference in speeds, a 56K modem can download a 3 megabyte file (the size of an average digital song) in 20 minutes. In comparison, a cable modem can download the same song in just a few seconds.

Some estimates place the growth rate in high speed Internet access at 88% annually, with the number of subscribers growing from 1.2 million in 1999 to 15 million in 2003. Although broadband access promises to deliver on the "need for speed", there are still some stumbling blocks that could slow the growth. In contrast to the fast-moving technology sector, the future of broadband access is closely tied to the slow-moving cable and telephone sector[4] and the political posturing that is currently in progress.

America Online and other Internet service providers are lobbying for open cable access, stating that cable is only the infrastructure or the pipe into the home, and the consumer should be given the choice of which service provider they wish. The cable companies counter that without being able to collect access revenues from consumers, it cannot afford and has no desire to upgrade the infrastructure for cable Internet access. Already, skirmishes have occurred on both fronts, and the battle could end up being long and drawn out, with the net effect that consumers will have to wait for cable access. However, the pending AOL/Time Warner merger could make this point moot. If the merger does go through as planned, AOL would effectively gain control of 20% of the cable subscribers in the US.

Another broadband technology that is slowly gaining ground is DSL, or digital subscriber line, which is being offered, albeit slowly, through the local telephone companies. DSL promises speeds ten times faster than the fastest modems and can reach speeds nearly as fast as cable modems. Currently, only 200,000 homes in the US have DSL Internet access, although that is expected to grow to 4 million by 2003. Ultimately, which technology or standard will win out is still unclear, as both have advantages and disadvantages. Cable modems are generally faster, although speeds can slow considerably the more people that are connected within a particular node. DSL is unaffected by that problem, but currently has a limited range of only 17,500 feet from a central office.

Far more likely as a driver for Internet connectivity will be the growth in Internet wireless devices including palmtop computers, cell phones and pagers. IDC, a technology research firm, estimates that by the year 2002, there will be an installed base of more than 151 million "information appliances." In 1999, 3Com and its Palm division rolled out a nationwide wireless service for a new generation of Palm devices that offer everything from online trading and mobile database connectivity to surfing the Web for news, movie reviews, restaurant guides, and shopping services. Cell phone manufacturers are also jumping into the fray and are expected to launch a series of new Web-enabled cell phones in early 2000.

---

[4] The Telecommunications Act of 1996 held the promise of greater choice for consumers in their local telephone company. Three years after its passage, though, little has changed.

Wireless connectivity does have its drawbacks, namely speed. A typical wireless Internet appliance such as the new Palm VII or a mobile phone can send and receive data at speeds of only 9.6 kilobits which is roughly six times as slow as the modems in most home computers. This may be fast enough for simple text messages, but is too slow to surf the Web. Many companies, including Sprint, will be rolling out faster wireless access over the next year. However, true high-speed wireless connectivity on par with today's fastest modems is still at least two years out.

The Ecommerce Factor – Are we Spending Yet?

Four years ago, the Web was being used as simple brochureware for businesses. Today, these businesses are using the Web to generate an estimated $82 billion in revenues either from consumers or from other businesses. Within another four years, ecommerce will grow to more than $1.2 trillion in revenues, a forty-fold increase from the estimated $32 billion spent in 1998, and coming close to rivaling the GDP of England. This is why businesses and investors are rushing so quickly to embrace the Internet. Ecommerce is the only sector of the economy experiencing a compound annual growth rate of over 100% per year.

What makes the growth in ecommerce spending even more telling, is the following fact: While it has taken England over 1000 years to reach $1.2 trillion in revenues (GDP), e-commerce will be able to achieve this level in only 10 years after the birth of the Web.

Who would also have thought a few short years ago that Amazon.com would become a $25 billion company merely by selling books and a few other items over the Internet. Or that a toy store (eToys) can go from $687,000 to $35 million in revenues in only one year – without opening a single store! Or that Dell would sell

Total E-Commerce Revenues
(US$ billions)

CAGR 126%

Year	Value
1995	2
1996	3
1997	9
1998	32
1999	82
2000	176
2001	357
2002	666
2003	1,200

Figure 1-7   Total E-Commerce Revenues
Source: Pegasus Research Intl

nearly $40 million a day over its Web site. From practically zero in 1994, consumers spent an estimated $23 billion on travel, books, music and other retail items over the Internet in 1999.

While 1998 was really the year that consumers tested the ecommerce waters, 1999 will be remembered as the year that consumers took the plunge, spending an estimated $23 billion on goods and services over the Internet. One of the things that surprised me during the holiday shopping season back in 1998, was how practically every morning show and news channel on TV was giving out online shopping tips and ideas almost as commonly as health and exercise or diet news. It seemed that hardly a day went by that either the Today show or Good Morning America didn't mention places to shop or pitfalls to avoid on the Web. It was then that I realized how quickly the Web had become mainstream. I even had parents asking me where they could go shopping for children's presents online. They were dreading going to the toy stores here in New York City during the mad holiday rush. This was even more amplified during the Christmas selling season of 1999 when consumers spent an estimated $9.4 billion on holiday gifts over the Internet. Even President Clinton joined the online shopping revolution that Christmas.

It's true that etailing, or business-to-consumer (B2C) ecommerce, is growing at an exponential pace, and it's easy to get caught up in the excitement on the for-

Figure 1-8 US E-Commerce as a % of US GDP
Source: Pegasus Research Intl

(in US$ billions)	1996	1997	1998	1999	2000	2001	2002	2003
US GDP	$7,661	$8,083	$8,510	$8,970	$9,454	$9,964	$10,502	$11,070
% change yoy	5.4%	5.5%	5.3%	5.4%	5.4%	5.4%	5.4%	5.4%
E-Commerce	$2.7	$9.4	$31.8	$82.0	$176.3	$356.9	$666.3	$1,200
% of GDP	0.04%	0.12%	0.37%	0.91%	1.87%	3.58%	6.34%	10.84%

Source: Pegasus Research Intl

est floor. However, let's put matters into perspective and take a helicopter view. Looking at the forest from this angle, we see that B2C ecommerce accounted for less than 0.3% of retail sales last year, and will account for less than 1% in 1999. How's the five year outlook? By then, B2C revenues are expected to be around $165 billion, yet this will still be less than 5% of total retail sales.

I have often compared electronic commerce to an iceberg, with the tip of the iceberg representing the most visible portion – B2C ecommerce. However, the bulk of ecommerce revenues is actually under the surface, less visible to both the media and investors. It is in this business-to-business (B2B) area that roughly 70% of all e-commerce revenue is being generated.

The Ecommerce Iceberg

Business-to-Consumer (B2C)

Business-to-Business (B2B)

Think of it this way, while the B2C ecommerce opportunity will be measured in the billions of dollars, B2B ecommerce will be measured in the trillions of dollars.

Organizations are finding that the Web can improve communications with their business partners, thus forming stronger business relationships as well as dramatically slashing costs and shortening sales and production cycles, which leads to higher profits and improved productivity.

Just think of something as simple as buying office supplies for a typical mid-sized company. The process is still very inefficient. An office assistant writes a paper purchase order, looks up the item and order number in a catalog, then gives it to a superior for approval. Once approved, the purchase order is passed on through the internal mail to the purchasing department, which re-writes or re-keys the order to send to one of its suppliers. The supplier then takes the purchase order and keys it into his system. If there are no errors, the supplier can fulfill the order – providing it has the items in inventory. If not, the supplier in many cases, mails back a letter stating that the item is out of stock. Then, the office assistant either waits until the item is in stock or goes through the process again, trying it with a substitute item. This type of scenario happens more often than many people realize.

Because of the steps involved in the transaction process, a typical purchase transaction can cost between $8 and $150, often more than the cost of the item itself. Some companies are running semi-automated or EDI (electronic data interchange systems however, because of the high cost and proprietary nature (i.e. software incompatibility), these solutions are not suitable for all the different suppliers or businesses. EDI, because of its high implementation and maintenance costs, is also out of the question for small- and mid-sized businesses, which comprise over 98% of all businesses in the US.

Now, the Internet changes all of that. Companies have a large-scale, flexible network that can connect tens of thousands of buyers and suppliers in giant trading exchanges with a common software interface. Purchases can be keyed in once in a simple browser environment, with inventory and order status instantly available. A Web-based procurement system can reduce costs up to 90%[5].

Recall our office assistant, who now can log into an office supply Web site, quickly search for the item needed, click on it once and have the order automatically approved and processed in a few seconds.

Leading the B2B revolution, is the rise in these trading communities or virtual marketplaces. These take the form of broad or horizontal exchanges that connect buyers with a broad array of suppliers, such as what Commerce One and Ariba provide, and vertical exchanges, such as Chemdex or eSteel, that focus on specific industries. How large is the market potential? Consider GM. It will be moving all of its purchasing online within two years. In other words, $80 billion worth of purchases. But if you include the purchasing power of its 30,000-plus suppliers, that figure blossoms to approximately $500 billion. No small change, and that's just for one company and its network of suppliers.

There are a number of other business processes that are being transformed through the Internet, including customer service, content management, workflow automation, data mining, supply chain management and more. B2C ecommerce, with the Amazon's and eBay's, may have received most of the media attention through 1999, but it is the B2B area that will receive most of the money. That's where the spending will be.

---

[5] According to Commerce One, the average cost of a purchase order is $79. A Web-based system that automates both the internal and external processes can reduce that cost to $6 per PO.
International Data Corporation, estimates that online or e-procurement systems can save corporations over $100 billion by 2003.

2

The Internet Playing Field

Much like the magic beans in Jack and the beanstalk, the Internet is a new industry that has emerged on the scene virtually overnight. Along with the emergence of this new and important sector of the economy have come a number of compelling investment opportunities. First, there was America Online, the grandfather of Internet stocks, which went public in March 1992, followed by CMGI and RSA Security which jumped onto the public stage in 1994.

The following year brought seven Internet companies to the public markets, including PSINet, Spyglass and Netscape. Over the following three years, 74 Internet companies entered the public limelight, and by the end of 1998, there were 88 publicly traded Internet companies. Then 1999 rolled around, and 250 companies jumped onto the public stage, bringing the total universe of Internet stocks to 326 companies at the end of 1999, with an aggregate market value of over $1.13 trillion dollars, greater than the GDP of Brazil, Canada, or Mexico.

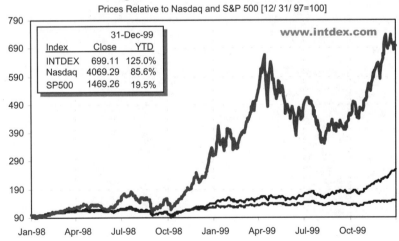

Figure 2-1 Pegasus Internet Index Performance
Source: Pegasus Research Intl

Internet Market Performance

It was in 1998 that Internet stocks began to reflect the underlying growth drivers in the sector, and the group substantially outperformed all major indices in the US. The Pegasus Internet INTDEX™, rose 210% in 1998, nearly eight times the performance of the broader S&P 500 and five times the Nasdaq's 40% performance. However, it sometimes did seem a little bit like lotto fever, with some investors scrambling to buying anything resembling Internet, in the hope of it being the next Amazon.com or Yahoo!. Companies like K-Tel or Zapata Holdings were only too happy to feed the market with press releases highlighting their Internet plans.

In 1999, Internet stocks started the year off strong, with the INTDEX™, climbing 115% before falling back in April in a solid round of consolidation. Highlighting the risk inherent in Internet investing (a point investors should always keep in mind), a number of dot-coms, including Amazon.com, fell 50% or more from their highs set in early April 1999 to their lows set that summer. Although a 50% drop may seem significant, it is important to put that drop into context. Many of these stocks had climbed +1,500% over the past 15 months, which was clearly unsustainable.

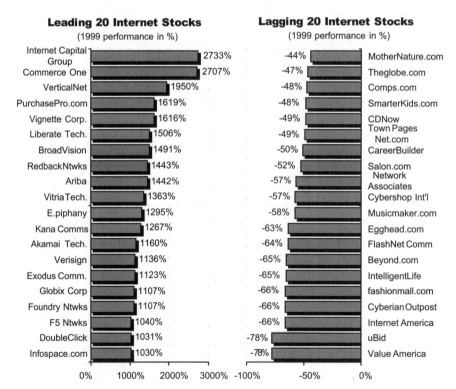

Leading 20 Internet Stocks
(1999 performance in %)

Stock	%
Internet Capital Group	2733%
Commerce One	2707%
VerticalNet	1950%
PurchasePro.com	1619%
Vignette Corp.	1616%
Liberate Tech.	1506%
BroadVision	1491%
RedbackNtwks	1443%
Ariba	1442%
VitriaTech.	1363%
E.piphany	1295%
Kana Comms	1267%
Akamai Tech.	1160%
Verisign	1136%
Exodus Comm.	1123%
Globix Corp	1107%
Foundry Ntwks	1107%
F5 Ntwks	1040%
DoubleClick	1031%
Infospace.com	1030%

Lagging 20 Internet Stocks
(1999 performance in %)

%	Stock
-44%	MotherNature.com
-47%	Theglobe.com
-48%	Comps.com
-48%	SmarterKids.com
-49%	CDNow
-49%	Town Pages Net.com
-50%	CareerBuilder
-52%	Salon.com
-57%	Network Associates
-57%	Cybershop Int'l
-58%	Musicmaker.com
-63%	Egghead.com
-64%	FlashNet Comm
-65%	Beyond.com
-65%	IntelligentLife
-66%	fashionmall.com
-66%	CyberianOutpost
-66%	Internet America
-78%	uBid
-78%	Value America

Figure 2-2 Leaders and Laggards in 1999
Source: Pegasus Research Intl

The consolidation lasted through the summer of 1999, giving many of these stocks a solid base to move forward again through the rest of the year, with the Pegasus Internet INTDEX™ finishing 1999 up 125%.

What was interesting to observe, was the shift in investor focus from the business-to-consumer (B2C) sector in 1998 and early 1999 to the business-to-business (B2B) sector in the latter part of 1999. In July, I had actually spoken at an Internet investor conference at the New York Society of Security Analysts (www.nyssa.org), and highlighted how the B2B space offered significant investment opportunities, and expected this group to do well throughout the rest of the year and into 2000.

Internet Market Statistics	
Internet universe (# stocks):	326
Total market value:	$1,129b
Average daily trading volume in Dec 99 (000s):	285,850
Internet volume as % of Nasdaq volume:	18.24%
Internet stocks as % of Nasdaq stocks:	6.52%
Volatilty (average daily absolute % ch):	5.27%
% of stocks with positive return in 1999:	79.4%
% of stocks with negative return in 1999:	20.2%

Bringing back our iceberg analogy, I explained how the bulk of the revenue potential was below the surface, less visible to investors. As this became more visible, the B2B sector began in August 1999 to outperform the broader Internet market, with the result that the group closed the year up 541%. Highlighting the strength in the B2B sector, all of the top 20 performers in 1999 were business-oriented Internet stocks.

Just as many of the best performing stocks in 1999 were in the B2B sector, most of the laggards in 1999 were second and third-tier B2C stocks. Many of these companies failed to gain market share and were unable to successfully differentiate their brand from stronger players in their respective space. With few of these companies generating profits, the ones that are unable to successfully reposition themselves could quickly fade from the investment scene.

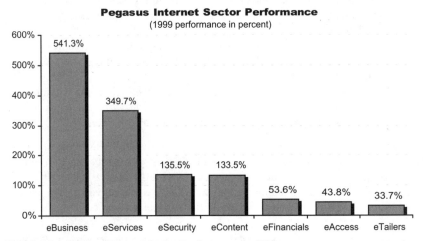

Figure 2-3 Pegasus Internet Sector Performance in 1999
Source: Pegasus Research Intl

The Pegasus Internet Index

To help investors track the performance of Internet stocks, our firm, Pegasus Research International, has developed the most comprehensive equity benchmark available for Internet investors. The Pegasus Internet Index or INTDEX™, is a market capitalization-weighted index of 50 stocks representing a complete cross-section of the Internet universe. It is also the first index to segment the Internet space into seven distinctive groups, allowing investors to make both performance and valuation comparisons among peer groups (i.e. apple-to-apple comparisons).

Broadly speaking, the Internet universe can be divided into two main groups, the business-to-consumer (B2C) segment and the business-to-business (B2B) segment. The B2C segment encompasses the online brokers, online retailers, content aggregators (portals), Internet access providers (ISPs), and other consumer-oriented companies. The B2B segment includes Internet security firms, Internet software and solutions providers, Internet services and other companies focused on the backend of the value-chain.

Specifically, the seven sectors are:

1. *eFinancials* – this includes the online brokers and investment banks, online banks and credit card issuers, and other financially-focused Internet companies.
2. *eContent* – these are the 21st Century media properties, and includes the larger horizontal portals or hubs that are in essence content aggregators, and the niche or vertical portals that are to a large extent content creators.
3. *eTailers* – these are the pure-play online retailers, running from the larger general merchandise companies to the specialty-focused online retailers.
4. *eAccess* – these are the gatekeepers to the Internet, and includes the Internet service providers and hosting companies that offer Internet access both to the consumer and to businesses.
5. *eBusiness* – these are the enablers, and includes the companies that provide Internet software solutions, infrastructure and business-to-business marketplaces.
6. *eSecurity* – is the insurance on the Web, and includes companies that provide firewalls, digital certificates and public key infrastructure, network security and antivirus software.
7. *eServices* – are the eclectic group, and includes the integrated solutions providers or iBuilders, measurement and analysis firms, audio/video streaming and delivery and Internet investment companies.

Companies are selected for inclusion in the Pegasus INTDEX™ based on a number of factors. Each firm must i) generate a majority of its revenues from the Internet or the majority of its business must be Internet-related; ii) generate a minimum of $10 million in annual revenues; iii) have a market value of at least $100 million; and iv) correlate closely with the Internet sector.[6]

---

[6] For those who are interested in a more detailed description of the methodology behind the Pegasus Internet INTDEX™, please visit the www.topinternetstocks.com Web site or www.intdex.com where our regularly updated INTDEX™ report and FAQ can be downloaded.

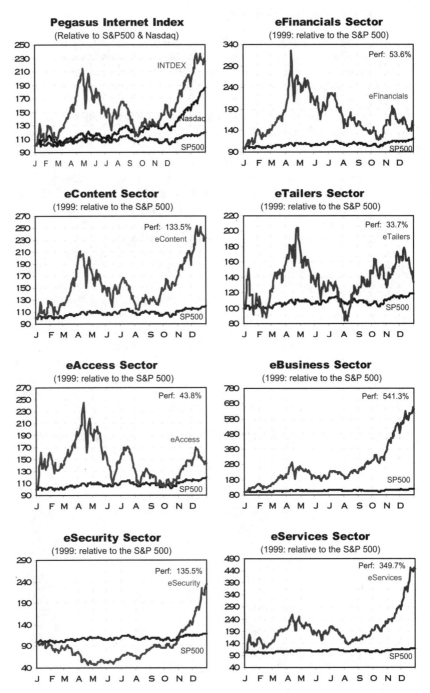

Figure 2-4   Internet sector performance in 1999
Source: Pegasus Research Intl

Internet IPOs: The Opening Act

Either way you slice it or dice it, 1999 was a busy year for Internet IPOs. During the year, 250 Internet companies went public, nearly ten times the number of Internet companies that came to market in 1998. The third quarter of 1999 set a record, as 83 Internet companies jumped onto the public stage. This was greater than all the Internet IPOs in the 1995-98 period.

One thing was clear in 1999, demand for Internet IPOs far outstripped the supply, with the average Internet IPO posting a first-day gain of over 85%. Sometimes the recipe seemed simple: start with a little music, throw in huge losses, add a dash of revenues, and voila, a successful IPO! Other times, it didn't matter if the company had revenues, as long as the concept sounded convincing. During the summer of 1999, four companies went public with no revenues prior to their IPO. Nevertheless, they were warmly greeted, all closing their first day on the public stage in positive territory.

The best performing IPOs in 1999 were in the B2B segment, with investor demand practically insatiable in this area. This group reported the strongest one-day gains, with the stocks in the group climbing 100% on average. Many of these companies including Akamai, Freemarkets and InterNAP Networks, came to market in the latter half of the year, finishing 1999 with multibillion dollar valuations.

For many of these Internet companies, 1999 was a strong year to tap the equity markets for capital in order to fund their growth plans. The 250 companies that went public in 1999 raised nearly $19.8 billion, five times the total amount raised between 1995 and 1998. However, these dot-coms also had the potential to raise nearly double that amount, with over $17.4 billion being left on the table. The amount left on the table is defined as the difference between the offering price and the opening price, times the amount of shares being offered.

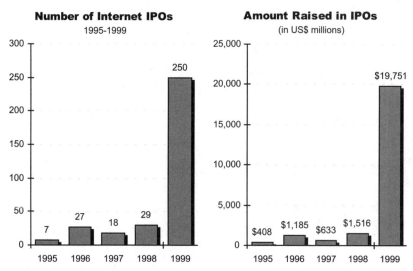

Figure 2-5 Number of Internet IPOs
Source: Pegasus Research Intl

Figure 2-6 Amount raised in Internet IPOs
Source: Pegasus Research Intl

   In theory, if stocks are accurately priced, the first-day gains should be marginal. Traditionally, securities are priced approximately 15% below the anticipated opening price in order to create enough demand for a full placement. In 1999, this wasn't the case, with the average Internet stock opening up 79% above its offering price. The first quarter of 1999 experienced the greatest mispricings, with the spread reaching 167%. This average was skewed by a few companies, including MarketWatch.com and Priceline.com, which opened over 400% above their offering prices. In the fourth quarter of 1999, the spread had the potential to be much greater, if not for the fact that many of the offering prices for B2B stocks were doubled shortly before going to the market.

   The eBusiness group gathered the most money in 1999, raising $6.5 billion, followed by the eTailers group which in aggregate, raised $3.3 billion. With only two IPOs during the year, the eSecurity group raised the least, at $131 million.

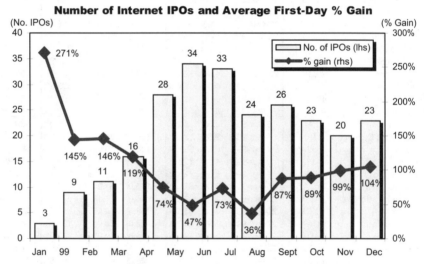

Figure 2-7   Number of Internet IPOs and average first-day percentage gain in 1999
Source: Pegasus Research Intl

Internet Initial Public Offerings in 1999

Company	Ticker	Offering Date	No. of shares*	Offering price	Amount Raised*	First day % gain	% ch since offer price	%ch from D1 close
MarketWatch.com	MKTW	15-Jan-99	2.75	$17.00	46.8	473.5%	114.7%	-62.6%
Allaire	ALLR	22-Jan-99	2.50	$20.00	50.0	118.8%	631.6%	234.4%
Tut Systems	TUTS	29-Jan-99	2.50	$18.00	45.0	219.4%	197.9%	-6.7%
M. M. Poppe Tyson	MMPT	5-Feb-99	2.60	$16.00	41.6	181.3%	339.8%	56.4%
Pacific Internet	PCNTF	10-Feb-99	2.50	$17.00	42.5	182.4%	176.1%	-2.2%
VerticalNet	VERT	11-Feb-99	3.50	$16.00	56.0	183.6%	1950.0%	622.9%
Healtheon	HLTH	11-Feb-99	5.00	$8.00	40.0	292.2%	368.8%	19.5%
Prodigy	PRGY	11-Feb-99	8.00	$15.00	120.0	87.5%	29.2%	-31.1%
WebTrends	WEBT	19-Feb-99	3.50	$13.00	45.5	108.2%	523.1%	199.3%
Vignette Corp.	VIGN	19-Feb-99	4.00	$19.00	76.0	124.7%	757.9%	281.8%
Intraware	ITRA	26-Feb-99	4.00	$16.00	64.0	18.0%	393.8%	318.5%
pcOrder	PCOR	26-Feb-99	2.20	$21.00	46.2	124.4%	142.9%	8.2%
RoweCom	ROWE	9-Mar-99	3.10	$16.00	49.6	53.1%	183.6%	85.2%
FlashNet Comm	FLAS	16-Mar-99	3.00	$17.00	51.0	156.6%	-63.6%	-85.8%
Multex.com	MLTX	17-Mar-99	3.00	$14.00	42.0	140.2%	168.8%	11.9%
iVillage	IVIL	19-Mar-99	3.65	$24.00	87.6	233.9%	-15.6%	-74.7%
AutoWeb.com	AWEB	23-Mar-99	5.00	$14.00	70.0	185.7%	-22.3%	-72.8%
MiningCo.com	BOUT	24-Mar-99	3.00	$25.00	75.0	90.0%	259.0%	88.9%
Onemain.com	ONEM	25-Mar-99	8.50	$22.00	187.0	79.8%	-31.8%	-62.1%
autobytel.com	ABTL	26-Mar-99	4.50	$23.00	103.5	75.0%	-34.0%	-62.3%
Critical Path	CPTH	29-Mar-99	4.50	$24.00	108.0	174.5%	293.2%	43.3%
Priceline.com	PCLN	30-Mar-99	10.00	$16.00	160.0	331.3%	196.1%	-31.3%
ZDNet Group	ZDZ	31-Mar-99	10.00	$19.00	190.0	89.5%	10.5%	-41.7%
Claimsnet.com	CLAI	6-Apr-99	2.50	$8.00	20.0	106.3%	25.0%	-39.4%
Rhythms Net Connect.	RTHM	7-Apr-99	9.38	$21.00	196.9	229.5%	47.6%	-55.2%
Value America	VUSA	8-Apr-99	5.50	$23.00	126.5	140.0%	-78.0%	-90.8%
iTurf	TURF	9-Apr-99	4.20	$22.00	92.4	161.1%	-43.5%	-78.3%
USinterNetworking	USIX	9-Apr-99	6.00	$21.00	126.0	173.8%	232.7%	21.5%
Worldgate Comm.	WGAT	15-Apr-99	5.00	$21.00	105.0	61.9%	126.5%	39.9%
Internet Financial Svs	IFSX	20-Apr-99	2.00	$7.00	14.0	57.1%	--	--
Proxicom	PXCM	20-Apr-99	4.50	$13.00	58.5	50.0%	856.3%	537.5%
Log On America	LOAX	22-Apr-99	2.20	$10.00	22.0	250.0%	102.5%	-42.1%
Launch Media	LAUN	23-Apr-99	3.40	$22.00	74.8	29.0%	-13.9%	-33.3%
NetPerceptions	NETP	23-Apr-99	3.65	$14.00	51.1	112.9%	200.0%	40.9%
Razorfish	RAZF	27-Apr-99	3.00	$16.00	48.0	109.4%	494.5%	184.0%
HearMe.co	HEAR	29-Apr-99	3.90	$18.00	70.2	181.3%	47.9%	-47.4%
Marimba	MRBA	30-Apr-99	4.00	$20.00	80.0	203.8%	130.3%	-24.2%
Applied Theory	ATHY	30-Apr-99	4.50	$16.00	72.0	28.1%	73.4%	35.4%
Town Pages Net.com	TPN	30-Apr-99	2.20	$10.00	22.0	16.3%	-48.8%	-55.9%
MapQuest.com	MQST	4-May-99	4.60	$15.00	69.0	49.2%	50.4%	0.8%
Flycast Comm.	FCST	4-May-99	3.00	$25.00	75.0	19.0%	419.8%	336.8%
Silknet Software	SILK	5-May-99	3.00	$15.00	45.0	134.2%	1005.0%	371.8%
NorthPoint Comm.	NPNT	5-May-99	15.00	$24.00	360.0	67.5%	0.0%	-40.3%
Comps.com	CDOT	5-May-99	4.50	$15.00	67.5	-5.0%	-47.5%	-44.7%
Portal Software	PRSF	6-May-99	4.00	$14.00	56.0	167.0%	634.8%	175.2%
AdForce	ADFC	7-May-99	4.50	$15.00	67.5	99.6%	375.8%	138.4%
Media Metrix	MMXI	7-May-99	3.00	$17.00	51.0	168.0%	110.3%	-21.5%
NetObjects	NETO	7-May-99	6.00	$12.00	72.0	8.3%	37.5%	26.9%
TheStreet.com	TSCM	11-May-99	5.50	$19.00	104.5	215.8%	1.0%	-68.0%
BiznessOnline.com	BIZZ	12-May-99	2.90	$10.00	29.0	18.8%	-30.0%	-41.1%
CareerBuilder	CBDR	12-May-99	4.50	$13.00	58.5	23.1%	-50.5%	-59.8%

* Number of shares in millions, amount raised in US$ millions
  Percentage gain from offering date to December 31, 1999

Company	Ticker	Offering Date	No. of shares*	Offering price	Amount Raised*	First day % gain	% ch since offer price	%ch from D1 close
Intelligent Life	ILIF	13-May-99	3.50	$13.00	45.5	0.0%	-65.4%	-65.4%
Copper Mountain	CMTN	13-May-99	4.00	$21.00	84.0	225.9%	364.3%	42.5%
Alloy Online	ALOY	14-May-99	3.70	$15.00	55.5	33.3%	5.0%	-21.3%
NextCard	NXCD	14-May-99	6.00	$20.00	120.0	67.5%	44.4%	-13.8%
Scient Corp.	SCNT	14-May-99	3.00	$20.00	60.0	63.2%	764.4%	429.8%
Redback Ntwks	RBAK	18-May-99	2.50	$23.00	57.5	265.8%	1443.5%	322.0%
OneSource Info. Svs	ONES	19-May-99	3.64	$12.00	43.6	18.8%	12.0%	-5.7%
eToys	ETYS	20-May-99	8.32	$20.00	166.4	282.8%	31.3%	-65.7%
@plan.inc	APLN	21-May-99	2.50	$14.00	35.0	14.3%	-29.5%	-38.3%
fashionmall.com	FASH	21-May-99	3.00	$13.00	39.0	0.0%	-65.9%	-65.9%
BarnesandNoble.com	BNBN	25-May-99	25.00	$18.00	450.0	27.4%	-21.2%	-38.2%
ZipLink	ZIPL	26-May-99	3.50	$14.00	49.0	-11.6%	-10.7%	1.0%
StarMedia Ntwk	STRM	26-May-99	7.00	$15.00	105.0	73.7%	167.1%	53.7%
Juno Online Svs	JWEB	26-May-99	6.50	$13.00	84.5	-10.5%	176.4%	209.0%
EDGAR Online	EDGR	26-May-99	3.60	$9.50	34.2	0.6%	-22.4%	-22.9%
DLJdirect	DIR	26-May-99	16.00	$20.00	320.0	50.0%	-32.2%	-54.8%
iXL Enterprises	IIXL	3-Jun-99	6.00	$12.00	72.0	49.0%	362.5%	210.4%
Wit Capital Group	WITC	4-Jun-99	7.60	$9.00	68.4	65.3%	88.9%	14.2%
Online Resources	ORCC	4-Jun-99	3.10	$14.00	43.4	0.4%	18.8%	18.2%
High Speed Access	HSAC	4-Jun-99	13.00	$13.00	169.0	56.8%	35.6%	-13.5%
F5 Ntwks	FFIV	4-Jun-99	3.00	$10.00	30.0	48.8%	1040.0%	666.1%
foreignTV.com	FNTV.OB	7-Jun-99	1.70	$6.00	10.2	4.2%	4.2%	0.0%
drkoop.com	KOOP	8-Jun-99	9.38	$9.00	84.4	82.7%	31.9%	-27.8%
BackWeb Tech.	BWEB	8-Jun-99	5.50	$12.00	66.0	64.1%	251.0%	113.9%
Phone.com	PHCM	11-Jun-99	4.00	$16.00	64.0	150.8%	624.6%	188.9%
onlinetradinginc.com	LINE	11-Jun-99	2.25	$7.00	15.8	41.1%	55.4%	10.1%
GenesisIntermedia.com	GENI	14-Jun-99	2.00	$8.50	17.0	-1.4%	-31.6%	-30.6%
CareInsite	CARI	16-Jun-99	5.65	$18.00	101.7	71.9%	347.2%	160.2%
Viant Corp	VIAN	18-Jun-99	3.00	$16.00	48.0	52.4%	518.8%	306.1%
Student Advantage	STAD	18-Jun-99	6.00	$8.00	48.0	0.0%	177.3%	177.3%
Streamline.com	SLNE	18-Jun-99	4.50	$10.00	45.0	-23.7%	-14.4%	12.2%
Mail.com	MAIL	18-Jun-99	6.85	$7.00	48.0	25.0%	167.9%	114.3%
GoTo.com	GOTO	18-Jun-99	6.00	$15.00	90.0	49.2%	291.7%	162.5%
AppNet Systems	APNT	18-Jun-99	6.00	$12.00	72.0	0.0%	264.6%	264.6%
Ramp Ntwks	RAMP	22-Jun-99	4.00	$11.00	44.0	52.3%	38.6%	-9.0%
Salon.com	SALN	22-Jun-99	2.50	$10.50	26.3	-4.8%	-52.4%	-50.0%
Netivation.com	NTVN	23-Jun-99	2.50	$10.00	25.0	-4.4%	-42.5%	-39.9%
TD Waterhouse	TWE	23-Jun-99	42.00	$24.00	1,008.0	6.8%	-31.3%	-35.6%
Ariba	ARBA	23-Jun-99	5.00	$23.00	115.0	291.3%	1442.5%	294.2%
Software.com	SWCM	24-Jun-99	6.00	$15.00	90.0	33.3%	540.0%	380.0%
quepasa.com	PASA	24-Jun-99	4.00	$12.00	48.0	42.8%	5.7%	-25.9%
CyberSource	CYBS	24-Jun-99	4.00	$11.00	44.0	29.5%	370.5%	263.2%
Juniper Ntwks	JNPR	25-Jun-99	4.80	$34.00	163.2	190.8%	900.0%	243.9%
US SEARCH Corp.com	SRCH	25-Jun-99	6.00	$9.00	54.0	-22.9%	-16.7%	8.1%
Persistence Software	PRSW	25-Jun-99	3.00	$11.00	33.0	25.5%	104.5%	62.9%
Stamps.com	STMP	25-Jun-99	5.00	$11.00	55.0	18.7%	278.4%	218.7%
Internet.com	INTM	25-Jun-99	3.40	$14.00	47.6	0.0%	273.2%	273.2%
Digital Island	ISLD	29-Jun-99	6.00	$10.00	60.0	18.8%	851.3%	700.7%
nFront	NFNT	29-Jun-99	3.90	$10.00	39.0	35.0%	100.0%	48.1%
E Loan	EELN	29-Jun-99	3.50	$14.00	49.0	164.3%	16.1%	-56.1%
Primus Knowledge	PKSI	1-Jul-99	4.15	$11.00	45.7	59.6%	311.9%	158.0%
Ask Jeeves	ASKJ	1-Jul-99	3.00	$14.00	42.0	363.9%	706.7%	73.9%

* Number of shares in millions, amount raised in US$ millions
Percentage gain from offering date to December 31, 1999

Company	Ticker	Offering Date	No. of shares*	Offering price	Amount Raised*	First day % gain	% ch since offer price	%ch from D1 close
Commerce One	CMRC	1-Jul-99	3.30	$21.00	69.3	190.5%	2707.1%	866.4%
Musicmaker.com	HITS	7-Jul-99	8.40	$14.00	117.6	71.0%	-58.0%	-75.5%
Interliant	INIT	8-Jul-99	7.00	$10.00	70.0	68.1%	160.0%	54.7%
Liquid Audio	LQID	9-Jul-99	4.20	$15.00	63.0	143.7%	75.0%	-28.2%
CommTouch Software	CTCH	13-Jul-99	3.00	$16.00	48.0	50.0%	203.5%	102.3%
China.com	CHINA	13-Jul-99	4.20	$20.00	84.0	235.6%	686.3%	134.3%
National Info Consortium	EGOV	15-Jul-99	13.00	$12.00	156.0	44.3%	166.7%	84.8%
Audible	ADBL	16-Jul-99	4.00	$9.00	36.0	133.3%	66.7%	-28.6%
Convergent Comm.	CONV	20-Jul-99	8.40	$15.00	126.0	43.3%	5.8%	-26.2%
Engage Tech.	ENGA	20-Jul-99	6.00	$15.00	90.0	173.3%	300.0%	46.3%
Talk City	TCTY	20-Jul-99	5.00	$12.00	60.0	14.1%	117.7%	90.8%
Art Tech Group	ARTG	21-Jul-99	5.00	$12.00	60.0	50.5%	967.7%	609.4%
Hoover's	HOOV	21-Jul-99	3.25	$14.00	45.5	57.1%	-37.5%	-60.2%
MP3.com	MPPP	21-Jul-99	12.30	$28.00	344.4	126.1%	13.2%	-49.9%
Voyager.net	VOYN	21-Jul-99	9.00	$15.00	135.0	0.4%	-38.8%	-39.0%
Tanning Tech	TANN	23-Jul-99	4.00	$15.00	60.0	22.9%	292.9%	219.6%
JFax.com	JFAX	23-Jul-99	8.50	$9.50	80.8	0.0%	-29.3%	-29.3%
VersaTel Telecom	VRSA	23-Jul-99	21.25	$10.50	223.1	31.0%	232.7%	154.1%
InsWeb	INSW	23-Jul-99	5.00	$17.00	85.0	85.6%	50.4%	-19.0%
Chemdex (Ventro)	VNTR	27-Jul-99	7.50	$15.00	112.5	70.0%	640.0%	335.3%
Quokka Sports	QKKA	28-Jul-99	5.00	$12.00	60.0	-5.2%	9.4%	15.3%
drugstore.com	DSCM	28-Jul-99	5.00	$18.00	90.0	179.2%	101.0%	-28.0%
Liberate Tech.	LBRT	28-Jul-99	6.30	$16.00	100.8	27.4%	1506.3%	1161.0%
Perficient	PRFT	29-Jul-99	1.00	$8.00	8.0	17.3%	59.4%	35.9%
Net2Phone	NTOP	29-Jul-99	5.40	$15.00	81.0	77.1%	206.3%	73.0%
Accrue Software	ACRU	30-Jul-99	3.90	$10.00	39.0	21.9%	441.3%	344.0%
Continuus Software	CNSW	30-Jul-99	3.10	$8.00	24.8	-1.5%	50.0%	52.3%
Digex	DIGX	30-Jul-99	10.00	$17.00	170.0	31.2%	304.4%	208.2%
N2H2	NTWO	30-Jul-99	4.50	$13.00	58.5	-1.5%	80.8%	83.5%
Pacific Softworks	PASW	30-Jul-99	0.95	$5.25	5.0	23.8%	8.3%	-12.5%
WatchGuard Tech.	WGRD	30-Jul-99	3.50	$13.00	45.5	-6.7%	132.7%	149.4%
BigStar Entertainment	BGST	3-Aug-99	2.50	$10.00	25.0	-18.4%	-22.5%	-5.0%
Quotesmith.com	QUOT	3-Aug-99	5.00	$11.00	55.0	-11.9%	3.4%	17.4%
Splitrock Services	SPLT	3-Aug-99	9.00	$10.00	90.0	-10.0%	98.8%	120.8%
The Cobalt Group	CBLT	5-Aug-99	4.45	$11.00	49.0	-24.5%	-14.8%	12.8%
HomeStore.com	HOMS	5-Aug-99	7.00	$20.00	140.0	13.8%	271.3%	226.4%
Internet Capital Group	ICGE	5-Aug-99	14.90	$12.00	178.8	103.7%	2733.3%	1291.2%
Pivotal	PVTL	5-Aug-99	3.50	$12.00	42.0	2.6%	252.1%	243.2%
Interactive Pictures	IPIX	6-Aug-99	4.20	$18.00	75.6	0.0%	29.5%	29.5%
Tumbleweed Comms	TMWD	6-Aug-99	4.00	$12.00	48.0	0.5%	606.3%	602.7%
Braun Consulting	BRNC	10-Aug-99	4.60	$7.00	32.2	0.9%	921.4%	912.7%
HotJobs.com	HOTJ	10-Aug-99	3.00	$8.00	24.0	-4.6%	446.1%	472.6%
US Interactive	USIT	10-Aug-99	4.60	$10.00	46.0	6.3%	330.0%	304.5%
InterWorld Corp	INTW	10-Aug-99	3.00	$15.00	45.0	18.3%	469.2%	381.0%
Mortgage.com	MDCM	11-Aug-99	7.06	$8.00	56.5	-10.5%	-27.3%	-18.8%
Active Software	ASWX	13-Aug-99	3.50	$11.00	38.5	27.3%	736.4%	557.1%
Quest Software	QSFT	13-Aug-99	4.40	$14.00	61.6	235.7%	628.6%	117.0%
SilverStream Software	SSSW	17-Aug-99	3.00	$16.00	48.0	96.9%	643.8%	277.8%
Headhunter.net	HHNT	19-Aug-99	3.00	$10.00	30.0	1.9%	25.6%	23.3%
Agile Software	AGIL	20-Aug-99	3.00	$21.00	63.0	89.9%	934.4%	444.7%
Lionbridge Tech.	LIOX	20-Aug-99	3.50	$10.00	35.0	26.3%	82.5%	44.5%
MyPoints.com	MYPT	20-Aug-99	5.00	$8.00	40.0	37.5%	825.0%	572.7%

* Number of shares in millions, amount raised in US$ millions
Percentage gain from offering date to December 31, 1999

Company	Ticker	Offering Date	No. of shares*	Offering price	Amount Raised*	First day % gain	% ch since offer price	%ch from D1 close
LookSmart	LOOK	20-Aug-99	9.00	$12.00	108.0	44.3%	125.0%	56.0%
Bamboo.com	BAMB	26-Aug-99	4.00	$7.00	28.0	150.9%	136.6%	-5.7%
ImageX.com	IMGX	26-Aug-99	3.00	$7.00	21.0	99.1%	498.2%	200.4%
PurchasePro.com	PPRO	14-Sep-99	4.00	$12.00	48.0	117.8%	1618.8%	689.3%
garden.com	GDEN	16-Sep-99	4.10	$12.00	49.2	58.8%	-27.6%	-54.4%
Luminant Worldwide	LUMT	16-Sep-99	4.06	$18.00	73.1	46.6%	152.8%	72.5%
Vitria Technology	VITR	17-Sep-99	3.00	$16.00	48.0	201.6%	1362.5%	385.0%
Broadbase Software	BBSW	22-Sep-99	4.00	$14.00	56.0	94.6%	703.6%	312.8%
E.piphany	EPNY	22-Sep-99	4.15	$16.00	66.4	182.4%	1294.5%	393.7%
Kana Comms	KANA	22-Sep-99	3.30	$15.00	49.5	243.3%	1266.7%	298.1%
Ashford.com	ASFD	23-Sep-99	6.25	$13.00	81.3	0.0%	-15.4%	-15.4%
Bluestone Software	BLSW	23-Sep-99	4.00	$15.00	60.0	25.0%	666.7%	513.3%
Cybergold	CGLD	23-Sep-99	5.00	$9.00	45.0	33.3%	96.5%	47.4%
eGain Comms	EGAN	23-Sep-99	5.00	$12.00	60.0	91.7%	214.6%	64.1%
yesmail.com	YESM	23-Sep-99	3.40	$11.00	37.4	18.7%	207.4%	158.9%
NetZero	NZRO	23-Sep-99	10.00	$16.00	160.0	82.1%	68.4%	-7.5%
Keynote Systems	KEYN	24-Sep-99	4.00	$14.00	56.0	94.6%	426.8%	170.6%
Webstakes.com	IWIN	24-Sep-99	3.58	$14.00	50.1	-17.9%	41.1%	71.7%
Foundry Ntwks	FDRY	28-Sep-99	5.00	$25.00	125.0	525.0%	1106.8%	93.1%
FreeShop.com	FSHP	28-Sep-99	3.20	$12.00	38.4	13.0%	300.0%	254.0%
ITXC	ITXC	28-Sep-99	6.25	$12.00	75.0	135.4%	180.2%	19.0%
Medscape	MSCP	28-Sep-99	6.60	$8.00	52.8	72.6%	25.0%	-27.6%
FTD.com	EFTD	29-Sep-99	4.50	$8.00	36.0	7.9%	-34.4%	-39.2%
InterNAP Ntwk Svs	INAP	29-Sep-99	9.50	$20.00	190.0	164.9%	765.0%	226.5%
perfumania.com	PF	29-Sep-99	3.50	$7.00	24.5	-3.6%	217.9%	229.6%
ShopNow.com	SPNW	29-Sep-99	7.25	$12.00	87.0	5.7%	57.8%	49.2%
Telemate.Net Software	TMNT	29-Sep-99	3.50	$14.00	49.0	1.4%	16.1%	14.5%
LoisLaw.com	LOIS	30-Sep-99	3.98	$14.00	55.7	3.6%	179.5%	169.8%
RADWARE	RDWR	30-Sep-99	3.50	$18.00	63.0	60.4%	139.6%	49.3%
Digital Insight	DGIN	1-Oct-99	3.50	$15.00	52.5	114.2%	142.5%	13.2%
AltiGen Comm.	ATGN	5-Oct-99	3.25	$10.00	32.5	60.0%	3.1%	-35.5%
DSL.net	DSLN	6-Oct-99	7.20	$7.50	54.0	13.7%	92.5%	69.3%
Breakaway Solutions	BWAY	6-Oct-99	3.00	$14.00	42.0	201.8%	421.4%	72.8%
PlanetRx.com	PLRX	7-Oct-99	6.00	$16.00	96.0	62.5%	-9.4%	-44.2%
Calico Commerce	CLIC	7-Oct-99	4.00	$14.00	56.0	300.0%	278.6%	-5.4%
VitaminShoppe.com	VSHP	8-Oct-99	4.55	$11.00	50.1	-11.4%	-17.0%	-6.4%
TriZetto Group	TZIX	8-Oct-99	4.20	$9.00	37.8	0.0%	418.1%	418.1%
Jupiter Comm.	JPTR	8-Oct-99	3.13	$21.00	65.7	69.0%	44.0%	-14.8%
Interwoven	IWOV	8-Oct-99	3.15	$17.00	53.6	141.2%	615.4%	196.6%
E-Stamp	ESTM	8-Oct-99	7.00	$17.00	119.0	31.6%	30.9%	-0.6%
iGo	IGOC	14-Oct-99	5.00	$12.00	60.0	17.2%	-24.5%	-35.5%
Netcentives	NCNT	14-Oct-99	6.00	$12.00	72.0	4.7%	419.3%	396.1%
NetRadio	NETR	14-Oct-99	3.20	$11.00	35.2	-9.1%	-25.0%	-17.5%
Cysive	CYSV	15-Oct-99	3.35	$17.00	57.0	122.1%	323.9%	90.9%
Women.com	WOMN	15-Oct-99	3.75	$10.00	37.5	85.0%	42.5%	-23.0%
ZapMe!	IZAP	20-Oct-99	9.00	$11.00	99.0	-13.6%	-21.6%	-9.2%
NaviSite	NAVI	22-Oct-99	5.50	$14.00	77.0	147.4%	614.3%	188.8%
Viador	VIAD	26-Oct-99	4.00	$9.00	36.0	23.7%	370.8%	280.7%
InterTrust Tech.	ITRU	27-Oct-99	6.50	$18.00	117.0	202.1%	553.5%	116.3%
Data Return	DRTN	28-Oct-99	6.30	$13.00	81.9	26.0%	311.5%	226.6%
Cavion Tech.	CAVN	29-Oct-99	1.20	$6.50	7.8	-7.7%	19.2%	29.2%
Akamai Tech.	AKAM	29-Oct-99	9.00	$26.00	234.0	458.4%	1160.1%	125.7%

* Number of shares in millions, amount raised in US$ millions
Percentage gain from offering date to December 31, 1999

Company	Ticker	Offering Date	No. of Shares*	Offering price	Amount Raised*	First day % gain	% ch since offer price	%ch from D1 close
Be Free	BFRE	3-Nov-99	5.60	$12.00	67.2	141.7%	499.0%	147.8%
Tickets.com	TIXX	4-Nov-99	6.70	$12.50	83.8	54.0%	14.5%	-25.6%
Webvan Group	WBVN	5-Nov-99	25.00	$15.00	375.0	65.9%	10.0%	-33.7%
Collectors Universe	CLCT	5-Nov-99	4.00	$6.00	24.0	0.0%	4.2%	4.2%
Netzee	NETZ	9-Nov-99	4.40	$14.00	61.6	5.8%	18.8%	12.3%
Expedia	EXPE	10-Nov-99	5.20	$14.00	72.8	281.7%	150.0%	-34.5%
iBasis	IBAS	10-Nov-99	6.80	$16.00	108.8	151.6%	79.7%	-28.6%
SonicWALL	SNWL	11-Nov-99	4.00	$14.00	56.0	86.1%	187.5%	54.5%
NetCreations	NTCR	12-Nov-99	3.30	$13.00	42.9	53.8%	238.5%	120.0%
Quintus	QNTS	16-Nov-99	4.50	$18.00	81.0	205.6%	154.9%	-16.6%
iManage	IMAN	17-Nov-99	3.60	$11.00	39.6	123.9%	192.0%	30.4%
Web Street	WEBS	17-Nov-99	3.50	$11.00	38.5	12.5%	12.5%	-0.0%
Retek	RETK	18-Nov-99	5.50	$15.00	82.5	117.1%	401.7%	131.1%
Exactis.com	XACT	19-Nov-99	3.53	$14.00	49.4	71.4%	73.7%	1.3%
LifeMinders.com	LFMN	19-Nov-99	4.20	$14.00	58.8	59.9%	312.5%	158.0%
Mediaplex	MPLX	19-Nov-99	6.00	$12.00	72.0	141.7%	422.9%	116.4%
SciQuest	SQST	19-Nov-99	7.20	$16.00	115.2	87.5%	396.9%	165.0%
Digital Impact	DIGI	23-Nov-99	4.50	$15.00	67.5	270.0%	234.2%	-9.7%
GetThere.com	GTHR	23-Nov-99	5.00	$16.00	80.0	53.1%	151.6%	64.3%
SmarterKids.com	SKDS	23-Nov-99	4.50	$14.00	63.0	0.0%	-48.2%	-48.2%
Mcafee	MCAF	2-Dec-99	6.25	$12.00	75.0	266.7%	275.0%	2.3%
Knot	KNOT	2-Dec-99	3.50	$10.00	35.0	50.0%	-15.6%	-43.8%
HealthCentral.com	HCEN	7-Dec-99	7.50	$11.00	82.5	-10.2%	-33.5%	-25.9%
E-Cruiter.com	ECRU	7-Dec-99	2.45	$6.00	14.7	42.7%	18.8%	-16.8%
Agency.com	ACOM	8-Dec-99	5.90	$26.00	153.4	192.3%	96.2%	-32.9%
NetRatings	NTRT	8-Dec-99	4.00	$17.00	68.0	64.7%	183.1%	71.9%
Preview Systems	PRVW	8-Dec-99	3.80	$21.00	79.8	298.8%	208.9%	-22.5%
Andover.Net	ANDN	8-Dec-99	4.00	$18.00	72.0	254.2%	97.9%	-44.1%
Fogdog	FOGD	9-Dec-99	6.00	$11.00	66.0	19.3%	-13.6%	-27.6%
El Sitio	LCTO	10-Dec-99	8.20	$16.00	131.2	108.2%	129.7%	10.3%
MedicaLogic	MDLI	10-Dec-99	5.30	$17.00	90.1	29.4%	23.5%	-4.5%
Freemarkets	FMKT	10-Dec-99	3.60	$48.00	172.8	483.3%	611.1%	21.9%
MotherNature.com	MTHR	10-Dec-99	4.10	$13.00	53.3	-20.7%	-43.8%	-29.1%
eBenX	EBNX	10-Dec-99	5.00	$20.00	100.0	124.4%	126.3%	0.8%
HealthExtras	HLEX	14-Dec-99	5.50	$11.00	60.5	-18.2%	9.1%	33.3%
Gric Communications	GRIC	15-Dec-99	4.60	$14.00	64.4	50.0%	81.3%	20.8%
Optio Software	OPTO	15-Dec-99	5.00	$10.00	50.0	63.1%	135.0%	44.1%
eCollege.com	ECLG	15-Dec-99	4.50	$11.00	49.5	29.5%	-0.6%	-23.2%
Xpedior	XPDR	16-Dec-99	8.50	$19.00	161.5	36.8%	51.3%	10.6%
C-Bridge Internet	CBIS	17-Dec-99	4.00	$16.00	64.0	150.4%	203.9%	21.4%
Egreetings.com	EGRT	17-Dec-99	6.00	$10.00	60.0	5.6%	1.3%	-4.1%
OnDisplay	ONDS	17-Dec-99	3.50	$28.00	98.0	175.0%	224.6%	18.0%
Streamedia Comm.	SMILU	21-Dec-99	1.00	$8.50	8.5	5.9%	1.5%	-4.2%

* Number of shares in millions, amount raised in US$ millions
  Percentage gain from offering date to December 31, 1999

3

Internet Investing 101

Sometimes it can feel like a jungle out there with the myriad of different metrics being touted for Internet stocks. Some of these measures attempt to capture the underlying value of Internet companies, and others are there merely to promote the hype and justify buys on companies that various firms have taken public. During the summer of 1999, a number of Internet music companies went public with valuations that by any means were extreme. Musicmaker.com was one of these companies. Prior to its initial public offering (IPO), the company had revenues over the prior 12 months of $74,000. It closed its first day on the public stage with a market value of over $700 million. That translates to a revenue multiple of over 10,000 times. In other words, for every dollar that the company sells, it was worth $10,000! Now, I'm not questioning Musicmaker.com's potential. After all, music over the Internet is just the next stage of digital distribution, but to justify to investors that the company is worth 10,000 times revenues is questionable at best.

I tend to use and recommend a rather simple approach. Start at the top, look at the big picture first, and ask a number of key questions. What industry is the company operating in? Is the industry growing quickly or maturing? How is the company positioned relative to its competition? Is market share growing or declining? Where are revenues coming from? How is the quality of revenues? Finally, how volatile is the stock? Can I afford the risk?

I am often asked what can justify such high valuation for Internet companies. One of the reasons is that these companies are in the early growth stage of their life cycle, where revenues are growing very quickly (see figure 2-1). In this period, companies traditionally seek to maximize growth at the expense of profits in the hopes of quickly capturing market share and reaching scale. The only difference with Internet companies is that the early life-cycle phase is often characterized by 200-500 percent revenue growth (or more) versus 20-50 percent for traditional companies.

> **Internet Valuation 101**
>
> 1. Understand the business model
> 2. Look at sales: (price/sales)
> 3. How's the growth:
>   (price/sales-to-growth)
> 4. Investing for the future:
>   (marketing expense as a % of sales)
> 5. A balancing act:
>   (GAAP vs GARP)
> 6. A crazy little thing called risk:
>   (volatility)

Understand the Business Model

- Define the market
- Understand the competition
- Understand the company

The first step in valuing companies – and Internet companies are no different – is to look at the business model and ask a number of key questions: What market or niche is the company operating in? Is it a new market that is rapidly growing or is growth slowing down as the market matures? Is the market fragmented, with a number of smaller players or consolidating, with just a few major players? Is the company defining the market or playing catch-up? What is it doing to maintain its lead? Is the company capturing market share or losing it to more nimble or larger competitors.

In other words, take a top-down approach, define the market, understand who the key competitors are and understand what the company is doing and how it is doing it better than its competitors.

For new companies that are planning IPOs and have recently entered the public markets, a more critical question would be to ask: Is the business model simply to do an IPO or to create a sustainable business that adds value to its customers? Sometimes, just stepping back and looking from a distance can be revealing.

Although nearly every Internet company promises to have a unique vision and business model that is substantially different from its competitors, the reality is a little different. In general, there are only four basic business models defining Internet companies: i. advertising-based; ii. ecommerce or transaction-based; iii. subscription-based; and iv. service-based.

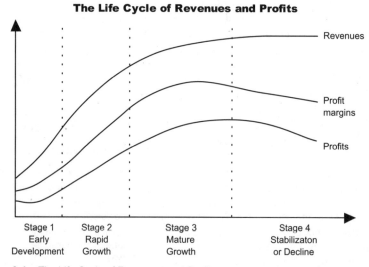

Figure 3-1   The Life Cycle of Revenues and Profits
Source: Pegasus Research Intl

In the advertising model, companies sell "real estate" on their various Web pages for a set fee (sponsorship) or for a fee based on the number of people that either visit that page and see the ad (impressions) or actually click on the ad (click-throughs). This is the basic model used by all the major portals or content aggregators, including Yahoo!, Lycos, CBS MarketWatch, About.com and others.

In the ecommerce or transaction-based model, companies either sell items over their virtual store front (Web site) much like a traditional retailer does, provide a forum or platform where buyers and sellers can meet, or license software. Examples of the new breed of eTailers include Amazon.com, barnesandnoble.com, and drugstore.com. Matching buyers and sellers, are companies like eBay, Priceline.com, Ariba and Commerce One. Charles Schwab and other eBrokers such as E*Trade and Ameritrade are also transaction-driven models.

In the subscription-based model, companies charge a monthly or annual fee for various services including Internet access, Web site hosting, and premium content. Under this category fall the Internet service providers and Web hosting companies such as PSINet, Concentric, Prodigy and Exodus.

Internet service companies are Internet consulting firms, or iBuilders[7], that charge either fixed or variable fees for consulting, designing and implementing Web strategies. These include companies like Razorfish, USWeb, and Scient. Other service-based models include ad management and marketing companies, such as DoubleClick and 24/7 Media, and Internet investment companies such as CMGI and Internet Capital Group.

Naturally, the lines are often blurred with several variations on each theme. America Online, for example, generates subscription, advertising and transaction revenues. Most Internet software companies generate licensing revenues (transaction), but also provide maintenance, training and other consulting services. Some

The Basic Business Models of the Web

Advertising	ECommerce	Subscription	Service
About.com	Amazon.com	America Online	DoubleClick
CNET	Buy.com	Concentric	CMGI
EarthWeb	Charles Schwab	Exodus	Internet Capital
GoTo.com	Chemdex	PSINet	Razorfish
Lycos	Commerce One	Prodigy	Sapient
SportsLine.com	drugstore.com	TheStreet.com	Scient
StarMedia	E*Trade		24/7 Media
Yahoo!	eBay		USWeb
ZDNet	priceline.com		

Figure 3-2   The Basic Business Models of the Web
Source: Pegasus Research Intl

---

[7] The term was first coined by the Internet news magazine, *The Industry Standard* in November 1999.

subscription-based models such as Dow Jones' The Wall Street Journal Interactive and TheStreet.com generate a combination of subscription and advertising revenues.

Define the Market

- Is it a new or established market?
- Is the market fragmented or consolidating?

This is really the first place to start. Take a look at the sector or industry that the company is operating in. Is the market a relatively new market with few competitors or an established market with many players? Now, in general, the Internet is a very new industry or sector of the economy that is just developing. However, even within this young sector, some markets are already establishing themselves, and the industry attractiveness may differ considerably. Take eTailers, for example. This is an industry that is characterized by relatively low barriers to entry, largely established players, high competition and low profit margins.

Although absolute revenue growth in dollar terms is still very high in the eTailing sector, growth rates in percentage terms is expected to slow marginally over the next few years. On this basis, a small company that is hoping to sell products below cost in the hopes of wresting market share from a much larger competitor in an industry where growth rates will begin to slow, may not have assessed the market attractiveness correctly. As Michael Porter, a well-regarded expert on industry analysis and competitive strategy has stated, "Many strategic planning concepts have ignored industry attractiveness and stressed the pursuit of market share, often a recipe for pyrrhic victories." [8]

Also look at whether the market is fragmented or consolidating. Several years ago we saw a problem of too many horizontal portals chasing too few ad dollars. This was a recipe for consolidation, and sure enough, the latter half of 1998 and 1999 was characterized by a round of merger activity in the sector. The same theme is likely to play out in the eTailing sector in 2000.

Understand the Competition

- Who are the key players?
- Is the company defining the market or playing catch-up?

Once the market has been assessed, look at the competition within the sector and try to decide who the key players are. From there, look at how the company is competing within its space. Is it defining the market or playing catch-up? Yahoo! pioneered the portal space and set the standard for other companies to follow. Although its model has now been copied by virtually every other portal, the company has still managed to stay ahead of the competition by adding new features and content that keep visitors at its collection of sites.

---

[8] Michael E. Porter, "Competitive Strategy: The Core Concepts," *Competitive Advantage: Creating and Sustaining Superior Performance*, The Free Press, 1985

Key to understanding the competition is understanding some of the competitive forces that define industries[9]. For example, in an etailing environment where the competition is literally "one click away", switching costs for consumers can be very low. On the other hand, in the online brokerage world, the cost (both in time and difficulty) of switching an online trading account is relatively high.

Or, consider barriers to entry. From a technical standpoint, entry barriers can be low on the Internet where virtually anyone with a $400 computer can set up shop. However, from a practical standpoint, entry barriers are often quite high. With over 1.2 billion pages out there in cyberspace, standing out from the crowd is a daunting challenge that often requires significant capital resource in order to be heard above the din.

Does a competitor enjoy a significant cost advantage or a much stronger brand identity? Two online music retailers, CDNow and N2K, Inc., ended up merging when Amazon.com started selling music and CDs. The two smaller companies knew they could not compete separately against Amazon.com with its much stronger brand identity.

In the end, it comes down to defining the competitive environment and understanding how a company intends to maintain a *sustainable competitive advantage*, which brings us to our next section.

Understand the Company

- Does it have first-mover advantage?
- Does it take a jujutsu approach?
- Is customer loyalty high or low?

The next step is to look at the company. Does it have first-mover advantage and can it maintain that lead? I like to borrow a phrase from Michael Porter called *sustainable competitive advantage*. What is the company doing to develop and maintain its competitive advantage over the long run? In the Internet world, first-mover advantage can give a company a significant lead over future competition, but it does not guarantee success. History is full of other companies that were first-to-market but failed to maintain that advantage. Anybody remember Willys Jeeps? It was one of the first makers of Jeeps under contract to the US Army during World War II. Technically, it was a superior Jeep to the other prototypes that were submitted for testing to the army. However, its design was quickly copied by the other competitors and the company went bankrupt just a few years later. Or take Apple. It was the first company to develop a widely popular graphical user interface (GUI) for operating systems with its Macintosh line of computers. Microsoft originally scoffed at, then copied the concept for its Windows operating system and now it is the de facto operating system for PCs. These are examples of companies that enjoyed first-mover advantage but failed to maintain that lead.

---

[9] Although beyond the scope of this book, these competitive forces include bargaining power of customers, bargaining power of suppliers, barriers to entry, threat of new entrants, threat of substitutes and intensity of rivalry within the industry. For those readers, interested in an excellent treatise on competitive strategy, I recommend reading *Competitive Strategy: Techniques for Analyzing Industries and Competitors*, by Michael E. Porter.

I have been involved with the martial arts – karate and jujutsu – for over two decades and have found the principles embodied within them to be very useful in helping to analyze companies. Principles like positioning, adaptability and leverage apply equally well in corporate strategy as they did on the battlefields of ancient Japan and during the conflicts of today.[10]

1. Positioning – as an instructor, one of the first principles that we teach students is to move out of the way of a direct attack. Don't compete head-to-head unless you have the resources to win. Sometimes it is more appropriate to let the opponent overextend himself and then counter. For companies, I look to see how they are positioning themselves vis- à-vis the competition.

2. Adaptability – a conflict is a rapidly changing environment. The student needs to be able to not just react quickly, but be proactive, adapting as the conflict changes. Similarly, companies must be able to adapt quickly to opportunities and threats. Nowhere is this more true than on the Internet where business models are in a constant state of flux, with the competitive landscape changing on an almost daily basis.

3. Leverage – as students progress, they learn to leverage their strengths in order to easily defeat the opponent. With companies, I look to see how they are leveraging their own strengths as well as their competitor's weaknesses.

On the Internet where competition is literally "one-click away", customer loyalty is very important. Granted, there is a certain commoditization with the Web, but branding is still important in building customer value. Branding is the intangible element that brings a customer to a site and keeps him there.

Take Amazon.com and barnesandnoble.com as an example. Although it could be argued that selling books on the Internet is a commodity, Amazon.com has been successful in generating repeat customers of 70% on average through much of 1999. It's nearest competitor, barnesandnoble.com, generated repeat customers that was 10% lower than Amazon.com. This is the power of branding – providing a customer experience that brings visitors or shoppers back to buy again and doing it more successfully than the competition.

The Jujutsu Approach to Corporate Strategy

1. Positioning:
   Is the company outmaneuvering its larger competitor?

2. Adaptability:
   Is the company proactive or reactive to the changing landscape?

3. Leverage:
   Is the company leveraging its strengths and its opponent's weaknesses?

---

[10]Two professors, David Yoffie of Harvard and Michael Cusumano of MIT, coined a phrase called judo strategy, which also takes the principles of the martial arts, judo in this case, and applies it to competitive strategy. The three principles that the two professors discuss are rapid movement, flexibility and leverage. The article, found in the *Harvard Business Review*, January-February 1999, is an excellent study of the Netscape-Microsoft Browser wars in the context of judo strategy.

Look at Revenues (Price/Sales)

- Where are the revenues coming from?
- Is it a one-product company or are revenues diversified?
- Price/sales is a key metric.
- Other metrics include: sales/customer, sales/employee.

After looking at the business model, the next area to look at is revenues. It may come as a surprise, but not all revenues are created equal. In the Internet world, barter revenue is a popular form of revenues, but is it really revenue? Barter revenue, sometimes known as reciprocal ad arrangements, usually involves exchanging ads on one Web site for the right to advertise on another medium, be it TV, print or another Web site. For example, 30% of StarMedia's revenues in 1999 were from reciprocal ad arrangements. Sometimes barter revenue can take an even more interesting form. Prior to theStreet.com's initial public offering (IPO), 17% of the subscriptions to its Web site came from people exchanging frequent flier mileage. Clearly there are differences in the quality of revenues. Cash is more valuable than a "place-an-ad-on-my-site-and-I'll-place-an-ad-on-yours" arrangement where no cash changes hands.

Having said that, barter revenue can be a useful tool for smaller companies looking to increase their exposure and to build market share; however, it is not cash and should not be valued accordingly. StarMedia used barter revenue successfully to build itself into one of the leading Internet portals in Latin America. As the number of regular visitors increased to the site, it could begin charging more for advertising, and the company began scaling back its proportion of barter revenues.

The other question to ask is, Where are revenues coming from? Is the company a "one-product" company or are revenues diversified? In other words, is the company earning money only by selling advertising or is it also attempting to capture a share of ecommerce revenues over its site. With portals, unless the company is a major player, significant ad revenues will be tough to come by. Currently, the 10 largest Web sites account for over 75% of Internet advertising revenues.

Also look at how effectively a company is at leveraging its existing customer base across multiple revenue categories. This is called cross-selling and is a good indicator of the depth of management experience in a company. Amazon.com is a good example of this. Last summer I went to Amazon's Web site to look for an Abbot and Costello video. After quickly searching and finding the video, the site also suggested a vintage Abbot and Costello poster from its auction site.

The most popular metric by far for evaluating Internet companies is the price/sales (P/S) ratio. If there are no earnings, price/earnings (P/E) ratios for Internet companies are meaningless. If there are earnings, management has considerable discretion in determining the amount of earnings to report, leading to sometimes substantial volatility in the earnings numbers. Hence, P/S is useful as a rough substitute. P/S gives a ballpark number for comparative valuations. Calculating the price/sales ratio is relatively easy. Simply take the current market value of a company and divide it by the revenues for the last 12 months.

The P/S ratio has the advantage that it can be used to value companies regardless of earnings and is a better indicator of "top-line" valuation. Unfortunately, by itself it tells us little about a company. What is the correct P/S ratio for Internet stocks, when the multiple can range from 1.5 to 150 or more? More importantly, are Internet stocks overvalued when most traditional stocks trade at 1-2x sales? If both the S&P 500 and the Nasdaq trade at around 2 times trailing revenues, does this make the Pegasus Internet INTDEX™ expensive at a 20x revenue multiple? This brings us to one of the limitations of using P/S as a valuation metric. Different companies have different growth rates, thus P/S gives you only an apples-to-oranges comparison.

Other revenue-based metrics that are useful in making comparable valuations are sales/customer and sales/employee. Sales per customer can tell you which companies can generate the most dollars from each customer. In other words, which companies are the most effective at monetizing the customers or visitors to its site. Sales per employee has the advantage in that it allows you to determine those companies that are more efficient at producing revenues from its key assets, namely its employees. Needless to say, this is an important metric for service-based companies. These two ratios should be used to compare companies only in their respective sectors. Obviously, eBrokers are fundamentally different from eTailers or even iBuilders, and comparative valuations should be made accordingly.

How's the Growth (Price/Sales-to-Growth)?

- How rapidly are revenues growing?
- Is this sustainable?
- Price/sales-to-growth allows apples-to-apples comparison.

Very few industries today are experiencing growth rates in excess of 100% per year. New customers in the form of new Internet users are jumping onto the Net at a rate of 20 every 10 seconds. E-commerce is growing at a rate of $258 million per day. Many Internet companies are doubling their revenues every six months – a phenomenal achievement by any means. The average year-over-year (yoy) growth rate for the universe of 326 Internet companies in 1999 was over 453%.

In the Internet world, most companies are in the early growth phase of their business life cycle where revenues are ramping up extremely quickly. Consider this, it took Amazon.com five years to generate $1.6 billion in sales. With Microsoft, it took 16 years, and Cisco took twelve years.

This is one of the reasons that Internet companies have been afforded much higher valuations than more traditional technology companies.

However, there are three constants in life – death, taxes and the law of large numbers. Growth will eventually slow down in the Internet sector. Otherwise, America Online will be providing Internet access to 80% of all US Web surfers within four years, and Charles Schwab and E*Trade will control all online brokerage accounts by 2003.

Clearly, these growth rates are unsustainable. However, the jury is still out on what the long-term sustainable growth rates are for the various Internet sectors and their respective companies. When Amazon.com first started selling books over the Internet, it was a fairly simple exercise to calculate the size of the online book market based on long-term revenue growth in the traditional book-selling market, then estimating Internet adoption and penetration rates, and calculating Amazon's market share. Now, the company is developing new revenue streams from areas like online auctions, an entire new industry that emerged on the scene just two years ago.

As I mentioned in the previous section, although price/sales is a useful starting metric to use in valuing Internet companies, it suffers from the apples-to-oranges shortfall as it does not adjust for different growth rates. Price/sales -to-growth (PSG) solves this problem by adjusting for the different growth rates, thus allowing apples-to-apples comparison.

To illustrate this, figure 3-2 shows the relationship between the P/S ratios and growth rates for the 50 stocks in the Pegasus Internet Index. As can be seen, the higher the growth rates, the higher the price/sales ratio and vice versa.

The PSG ratio is calculated by taking the price/sales ratio and dividing it by the most recent annual revenue growth rate for the last 12 months.

Now, let's look at a quick example. If we were to make the comparison between the Pegasus Internet Index and the Nasdaq index, the Pegasus Internet Index trades at a 15 times revenue multiple, yet it has been growing at nearly 80% over the past year. On the other hand, the Nasdaq index trades at a 2.1 times revenue multiple, with a 9.5% growth rate. For the INTDEX™, the PSG ratio is 18.7, while the Nasdaq has a PSG ratio of 21.1. On this basis, the INTDEX™ is undervalued relative to the Nasdaq index.

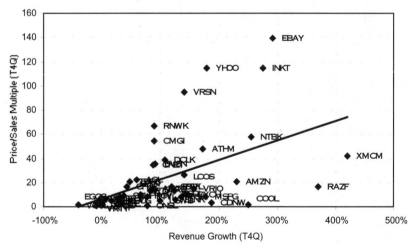

Figure 3-2   Price/Sales and Revenue Growth Valuation Matrix
Source: Pegasus Research Intl

Investing for the Future (Marketing Expense as a % of Sales)

- It's hard to be noticed.
- Market expense as a % of sales.

Before a company can even begin to earn money over the Web, it needs to be able to get people to notice its site. Hanging up a virtual shingle and hoping that customers (or visitors) will stumble by its Internet site doesn't cut it anymore. With an estimated 1.5 billion Web pages out there in cyberspace, the chances of a customer finding an emerging company's virtual storefront or newsroom is like an ant trying to capture the attention of an elephant from the floor of the jungle. Good luck.

In the great land grab of the Internet, companies have been spending aggressively on advertising and marketing in a frantic race to capture the most visitors and turn them into customers. This is a process that I call investing for the future. Companies are "spending for growth", hoping to quickly capture market share and then extend that lead.

As in traditional sectors of the economy, in the Internet space, a few winners will emerge that will dominate each particular sector. Spending aggressively on marketing is one way that companies are hoping to capture customers quickly in order to build scale and dominate their particular arena.

Some of the metrics that are used as indicators of future growth are marketing expenses as a percentage of sales and acquisition costs/customer. This is similar to R&D spending in traditional technology industries. Is this reliable? Not perfectly, but look at Amazon.com and America Online. Both spent heavily on marketing, and both have managed to define their respective industries. Everyone else seems to be playing catch-up.

A Balancing Act: GAAP versus GARP[11]

- Growth is good, but at what cost?
- Growth at any price vs growth at a reasonable price.

It is important to quickly capture market share, but at what cost? In 1998 and early 1999, most companies were following a strategy I call GAAP – "*growth at any price*". The key consideration was to spend heavily on advertising in order to quickly capture market share, and this was exemplified by some companies spending over 100% of their annual revenues on selling and marketing expenses.

One company that stood out was Hotjobs.com, an online job board. The company took the unprecedented move of being one of the first Internet companies to advertise on the Superbowl, paying $1.3 million for a 30-second spot. This may not seem like much compared to some companies like Coca Cola and Procter & Gamble that spend between $1.6 billion to $3.7 billion each year on advertising. However, for this tiny Internet company, the $1.3 million it paid for this one-time exposure was 40% of its annual revenues at that time.

---

[11] Not to be confused with the GAAP acronym used for Generally Accepted Accounting Principles.

As 1999 developed, consumer-centric Internet companies began to switch their focus from GAAP to GARP – or *"growth at a reasonable price"*. It was still important to capture market share, but having built a base of customers, the focus for many of the larger Internet companies began to shift towards maximizing revenues from that customer base. In the end, profits do matter, and it comes down to cash left over at the end of the day.

Investors should focus on how both gross and operating margins are developing for Internet companies and compare it to revenue growth. If a company is spending aggressively and experiencing declining margins with no appreciable growth in revenues, this should be considered a red flag. This is particularly true in more mature areas of the Internet economy (B2C).

A Crazy Little Thing Called Risk

- Can I buy and sell when I want?
- What is the volatility?

Sometimes in the excitement of investing in Internet stocks, risk is one area that is often neglected. Unfortunately, it is perhaps the most important factor to keep in mind with Internet stocks. Because, no matter how you slice it or dice it, investing in Internet stocks is risky business.

Just browsing through the prospectuses (SEC filings) of most of these Internet companies highlights a common theme: 1. they are young companies with a short or limited operating history; 2. their business model is unproven; 3. it is not known if there is a market for their products or services; 4. they are likely to generate considerable losses in the foreseeable future; and 5. the list goes on.

Risk and return are two sides of the same coin. Just as Internet stocks can move up 1,000% to 2,000% in a year, they can easily fall 50% or more in a matter of months, if not days. Small consolation for the investor who may have bought shares in Value America at $50 in April 1999 only to see it fall to $25 a share barely a month later, and close the year out at $5 a share.

Volatility or risk can be measured in one of two ways: in standard deviation of returns or in absolute daily percentage change. Typically I like to refer to volatility in terms of absolute daily percentage change as this is easier for most investors to visualize. In other words, on any particular day, a stock will move up or down X percent on average. And what is the volatility for the average Internet stock? Out of a universe of 326 Internet stocks, the average stock moves up or down 5.27% each day on average. However, it is not unusual to see price swings of 25% or more in one day for many Internet stocks. In fact, from October 1999 through February 2000, more than 85% of all Internet stocks had experienced at least one day of +/- 25% price swings!

One of the reasons Internet stocks have high volatility is because of the small free float that many of these companies have. The free float is the number of shares available to the public and is something I call the tradable market cap. This is effectively what investors can buy and sell into. With Internet stocks – or those sometimes touted as I-stocks – the free float can often be very small, making it difficult to buy or sell the stock when you want without sometimes significant price fluctuations. Remember K-Tel? As soon as the company announced that it was moving to the Web in late 1998, the stock quadrupled. However, with a float of only 1.9 million shares and a price of around $10/share prior to its 400% move, the company had a "tradable" market value of only $20 million. This is peanuts compared to the hundreds of billions of dollars that were flowing into the Internet sector at the time.

It goes without saying, that the lower the free float, the higher the volatility of a stock. And in general, the stocks of companies with low free floats are driven less by any fundamental measures than by capital flows. Sometimes, as in the case of K-Tel, it just takes a press release to drive the stock up leaving individual investors holding the short end of the stick, watching the stock fall on the downside.

How does liquidity measure up for the Internet universe as a whole? The average free float is 33% for the 326 stocks in the Internet universe. In other words, although the total market capitalization for the Internet universe was $1,129 billion at the end of 1999, the "tradable" market value was only $345 billion. Another point to keep in mind is that half of all Internet stocks have a free float of less than 25% of total shares outstanding. This highlights just how illiquid most Internet stocks are. And as far as liquidity is concerned, it boils down to one simple question: Can I buy and sell when I want?. For many Internet stocks, this may not always be the case.

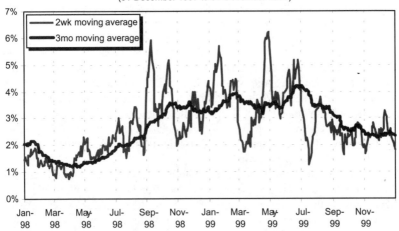

Daily Absolute % Change in the Pegasus INTDEX
(31-December 1997 to 31-December 1999)

Figure 3-3   Daily absolute percentage change in the Pegasus INTDEX™
Source: Pegasus Research Intl

Common Valuation Metrics for Internet Companies

Market-Related Metrics

Market value/sales, also known as price/sales
Market value/customer
Market value/account
Market value/subscriber
Market value/visitor
Market value/page view
Market value/employee
Market value/POP

Revenue-Related Metrics

Revenues/customer
Revenues/account
Revenues/subscriber
Revenues/visitor
Revenues/page view
Revenues/employee

Expense-Related Metrics

Marketing expense/sales
Acquisition costs/customer

Profitability-Related Metrics

Gross margin
Operating margin
Operating margin (excluding marketing expenses)
Return on equity

Risk-Related Metrics

Burn rate
Free float
Absolute daily % change
Annualized standard deviation

4

The Company List

Selecting the list of the top 100 Internet companies for this book was not an easy task by any means. The landscape of the Internet sector was constantly changing with new companies going public, and others merging – sometimes after only a few months on the public markets.

At the beginning of 1999, there were 78 publicly traded Internet companies. By the end of 1999, 250 Internet companies had completed their initial public offerings, bringing the total number of Net companies to 324. And as new companies were coming to the public markets, others were merging or being acquired. In the first half of 1999 alone, Thomson Financial Securities Data reported 617 M&A (merger and acquisition) deals, most of them among private companies.[12] Nevertheless, it has been a challenging and rewarding effort to put together this comprehensive list.

This book is meant as a reference work to Internet investing, providing investors with a guide to the key companies in the emerging Internet sector. The companies are organized alphabetically.

Methodology

There were a number of factors that were considered when constructing the list of the top Internet stocks. Key of course, was that the company generated the majority of its revenues over the Internet, or that its revenues were Internet-related. Although this may seem obvious at first glance, it is not always so. In late 1998, a number of companies were touted as Internet stocks even though their only relationship with the Internet was a press release announcing that they were setting up a Web site.

Others were a little less obvious. Cisco Systems, Dell Computer, Intel and Microsoft could all be considered Net companies as they all have substantial Internet-related components to their business. However, one of the factors that was considered in drawing up the list of the 100 top Internet companies was the correlation of stock returns. In other words, how closely a particular group of stocks move in unison. The higher the correlation, the closer the stocks move to-

---

[12] *The Industry Standard*, August 16-23, 1999.

gether as a group, and vice versa. Under this criteria, Cisco, Dell and the others are not classified as Net stocks.

Another factor that was taken into account was that the companies also had to be publicly traded for several months. This served one important purpose. Flush with cash from the IPO, it enabled us to better evaluate the company's growth strategy. In the glare of the public spotlight, it has not been uncommon for a few potential high-fliers to falter.

Next, only companies with annual revenues in excess of $5 million dollars – with two exceptions – were considered. Anything less than that is just too small for most investors. The companies that have not yet passed that threshold tend to be synonymous with extremely high risk and should in general be avoided by all but the most sophisticated investors, or at least those that can stomach the high volatility. The two exceptions were Akamai and InterTrust with annual revenues of $4.0 million and $1.5 million respectively.

Once that was taken care of, it was time to get down to the number crunching, comb through the SEC filings, talk to the companies, look at the intangible factors that are so important with Internet stocks, and then run the list through a screen and rank them according to four different factors.

- Market value – this is a measure of how successful a company has been in creating shareholder return.
- Revenues – those companies that have generated the most revenues should be the companies that have the greatest chance at being around for the long term.
- Absolute revenue growth – some companies like AOL may no longer be growing at 100% to 200% annually, but it adds $1.7 billion each year in new revenues – more than 50 of the top 100 companies earn in total revenues.
- Percentage revenue growth – the Internet is about scalability, and this measures how successful a company is in quickly ramping up revenues.

It was a long and arduous task to filter through more than 300 Internet companies and create the most comprehensive list of the top 100 Internet stocks for the new millennium. There were many Internet companies that I would have liked to have included, but for one reason or another, they did not make the list. Usually, it was a combination of factors including lower shareholder return, low revenues and/or slower revenue growth than other comparably sized companies.

Finally, the one general caveat that I would add for Internet companies is that most are still losing money – some substantially – and are thus a far riskier investment than traditional companies. A study that Pegasus Research conducted with *Barron's* in March 2000, found that three-quarters of all Internet companies were still operating at a loss. Needless to say, financial risk is an important risk factor that investors should keep in mind when investing in Internet stocks.

And on that note, it's time to introduce the top 100 Internet companies of the new millennium.

The Top 100 Internet Companies

Rank	Company Name	Ticker	Price 20-Apr	Mkt Value[1]	Sales 1999[1]	Sales gr yoy	P/S TTM	PSG TTM	Sector
1	America Online	AOL	60.00	136,906	$5,718.0	48.6%	23.9	49.2	eContent
2	Charles Schwab	SCH	44.00	36,837	$3,944.8	44.2%	9.3	21.1	eFinancials
3	Yahoo! Inc.	YHOO	123.13	66,889	$588.6	140.2%	113.6	81.1	eContent
4	Amazon.com	AMZN	52.38	18,306	$1,639.8	168.9%	11.2	6.6	eTailers
5	priceline.com	PCLN	67.88	11,547	$482.4	1269.0%	23.9	1.9	eTailers
6	TD Waterhouse Group	TWE	20.00	7,528	$1,126.7	59.8%	6.7	11.2	eFinancials
7	Internet Capital Group	ICGE	43.75	11,562	$16.5	427.5%	699.2	163.6	eServices
8	CMGI	CMGI	57.69	16,144	$376.5	212.5%	42.9	20.2	eServices
9	Akamai Technologies	AKAM	86.94	8,091	$4.0	na	2029.8	na	eBusiness
10	ExciteAt Home	ATHM	17.94	6,902	$337.0	601.3%	20.5	3.4	eContent
11	Commerce One	CMRC	55.00	8,513	$33.6	1209.3%	253.7	21.0	eBusiness
12	E*TRADE Group	EGRP	20.13	5,818	$751.5	89.0%	7.7	8.7	eFinancials
13	EarthLink Network	ELNK	14.06	1,662	$670.4	130.7%	2.5	1.9	eAccess
14	Exodus Commun.	EXDS	107.69	19,853	$242.1	359.1%	82.0	22.8	eAccess
15	PSINet	PSIX	23.13	3,642	$554.7	113.6%	6.6	5.8	eAccess
16	USWeb (marchFIRST)	MRCH	24.13	3,494	$510.9	123.5%	6.8	5.5	eServices
17	Scient Corp.	SCNT	43.19	3,050	$99.3	765.7%	30.7	4.0	eServices
18	Homestore.com	HOMS	24.63	1,847	$62.6	na	29.5	3.0	eContent
19	Vignette Corp.	VIGN	52.75	10,071	$89.2	450.4%	112.9	25.1	eBusiness
20	Ariba	ARBA	69.00	13,263	$62.0	321.0%	213.9	66.6	eBusiness
21	Redback Networks	RBAK	63.00	5,561	$64.3	598.2%	86.5	14.5	eBusiness
22	Covad Commun.	COVD	30.69	4,804	$66.5	1148.4%	72.3	6.3	eAccess
23	Chemdex (Ventro)	VNTR	29.69	1,328	$30.8	nm	43.1	na	eBusiness
24	eBay Inc.	EBAY	150.25	19,560	$224.7	160.9%	87.0	54.1	eTailers
25	DoubleClick	DCLK	55.44	6,597	$258.3	86.2%	25.5	29.6	eServices
26	Ask Jeeves	ASKJ	29.38	1,027	$22.0	2652.0%	46.6	1.8	eBusiness
27	MyPoints.com	MYPT	16.75	481	$24.1	1777.1%	19.9	1.1	eServices
28	VeriSign	VRSN	118.50	12,297	$84.8	117.8%	145.0	123.2	eSecurity
29	VerticalNet	VERT	41.63	3,055	$20.8	562.2%	147.2	26.2	eBusiness
30	Critical Path	CPTH	45.13	2,614	$16.2	1701.2%	161.8	9.5	eServices
31	GoTo.com	GOTO	35.88	1,758	$26.8	3161.4%	65.6	2.1	eContent
32	BroadVision	BVSN	36.56	9,081	$115.5	126.9%	78.6	62.0	eBusiness
33	Wit Capital Group	WITC	10.88	953	$48.6	2285.8%	19.6	0.9	eFinancials
34	drugstore.com	DSCM	8.06	419	$34.8	na	12.0	na	eTailers
35	NetZero	NZRO	8.28	868	$24.5	nm	35.5	0.2	eAccess
36	NorthPoint Commun.	NPNT	15.00	1,923	$21.1	2170.7%	90.9	4.2	eAccess
37	ITXC Corp.	ITXC	34.50	1,310	$25.4	1243.8%	51.6	4.1	eServices
38	InterNAP Network Svs.	INAP	34.94	4,751	$12.5	539.8%	379.5	70.3	eBusiness
39	NextCard	NXCD	12.63	651	$26.6	2115.2%	24.5	1.2	eFinancials
40	Rhythms NetConnections	RTHM	20.81	1,608	$11.1	2000.2%	145.0	7.3	eAccess
41	Ameritrade Holding	AMTD	16.00	2,794	$327.1	102.7%	8.5	8.3	eFinancials
42	iXL Enterprises	IIXL	20.00	1,437	$218.3	237.1%	6.6	2.8	eServices
43	Interliant	INIT	19.50	922	$47.1	860.5%	19.6	2.3	eServices
44	USinternetworking	USIX	21.44	2,065	$35.5	762.0%	58.2	7.6	eServices
45	InterTrust Tech.	ITRU	32.88	2,691	$1.5	913.8%	1746.4	191.1	eSecurity
46	Sapient Corp.	SAPE	66.25	3,851	$276.8	67.9%	13.9	20.5	eServices
47	Kana Communications	KANA	40.00	2,432	$14.1	499.4%	173.0	34.6	eBusiness
48	E.piphany	EPNY	72.25	2,334	$19.2	468.0%	121.7	26.0	eBusiness
49	Network Solutions	NSOL	128.19	9,277	$220.8	135.8%	42.0	30.9	eServices
50	Portal Software	PRSF	45.38	7,176	$103.0	286.2%	69.7	24.3	eBusiness

1 Market value and sales in US$ millions, sales for trailing four quarters or calendar year 1999.

The ranking was compiled based on year-end 1999 data.

Rank	Company Name	Ticker	Price 20-Apr	Mkt Value[1]	Sales 1999[1]	Sales gr yoy	P/S TTM	PSG TTM	Sector
51	F5 Networks	FFIV	52.75	1,115	$44.3	557.1%	25.2	4.5	eBusiness
52	AppNet	APNT	20.06	681	$112.3	535.7%	6.1	1.1	eBusiness
53	InfoSpace.com	INSP	57.56	12,467	$36.8	282.8%	338.4	119.7	eContent
54	Phone.com	PHCM	67.69	4,662	$31.6	486.0%	147.6	30.4	eBusiness
55	eToys	ETYS	6.00	723	$134.1	457.4%	5.4	1.2	eTailers
56	Vitria Technology	VITR	42.75	5,408	$31.5	313.5%	171.5	54.7	eBusiness
57	Lycos	LCOS	36.06	3,964	$203.7	125.3%	19.5	15.5	eContent
58	Verio	VRIO	27.63	2,175	$258.3	114.1%	8.4	7.4	eAccess
59	EarthWeb	EWBX	10.50	106	$31.1	827.1%	3.4	0.4	eContent
60	uBid	UBID	14.94	174	$204.9	324.9%	0.8	0.3	eTailers
61	Copper Mountain Ntwk	CMTN	76.06	3,641	$112.7	416.6%	32.3	7.8	eServices
62	Inktomi Corp.	INKT	129.13	9,620	$98.8	232.7%	97.4	41.9	eBusiness
63	RealNetworks	RNWK	37.69	5,818	$131.2	97.7%	44.3	45.4	eServices
64	Barnesandnoble.com	BNBN	8.56	259	$202.6	227.6%	1.3	0.6	eTailers
65	Check Point Software	CHKP	161.69	12,078	$219.6	54.7%	55.0	100.6	eSecurity
66	About.com	BOUT	27.38	453	$27.0	624.4%	16.8	2.7	eContent
67	Digital Island	ISLD	32.38	2,089	$18.6	440.3%	112.1	25.4	eBusiness
68	PurchasePro.com	PPRO	32.00	997	$6.0	260.3%	165.7	63.7	eBusiness
69	Razorfish	RAZF	18.50	1,765	$170.2	102.9%	10.4	10.1	eServices
70	FreeMarkets	FMKT	59.81	2,122	$20.9	167.7%	101.6	60.6	eBusiness
71	S1 Corporation	SONE	44.94	2,293	$92.9	284.2%	24.7	8.7	eBusiness
72	CheckFree Holdings	CKFR	33.56	1,762	$275.7	14.1%	6.4	45.4	eBusiness
73	DLJdirect	DIR	10.44	1,071	$238.1	101.9%	4.5	4.4	eFinancials
74	LookSmart Ltd.	LOOK	17.50	1,538	$48.9	456.2%	31.5	6.9	eContent
75	Go2Net	GNET	51.75	1,582	$33.8	293.5%	46.7	15.9	eContent
76	Engage Technologies	ENGA	24.00	2,600	$32.8	406.5%	79.2	19.5	eServices
77	24/7 Media	TFSM	18.94	492	$90.0	331.3%	5.5	1.6	eServices
78	Healtheon/WebMD	HLTH	18.94	3,416	$102.1	109.2%	33.4	30.6	eBusiness
79	CNET	CNET	38.06	3,222	$112.3	95.5%	28.7	30.0	eContent
80	RSA Security	RSAS	50.88	2,023	$218.1	27.3%	9.3	34.0	eSecurity
81	NBC Internet	NBCI	20.19	1,137	$35.6	327.8%	32.0	9.8	eContent
82	Quest Software	QSFT	47.25	4,029	$70.9	103.7%	56.8	54.8	eBusiness
83	Agency.com	ACOM	18.50	647	$87.8	231.9%	7.4	3.2	eServices
84	NaviSite	NAVI	39.88	2,240	$21.7	257.3%	103.1	40.1	eServices
85	Silknet Software	SILK	--	--	$22.4	161.9%	--	--	eBusiness
86	Concentric Network	CNCX	40.94	2,112	$147.1	77.6%	14.4	18.5	eAccess
87	Prodigy Commun.	PRGY	12.38	799	$189.0	38.9%	4.2	10.9	eAccess
88	StarMedia Network	STRM	20.75	1,349	$20.1	248.9%	67.1	27.0	eContent
89	Entrust Technologies	ENTU	42.63	2,480	$85.2	73.9%	29.1	39.3	eSecurity
90	ZDNet	ZDZ	12.56	943	$104.2	85.6%	9.1	10.6	eContent
91	MarketWatch.com	MKTW	16.50	233	$24.9	254.8%	9.3	3.7	eContent
92	Retek	RETK	19.63	913	$69.2	25.7%	13.2	51.4	eBusiness
93	Expedia	EXPE	16.75	653	$57.9	119.5%	11.3	9.4	eTailers
94	Cobalt Group	CBLT	10.13	171	$23.3	272.9%	7.3	2.7	eServices
95	SportsLine.com	SPLN	22.13	574	$60.3	97.3%	9.5	9.8	eContent
96	Open Market	OMKT	9.00	415	$83.0	28.6%	5.0	17.5	eBusiness
97	Verity	VRTY	26.63	832	$72.5	37.4%	11.5	30.7	eBusiness
98	Cylink Corp.	CYLK	11.63	354	$59.7	39.5%	5.9	15.0	eSecurity
99	AXENT Technologies	AXNT	16.75	482	$112.8	11.7%	4.3	36.6	eSecurity
100	Spyglass	SPYG	40.63	694	$32.1	41.3%	21.7	52.5	eBusiness

1 Market value and sales in US$ millions, sales for trailing four quarters or calendar year 1999.

The ranking was compiled based on year-end 1999 data.

About.com, Inc.

http://www.about.com   eContent

Address:
220 E. 42nd St., 24th Fl.   Phone: 212.849.2000
New York, NY 10017   Fax: 212.818.1376
Management:
Chairman & CEO: Scott P. Kurnit
President & COO: William C. Day
CFO: Todd B. Sloan

Description

It's all about mining the Web for information. About.com originally started as General Internet in June 1996, changed its name to the MiningCo. in December 1998 and changed it again to About.com shortly after going public in March 1999. What sets About.com apart from the other content sites and search directories is its collection of 700 topic-specific (i.e. vertical) Web sites aggregated in 30 different channels, each overseen by a human guide. These human guides mine the Web for interesting and relevant links to add to their niche channels, as well as creating content and running communities. Revenues are generated from advertising and sponsorship fees. Barter transactions accounted for less than 10% of total revenues in 1999.

Opportunities

- The money spent on Internet advertising is expected to grow significantly in the next few years, from $2.9 billion in 1999 to more than $12.5 billion in 2003 according to estimates by Pegasus Research. Internet advertising has grown so quickly since its humble beginnings in 1995 that in 1998, it surpassed outdoor advertising in total revenues.
- About.com has been one of the fastest growing Web properties in terms of traffic or unique visitors. In the last quarter of 1999, traffic grew over 50% to 12.6 million visitors. The steady climb in popularity has moved About.com up to the 9th most visited Web property in December 1999 from 20th in June and 29th in February 1999.
- About.com is planning to capture revenues as a faciliator of ecommerce, thus leveraging its core base of loyal visitors.

Challenges

- The portal or eContent space is a hyper-competitive environment with low barriers to entry. If About.com fails to differentiate itself from the myriad of other portal sites, traffic growth could decline, leading to lower advertising revenue growth. It competes for ad dollars against Yahoo!, Microsoft's MSN, AOL, Lycos and other general interest eContent sites.
- Because About.com relies on human guides to provide it with its content, content and page growth (which is important in order to create inventory to sell ads) is tied to an extent to the growth in human guides.

The Bottom Line

It's all about the human touch. About.com has been successful in differentiating itself from the dozens if not hundreds of other content sites by using human guides to filter and select information and links on its sites. This is a strategy that has paid off well for About.com, as reflected in the strong traffic growth it has witnessed in 1999, rising to ninth place in the Media Metrix rankings . Looking ahead, the key issue for About.com is whether it can continue to capture mindshare in a competitive environment dominated by AOL, Yahoo! and a host of other hungry portals. Differentiation is the key to long-term success, and About.com has been able to successfully achieve that.

Key Statistics	BOUT
Market Cap (4/20/00):	$453.4m
Free Float:	59.8%
IPO Date:	3/24/99
Offer Price:	$25.00
Price (4/20/00):	$27.38
52 week high:	$105.81
52 week low:	$19.50
Volatility: (avg. daily % ch)	6.7%
Price/Sales:	16.8
Price/Sales-Growth:	2.7

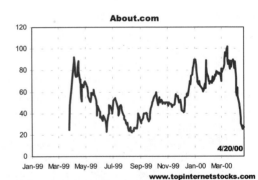

About.com

www.topinternetstocks.com

Annual Financial Data ($ m)	12/1994	12/1995	12/1996	12/1997	12/1998	12/1999
Revenues	--	--	--	0.39	3.72	26.96
Operating Profit	--	--	-2.38	-8.34	-14.89	-58.47
Net Income	--	--	-2.44	-8.64	-15.58	-55.10
Unique Visitors (m)	--	--	--	--	--	12.61
Key Ratios:						
Gross Margin	--	--	--	-393.9%	-13.3%	34.7%
Operating Margin	--	--	--	-2133.2%	-400.1%	-216.9%
Net Margin	--	--	--	-2209.7%	-418.5%	-204.3%
Marketing as % of Revenues	--	--	--	450.4%	212.0%	180.2%

Agency.com Ltd

http://www.agency.com   eServices

Address:
20 Exchange Place   Phone: 212.358.2600
New York, NY 10005   Fax: 212.358.2604
Management:
Chairman & CEO: Chan Suh
Co-founder & CCO: Kyle Shannon
CFO: Charles Dickson

Description

Agency.com may be one of the newest additions to the public list of interactive agencies, but it is an old hat in this area. The company was originally launched in February 1995 by co-founders Chan Suh and Kyle Shannon and grew quickly through a combination of acquisitions and internal growth before going public in December 1999. Agency.com provides strategic consulting, interactive design, and Web integration, taking the clients from concept to launch and operation of their Internet businesses. The company has over 200 clients including British Airways, Compaq, FT Group, Sprint and Unilever. Its ten largest clients accounted for more than 42% of total revenues in 1999 with British Airways accounting for roughly 13%.

Opportunities

- IDC estimates that the Internet professional services market will grow tenfold over the next few years to $78 billion by 2003 from $7.8 billion in 1998. Driving this growth is corporate America's rush to develop and roll out their eBusiness strategies.
- Agency.com has been aggressively expanding overseas through a series of strategic acquisitions in Europe and investments in Asia. Both these regions are young in terms of their Internet adoption, presenting faster growth opportunities than in the US.
- The company has recently launched its broadband practice based in Europe, where interactive TV is further ahead than in the US. Agency.com is one of the few firms that can offer broadband design and integration.

Challenges

- The Internet professional services arena is very competitive, populated with hundreds of "me too" firms offering virtually the same services. These can range from smaller, one-man garage shops to aggressive competitors like Razorfish, Scient and Sapient and large consulting firms like Andersen Consulting and PricewaterhouseCoopers.
- Internet services, or what the *Industry Standard* calls the iBuilders, is not as scalable as other Internet business models. Revenue growth is largely a function of billable employee growth.

The Bottom Line

Agency.com represents the new breed of interactive ad agencies turned Web-consultant/integrator/partner. It is one of the faster growing companies in the iBuilders arena with a strong international presence. Although the market that Agency.com operates in is fiercely competitive with a host of "me too" competitors, the firm has been able to successfully differentiate itself from the rest of the pack. This is evident both in the strong revenue growth the company has been experiencing and its blue-chip roster of clients. In addition, Agency.com's growth strategy in Europe and Asia should help the company establish an early market leadership position in two markets that are just beginning to develop and offer growth rates substantially higher than in the US.

Key Statistics	ACOM
Market Cap (4/20/00):	$647.4m
Free Float:	26.9%
IPO Date:	12/08/99
Offer Price:	$26.00
Price (4/20/00):	$18.50
52 week high:	$98.00
52 week low:	$14.25
Volatility:	16.0%
(avg. daily % ch)	
Price/Sales:	7.4
Price/Sales-Growth:	3.2

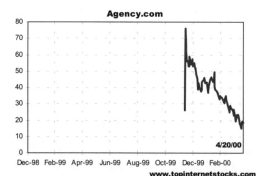

www.topinternetstocks.com

Annual Financial Data ($ m)	12/1994	12/1995	12/1996	12/1997	12/1998	12/1999
Revenues	--	2.16	6.10	12.98	26.45	87.79
Operating Profit	--	0.87	2.86	2.06	-3.05	-9.82
Net Income	--	0.79	1.50	1.18	-2.48	-12.88
Customers	--	--	--	--		
Key Ratios:						
Gross Margin	--	69.9%	63.6%	52.2%	39.8%	48.2%
Operating Margin	--	40.1%	47.0%	15.8%	-11.5%	-11.2%
Net Margin	--	36.6%	24.6%	9.1%	-9.4%	-14.7%
Marketing as % of Revenues	--	5.5%	--	4.1%	2.3%	5.3%

Akamai Technologies, Inc

http://www.akamai.com   eBusiness

Address:
201 Broadway   Phone: 617.250.3000
Cambridge, MA 02139   Fax: 617.250.3001
Management:
Chairman & CEO: George H. Conrades
President & COO: Paul Sagan
CFO: Timothy Weller

Description

Akamai's business is speed, speeding up the Net that is. Akamai, pronounced "AH-kuh-my" (Hawaiian for intelligent, clever or cool), grew out of a research project that the founders, Tom Leighton and Daniel Lewin developed at MIT in 1995. The company was launched in August 1998 and went public in October 1999. Akamai's technology speeds the distribution of content over the Internet through a series of 1,700 local servers and algorithms that can identify and deliver content that is closest to a particular user. The company's flagship service, FreeFlow, is designed to reduce the impact of "flash crowds", one of the major bottlenecks on the Internet. Flash crowds are caused by infrequent, but sudden demand for particular sites (i.e. 100 million Superbowl fans descending on the Victorias' Secret Web site during a commercial break). Customers include Apple Computer, Britannica.com, Yahoo!, VerticalNet and CNN Interactive.

Opportunities

- As more people log on to the Net, and the Internet becomes more bandwidth intensive, bottlenecks will become more of an issue. Akamai's technology can double the delivery speed of Web content to Net users, and in some cases improve speeds tenfold. Akamai signed up Yahoo! as a customer after tests showed that the FreeFlow service improved Yahoo!'s performance by 50%.

- Akamai is moving into the application delivery market with its new EdgeAdvantage service. The new service is designed to help speed the access and delivery of a wide variety of application processes including e-commerce transactions and targeted advertising.

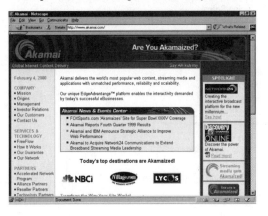

Challenges

- Akamai competes in the Web caching market against more established competitors such as Inktomi, Network Appliance and Exodus. New entrants are quickly moving in, and similar to the development in the Web search engine arena, companies can come onto the scene virtually overnight with a better technology and quickly capture market share.
- Apple Computer represents roughly 45% of Akamai's revenues, which represents a potentially substantial risk. Needless to say, if Apple were to terminate the contract, Akamai's revenues growth could be slowed substantially.
- Akamai is just now beginning to widely deploy its technology, and its concept is unproven under heavy Web traffic conditions. If Akamai cannot effectively manage the unanticipated strong demand for its customer's Web sites under heavy loads, it could lose those customer relationships.

The Bottom Line

When it comes to speeding up the Internet, "AH-kuh-my" is cool. Its technology is quickly being adopted as the solution for improving Web site loading times, one of the key complaints of the Internet. It also helps that the company has such heavyweight partners as Cisco and Microsoft. However, the playing field, while still relatively young, is quickly becoming crowded. In addition, Akamai is also competing against established players in the network caching area. But for now, it happens to be the speed demon of the Internet.

Key Statistics	AKAM
Market Cap (4/20/00):	$8,091m
Free Float:	9.8%
IPO Date:	10/29/99
Offer Price:	$26.00
Price (4/20/00):	$86.94
52 week high:	$345.50
52 week low:	$56.62
Volatility: (avg. daily % ch)	15.5%
Price/Sales:	2,029.8
Price/Sales-Growth:	--

Akamai

www.topinternetstocks.com

Annual Financial Data ($ m)	12/1994	12/1995	12/1996	12/1997	12/1998	12/1999
Revenues	--	--	--	--	--	3.99
Operating Profit	--	--	--	--	-0.90	-56.44
Net Income	--	--	--	--	-0.89	-57.56
Customers	--	--	--	--	--	227
Key Ratios:						
Gross Margin	--	--	--	--	--	-125.9%
Operating Margin	--	--	--	--	--	-1415.9%
Net Margin	--	--	--	--	--	-1444.1%
Marketing as % of Revenues	--	--	--	--	--	--

Amazon.com

http://www.amazon.com   eTailer

Address:
1200 12th Ave. South, Ste 1200   Phone: 206.266.1000
Seattle, WA 98144   Fax: 206.266.6996
Management:
Chairman & CEO: Jeffrey P. Bezos
President & COO: Joseph Galli
CFO: Warren Jenson

Description

Amazon.com has been one of the classic success stories of the new Internet era. The company set up its shingle in cyberspace in July 1995, with the goal of selling books over a new medium called the World Wide Web. In the five short years Amazon.com has been operating on the Internet, it has grown out of a garage to be the third largest bookseller in the US with revenues of over $1.6 billion in 1999. In late 1998, the company set its sights on other retailing categories, offering CDs and videos – where it quickly grew to number one – toys, electronic games, auctions and recently, home improvement. Amazon.com currently has more than 17 million customers in over 65 countries, with 20% of its revenues coming from outside the United States. In addition, more than 200,000 other Web sites are part of the company's associate program, selling books and other items for Amazon.com.

Amazon.com has also built up a family of Web sites through strategic investments in other online retailers with the goal of providing a greater selection and shopping experience for online consumers. These partner sites include: drugstore.com, an online pharmacy that also sells health, beauty and personal care items; HomeGrocer.com, an Internet grocer and home-delivery service; Pets.com, an online pet supply company; luxury goods eTailer, Ashford.com; living.com, a site for home furniture, lightings, linens and more; and Gear.com, an online sporting-goods company.

Rapid growth has not come without a price. The company has yet to generate a profit, opting to spend heavily in order to quickly capture market share. In 1999, the company posted a net loss of $605.8 million, with the bulk of those losses attributable to marketing expenses. During the year, Amazon.com spent more than $413 million on sales and marketing expenses in order to build its brand and grow its customer base.

Opportunities

- Book selling on the Internet has often been defined as a commodity business where the barriers to entry are low. Granted, hanging a virtual shingle is no more complicated than setting up a Web site for a few dollars, yet the ability to attract and keep customers at a virtual store is often difficult to do with the competition just a "mouse click away". Amazon.com has proven that it has the ability to do just that. The company's site is intuitive and easy to navigate. Other features on Amazon.com's site are also targeted at building a base of loyal customers. Reviews, recommendations, personalization and e-mail notifications have helped the company distinguish itself from the pack. This is reflected by the percentage of loyal, or repeat customers which stands at 73% compared to 66% for its closest competitor, Barnesandnoble.com.

- However, building a loyal base of customers is only half the battle, the other half is maximizing revenues from each customer that shops at its site. This is another area where Amazon.com is setting the standard for online retailers. Through intelligent software, the company can successfully cross-sell merchandise from the different product categories.

- Amazon.com is positioning itself to be the Wal-Mart of online retailing, in essence to be the first stop for consumers as they go online to shop. Recent acquisitions highlight this strategy, and more are sure to come as the company positions itself to offer everything from books to pet supplies, drugs, and even hammers.

Challenges

- Amazon.com faces stiff competition from other Internet retailers as well as traditional retailers moving into the online world. Although being first in the marketplace is a strong competitive advantage, it does not guarantee that advantage.

- As the competition intensifies and competitors become more successful at carving away at Amazon.com's pedestal, the one area that could be affected is gross margins. More competition invariably means lower prices for consumers and tighter margins for retailers. With profits already well in the red zone, any pressure on gross margins could magnify itself on the company's bottom-line, increasing losses further.

- The major challenge for Amazon.com is profitability. Since the company began selling books on the Internet in 1995, it has an accumulated deficit of more than $882 million. In 1999 alone, the company posted a net loss of more than $605 million. Eventually, the company will need to scale back expenses if it expects to generate profits. In the GAAP vs GARP[13] debate, the pendulum for Amazon.com will need to shift towards GARP. Investors want to see a glimmer of light at the end of the profitability tunnel.

- As Amazon.com moves from books to consumer electronics and other larger ticket items, the challenge will be to manage customer returns smoothly. With books and CDs, returns are less of an issue as return rates are typically very low. However, other items can see return rates running from 5% to as high as 20%. This could put further pressure on margins

---

[13] GAAP is "growth at any price" and GARP is "growth at a reasonable price".

The Bottom Line

Amazon.com understands branding on the Web better then most companies operating in cyberspace. Branding is about building customer value, bringing shoppers to your door and monetizing that traffic. This is where Amazon.com has taken the lead and is setting the standard for other companies to follow.

Amazon.com's move into other retailing categories is a bold strategic move that can also help the company improve gross margins. Selling CDs and books at a discount is a low margin business yet a great way to build a following of loyal, repeat customers and track their shopping habits. The next step is to use the personalization features on its Web site and its detailed customer database to suggest or recommend higher-margin items such as toys, drugs, health care products, etc.

Eventually Amazon.com will need to generate a profit – that is a sad fact of life for many Internet companies. Fortunately, online retailing – as Amazon.com is defining it – is a scalable business with potentially attractive profit margins. In the last quarter of 1999, Amazon.com did reach profitability in its online book business, giving a hint that it is beginning to focus on profitability. As the company reaches market dominance in other retailing categories, look for it to slowly ramp back marketing and infrastructure costs leading to more of a GARP approach.

When it comes to online retailing, few companies can be expected to replicate Amazon.com's success. If Amazon can bring profitability into the picture, the company will be the standard bearer for the retailing industry for years to come.

Key Statistics	AMZN
Market Cap (4/20/00):	$18,306m
Free Float:	39.0%
IPO Date:	5/15/97
Offer Price (adj):	$1.50
Price (4/20/00):	$52.38
52 week high:	$113.00
52 week low:	$40.81
Volatility: (avg. daily % ch)	5.0%
Price/Sales:	11.2
Price/Sales-Growth:	6.6

Amazon.com

www.topinternetstocks.com

Annual Financial Data ($ m)	12/1994	12/1995	12/1996	12/1997	12/1998	12/1999
Sales	--	0.51	15.75	147.79	609.82	1,639.84
Operating Profit	-0.05	-0.30	-6.44	-32.60	-109.06	-605.76
Net Income	-0.05	-0.30	-6.25	-31.02	-124.55	-719.97
Customers (m)	--	--	0.18	1.50	6.20	16.90
Key Ratios:						
Gross Margin	--	20.0%	22.0%	19.5%	21.9%	17.7%
Operating Margin	--	-59.5%	-40.9%	-22.1%	-10.3%	-36.9%
Net Margin	--	-59.3%	-39.7%	-21.0%	-20.4%	-43.9%
Marketing as % of Sales	--	39.1%	38.7%	27.4%	21.8%	25.2%

America Online, Inc

http://www.aol.com   eContent

Address:
22000 AOL Way   Phone: 703.265.1000
Dulles, VA 20166   Fax: 703.265.1101
Management:
Chairman & CEO: Stephen M. Case
President & COO: Robert W. Pittman
CFO: J. Michael Kelly

Description

America Online is to the Internet economy what Intel is to the PC industry. What started out as a small online service, eclipsed by CompuServe and Prodigy in the early 1990's, quickly grew to be the number one online service with a customer base of more than 23 million subscribers by year-end 1999. Along the way to ISP domination, AOL bought its early rival, CompuServe. But, more than just an online service, America Online and its family of Web properties is also the number one destination spot on the Internet for 54 million Web surfers.

AOL is the grandfather of Internet stocks, starting out as a proprietary online service called Q-Link back in 1985. Up until 1991, when it changed its name to America Online, the company had fewer than 180,000 members. It wasn't until 1994 that AOL broke the one million member mark. Since then, the company has grown its subscriber base at over 46% compounded annually to 23 million members at the end of 1999. Key to the company's strong growth has been its marketing strategy of blanketing the United States first with floppy disks, then with CDs.

AOL has been busy extending its reach, buying Mirabilis and its instant messaging service, ICQ, in 1997. ICQ has grown quickly and now has more than 53 million users, sending more messages over its network than the US post office sends in first-class mail. In early 1999, AOL acquired Netscape Communications in a move that further extended its reach into cyberspace.

In January 2000, America Online and Time Warner announced plans to join forces in order to create a new media powerhouse combining AOL's Internet experience and consumer savvy with Time Warner's content and broadband platform. The merger, if approved by shareholders, should close by year-end 2000.

Roughly 65% of AOL's revenues come from providing Internet access. The other 35% is split between advertising, e-commerce and enterprise solutions (through Netscape). America Online went public in March 1992 and made headlines in 1998 when it became the first Internet stock to be listed on the New York Stock Exchange.

Opportunities

- America Online has a compelling business model: build a strong customer base, then leverage that base to generate multiple revenue streams. Imagine it this way: AOL owns a cyber-town on the entrance to a busy freeway and it collects a toll from residents for access to that town and the nearby freeway (subscriptions), charges merchants rent to set up shop (advertising), and collects a percentage of anything sold in that town (ecommerce).
- With 54 million people visiting its various Web properties, AOL can afford to charge top dollar in advertising fees. First it was $25 million, then $75 million, then $150 million, and then last February, First USA agreed to pay $300 million over five years to advertise on AOL's site. As AOL continues to grow and be the destination of choice for Web users, the company could see a $500 million deal within the next year.
- America Online is beginning to focus on international markets as a source of subscriber growth. AOL Europe has grown to over 3.1 million members and has become one of the largest ISPs in Europe. The company has also teamed up with the Cisneros Group in entering Latin America, and it is working with Mitsui and Nikkei to offer services in Japan. In addition, AOL invested in China.com, a Chinese language portal site.
- Broadband access will soon be the access of choice for consumers. In the US. AOL has been preparing for broadband access on three fronts: forming strategic partnerships with local telephone companies to offer high-speed (DSL) Internet service, teaming with Hughes Electronics to develop Internet services delivered by satellites, and aggressively lobbying on Capitol Hill to force open access of cable systems.
- The planned merger between America Online and Time Warner would give AOL a strong platform to speed broadband penetration in the US. Time Warner through its cable properties, controls 20% of the US cable market.

Challenges

- One of AOL's greatest successes is also one of its greatest challenges. With the law of large numbers setting in, subscriber growth is slowing in the US. From 230% annual growth in the mid 1990's, AOL's membership growth over the past year has slowed to around 50%. In international markets, AOL does not have the same strong brand recognition as in the US, and local competition can be strong. In Europe, AOL has been overshadowed in the UK by FreeServe and by T-Online in Germany. In Latin America, AOL is up against stiff competition in Brazil from UOL, IG.com and the local banks that are also beginning to offer Internet access to their customers.

- Free Internet access is another issue that AOL is facing. It has been gaining ground in Europe and has recently jumped the pond with AltaVista, Kmart, NetZero and others offering free access in the US. If free Internet access does become as popular in the US as it is in Europe, it could slow or even erode AOL's dial-up subscriber growth.
- The AOL/Time Warner merger could present substantial integration risk for America Online. Although AOL has been successful in integrating a number of smaller acquisitions into its fold, larger acquisitions such as Netscape, have proved a bit more challenging. If AOL runs into difficulty integrating Time Warner, revenue and profitability growth could slow.

The Bottom Line

America Online is the blue chip of Internet stocks and one of the longest surviving Internet companies. The company's greatest strength is its established customer base and its ability to leverage that base across multiple revenue streams. In addition to generating subscription revenues, which provide a stable source of cash flow from its 23 million-plus subscribers, AOL also generates significant advertising and ecommerce revenues as the leading destination on the Web.

Although AOL has been entering foreign markets, including Europe and Latin America, it is up against stiff competition from better established local players, and it will likely enjoy only moderate success in these markets. The planned AOL/Time Warner merger if successfully implemented, could speed AOL's broadband plans, giving the company a new source of accelerated revenue growth and establishing AOL as the new model for media companies well into the new millennium.

Key Statistics	AOL
Market Cap (4/20/00):	$136,906m
Free Float:	98.0%
IPO Date:	3/19/92
Offer Price (adj):	$0.09
Price (4/20/00):	$60.00
52 week high:	$95.81
52 week low:	$38.47
Volatility: (avg. daily % ch)	3.5%
Price/Sales:	23.9
Price/Sales-Growth:	49.2

America Online

www.topinternetstocks.com

Annual Financial Data ($ m)	6/1995	6/1996	6/1997	6/1998	6/1999	12/1999*
Revenues	425.00	1,323.00	2,197.00	3,091.00	4,777.00	3,088.00
Operating Profit	-41.00	64.00	-485.00	-120.00	458.00	746.00
Net Income	-55.00	35.00	-485.00	-74.00	762.00	455.00
Subscribers (m)	3.00	6.20	8.60	14.50	19.60	23.00
Key Ratios:						
Gross Margin	44.4%	46.1%	47.1%	41.4%	44.4%	47.5%
Operating Margin	-9.6%	4.8%	-22.1%	-3.9%	9.6%	24.2%
Net Margin	-12.9%	2.6%	-22.1%	-2.4%	16.0%	14.7%
Marketing as % of Revenues	0.0%	16.6%	27.7%	20.2%	16.9%	15.2%

* Six months ended 12/31/99

Ameritrade Holding Corporation

http://www.ameritrade.com   eFinancials

Address:
4211 South 102nd Street
Omaha, NE 68127

Phone: 402.331.7856
Fax: 402.597.7789

Management:
Chairman & Co-CEO: J. Joe Ricketts
Co-CEO: Thomas K. Lewis
Senior Finance Manager: William J Gerber

Description

Ameritrade has been at the forefront of the discount brokerage business,
opening its doors back in 1971 as First Omaha Securities. With the advent of the
Internet, the company jumped onto the Web, opening its Web site in 1994. Ameritrade went public in March 1997, and in 1998, began advertising heavily to capture market share, spending $43 million to promote its low-cost $8 commissions
for online trades. At the end of 1999, Ameritrade was the third largest discount
online broker with 686,000 online accounts and $31.6 billion in customer assets.
The company's retail brokerage services are provided under the Ameritrade and
Accutrade brands. In addition, Ameritrade also provides clearing services for securities brokers. The company recently launched its *OnMoney* personal finance
portal which provides content, tools and services in four channels: investment,
banking, financial planning and insurance. *OnMoney* is expected to generate revenues through advertising and transaction fees.

Opportunities

- Online trading has taken the investment world by storm, with more than 8
  million investors buying and selling stocks online. Within four years, 60% of
  all investors, or 25 million people, are expected to be trading on the Internet.
- With its $8 trades, Ameritrade has been successful at establishing itself as the
  leading deep discount on-
  line broker.
- Ameritrade is repositioning
  itself not just as a deep discount online broker, but
  also as a financial portal
  with its *OnMoney* site.
  This should help diversify
  revenues away from volatile trading commissions.

Challenges

- The online discount brokerage industry is a very competitive environment with more than 160 brokers competing for online investors. Customer acquisition costs within the industry have been moving up while trading commissions have been trending down. This creates pressure on margins and profitability.
- With the strong growth in customer accounts, Ameritrade has suffered from system outages and the inability of its customers to trade during busy market periods. This could potentially lead to customer losses and class-action lawsuits if not addressed.
- Ameritrade's customers trade more actively than either Charles Schwab's or E*Trade's customers. Most of this activity is in volatile Internet and small cap stocks, which are more vulnerable to any market corrections or downturns.

The Bottom Line

Ameritrade has defined the deep discount online brokerage industry with its $8 commission trades. The company has also been one of the fastest growing eBrokers, with revenues and customer accounts growing 51% and 78% annually over the last three years. Heading forward, the competition is intensifying, which in turn, will put pressure on margins and profitability. The challenge will be to see how well the company can improve its technology to handle heavy trading activity. Notwithstanding the challenges, Ameritrade has a strong chance of remaining one of the leading eBrokers heading the online investor revolution.

Key Statistics	AMTD
Market Cap (4/20/00):	$2,794m
Free Float:	24.5%
IPO Date:	3/04/97
Offer Price (adj):	$1.25
Price (4/20/00):	$16.00
52 week high:	$48.12
52 week low:	$12.31
Volatility: (avg. daily % ch)	6.4%
Price/Sales:	8.5
Price/Sales-Growth:	8.3

www.topinternetstocks.com

Annual Financial Data ($ m)	9/1994	9/1995	9/1996	9/1997	9/1998	9/1999
Net Revenues	27.45	35.02	54.34	77.24	134.92	268.35
Operating Profit	7.45	10.83	18.42	21.43	0.53	18.11
Net Income	4.83	7.03	11.16	13.82	0.21	11.54
Active Accounts (m)	0.02	0.04	0.05	0.10	0.31	0.56
Key Ratios:						
Gross Margin	--	--	--	--	--	--
Operating Margin	27.1%	30.9%	33.9%	27.7%	0.4%	6.7%
Net Margin	17.6%	20.1%	20.5%	17.9%	0.2%	4.3%
Marketing as % of Revenues	21.8%	13.8%	13.9%	18.1%	32.3%	22.3%

AppNet, Inc.

http://www.appnet.com   eServices

Address:
6707 Democracy Blvd.   Phone: 301.493.8900
Suite 1000, Bethesda, MD 20817   Fax: 301.581.2488
Management:
Chairman, President & CEO: Ken S. Bajaj
Executive VP, Operations   Toby Tobaccowala
CFO: Jack Pearlstein

Description

AppNet brings the power of eBusiness to companies. Founded in November 1997, the company provides end-to-end Internet solutions for corporations. This includes strategy consulting and interactive marketing, as well as back-office eBusiness applications, integration and outsourcing. AppNet has been growing rapidly through an aggressive acquisition strategy. In 1998 and 1999, it acquired 12 companies, barely pausing in June to complete its IPO. Customers include Ford, Burton Snowboards, AOL/Cisneros and Toshiba. In January 2000, AppNet was awarded a contract by the Uniform Code Council (UCC) to build and maintain a real time information and electronic marketplace for the food and consumer packaged goods sector.

Opportunities

- As corporate America rushes to embrace the Internet, the strong growth for experienced iBuilders is expected to continue. According to IDC, the Internet professional services market, is expected to grow at more than 58% compounded annually to $78 billion in 2003 from an $7.8 billion in 1998.
- The demand for high-quality iBuilders is likely to outpace the supply over the next few years, leading to strong revenue growth for the market leaders. AppNet has been capturing market share as it grows faster than the industry average.
- AppNet is teaming up with the UCC to build a B2B real-time marketplace between grocers and packaged goods companies. Companies representing $400 billion in supply chain revenues have agreed to use the new service.

Challenges

- AppNet operates in an industry that the *Industry Standard* calls the iBuilders arena. This is an intensely competitive arena, where the barriers to entry are virtually non-existent. Hundreds of companies compete in a "me too" environment, all promoting similar core competencies. Competitors include Scient, Razorfish, USWeb, Andersen Consulting and PricewaterhouseCoopers.
- Although a high growth industry, the Internet consulting market is not as scalable as other Internet business models. Revenue growth is tied to employee growth.
- AppNet, similar to most of its successful competitors, has been growing quickly through acquisitions. The downside of this strategy is that the company could have difficulties quickly integrating new and existing acquisitions which could lead to high turnover and lost clients.

The Bottom Line

AppNet has been quickly growing its reputation and its customer base as one of the leaders in the Internet professional services market. In an industry where, like Godzilla, size does matter, AppNet has been staying near the front of the pack through an aggressive acquisition strategy and strong organic growth. Competition is intense, but the main challenge for AppNet will be to seamlessly integrate any future acquisitions without losing key personnel and customers. If it can continue to accomplish that, AppNet has a strong future ahead of itself.

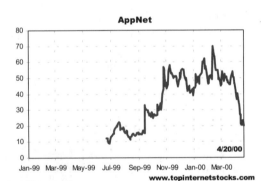

Key Statistics	APNT
Market Cap (4/20/00):	$680.8m
Free Float:	63.1%
IPO Date:	6/18/99
Offer Price:	$12.00
Price (4/20/00):	$20.06
52 week high:	$71.62
52 week low:	$8.62
Volatility: (avg. daily % ch)	6.6%
Price/Sales:	6.1
Price/Sales-Growth:	1.1

www.topinternetstocks.com

Annual Financial Data ($ m)	12/1994	12/1995	12/1996	12/1997	12/1998	12/1999
Revenues	--	--		--	17.67	112.34
Operating Profit	--	--		--	-12.80	-5.53
Net Income	--	--	--	--	-14.38	-76.59
Customers	--	--	--	--	--	--
Key Ratios:						
Gross Margin	--	--	.	--	33.8%	43.7%
Operating Margin	--	--	--	--	-72.4%	4.9%
Net Margin	--	--	--	--	-81.4%	-68.2%
Marketing as % of Revenues	--	--	--	--	5.5%	8.0%

Ariba, Inc.

http://www.ariba.com   eBusiness

Address:
1565 Charleston Rd.   Phone: 650.930.6200
Mountain View, CA 94043   Fax: 650.930.6300
Management:
Chairman, President & CEO: Keith Krach
CFO: Edward P. Kinsey

Description

Ariba aims to be the holy grail of corporate buyers, by automating the purchasing or procurement process. The company was founded in September 1996 by a group of entrepreneurs in residence at two venture capital firms.

Ariba is one of the leading companies in the growing B2B sector, providing an ecommerce platform that automates and integrates the internal and external purchasing process of buyers and suppliers. This spans the entire procurement process from the purchase order to selection and approval through to fulfillment. At the end of 1999, Ariba had 40 clients including 14 percent of the Fortune 100 companies.

In November 1999, Ariba acquired TRADEX, a company that develops Internet trading exchanges for Web marketplaces. In December 1999, Ariba partnered with American Management Systems (AMS) to help improve operating efficiencies in the government-to-business (G2B) marketplace.

Opportunities

- The corporate procurement process is highly inefficient, with organizations spending roughly 30%-38% of total revenues on operating resources. The cost of a corporate purchase transaction can run from $8 to $150 or more because of the manual cost, error and lack of economies of scale (bulk purchasing). Automating the process both internally and externally can lead to a 5% to 25% reduction in operating expenses.

- Ariba has a strong client list which comprises fourteen percent of the Fortune 100. In aggregate, Ariba's customers spend more than $140 billion each year on operating resources.
- The AMS partnership opens up the $200 billion government procurement market to Ariba, and AMS

controls approximately $100 billion of those funds through its contracts with various federal agencies.

Challenges

- Although the competition is currently limited to a handful of players, including Commerce One, Oracle and SAP, barriers to entry are relatively low, and new competitors could quickly appear.
- Quarterly revenues could be extremely volatile as Ariba sells small numbers of relatively large orders. This also tends to lead to long sales cycles. If the company cannot close one or more sales in a particular quarter because of timing issues, revenues could be severely impacted.

The Bottom Line

Arriba Ariba! When it comes to helping organizations save money and improve their bottom line, Ariba is one of the companies at the forefront. With a blue chip roster of customers including Motorola, Dow Chemical and MCI, reaching critical mass should not be an issue. It also helps to be in a market that is expected to double every year[14]. However, as the company looks to expand into other B2B markets, the challenge is to not lose focus, particularly when its two rival competitors, Commerce One and Oracle, are eagerly awaiting any missteps.

Key Statistics	ARBA
Market Cap (4/20/00):	$13,263m
Free Float:	41.0%
IPO Date:	6/23/99
Offer Price (adj):	$5.75
Price (4/20/00):	$177.38
52 week high:	$183.31
52 week low:	$15.25
Volatility: (avg. daily % ch)	6.6%
Price/Sales:	213.9
Price/Sales-Growth:	66.6

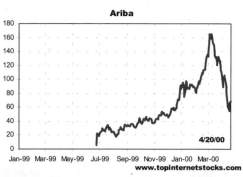

Ariba

www.topinternetstocks.com

Annual Financial Data ($ m)	9/1994	9/1995	9/1996	9/1997	9/1998	9/1999
Revenues	--	--	--	0.76	8.36	45.37
Operating Profit	--	--	--	-4.95	-11.52	-31.42
Net Income	--	--	--	-4.68	-10.95	-29.30
Customers	--	--	--	--	--	--
Key Ratios:						
Gross Margin	--	--	--	-23.7%	81.6%	80.6%
Operating Margin	--	--	--	-651.6%	-137.8%	-69.3%
Net Margin	--	--	--	-615.7%	-131.0%	-64.6%
Marketing as % of Revenues	--	--	--	294.1%	123.3%	74.6%

---

[14] IDC expects the eProcurement application market to grow 114% CAGR to $8.5 billion by 2003.

Ask Jeeves, Inc.

http://www.askjeeves.com

eBusiness

Address:
5858 Horton St., Ste. 350
Emeryville, CA 94608
Management:
Chairman:
President & CEO:
CFO:

Phone: 510.985.7400
Fax: 510.985.7410

Roger A. Strauch
Robert Wrubel
M. Bruce Nakao

Description

Ask Jeeves is the butler to the Web. The company was founded in June 1996 to provide a more natural way of searching for information on the Web. It launched its first Web site in April 1997 and began its corporate licensing program in October of that year. The company went public in July 1999. Ask Jeeves' natural language question answering services has proven to be a big hit with corporations and has moved the company from a "just-another-search-engine" concept to a major provider of customer service solutions for Fortune 500 companies. In the fourth quarter of 1999, Ask Jeeves' corporate licensing revenues climbed to 35% of total revenues from less than 3% in 1998. Major customers include Microsoft, Dell, Office Depot, E*Trade and Nike.

Opportunities

- Along with the explosive growth in Web usage comes the growth in the number of Web pages in cyberspace. Forrester Research estimates that 1.5 million new pages are being added to the Internet each day, and Pegasus Research estimates that there are over 1.5 billion Web pages in cyberspace.
- While most search engines require users to know Boolean logic in order to improve results, Ask Jeeves' technology can answer plain-English questions, from a knowledge database that learns and grows query by query.
- As corporations turn to the Web for more of their customer service functions, there is a growing need to develop an interface that can answer questions in plain language from the thousands of pages on a large corporate site. Ask Jeeves is aggressively targeting this growing B2B area and has a significant early lead.

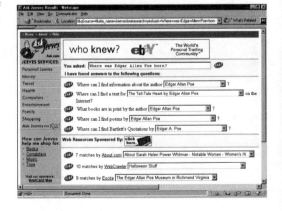

Challenges

- Ask Jeeves competes on the consumer front with a multitude of other search engines and directories including Yahoo!, Inktomi, Lycos and Hotbot.com. The company still lags behind these search engines in audience reach. In December 1999, askjeeves.com was in 10th place for search sites according to Media Metrix.
- Ask Jeeves has significant up-front costs associated with implementing corporate solutions, while revenues are generated over the life of the contract. This means that as the company aggressively grows its corporate business, losses could widen substantially in the near term, putting a strain on capital resources.

The Bottom Line

Have a question? Ask Jeeves. It is the leader in natural language search technology. Its plain English answers to the questions on the Web have proven very popular, with the site attracting over 6 million visitors every month. However, as a search engine, it is competing for consumer's eyeballs and advertising dollars with a number of stronger players including Yahoo!, Go.com, Lycos and AltaVista . Where the company shines, is in its corporate solutions, which helps major organizations provide a more human-like interface to Web-based customer support functions. B2B is where the real potential going forward is, and it is there that Ask Jeeves is smartly positioning itself.

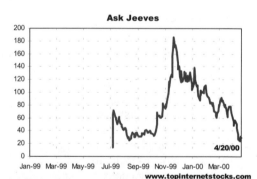

Key Statistics	ASKJ
Market Cap (4/20/00):	$1,027m
Free Float:	65.2%
IPO Date:	7/01/99
Offer Price:	$14.00
Price (4/20/00):	$112.94
52 week high:	$190.50
52 week low:	$22.12
Volatility: (avg. daily % ch)	9.2%
Price/Sales:	46.6
Price/Sales-Growth:	1.8

Ask Jeeves

www.topinternetstocks.com

Annual Financial Data ($ m)	12/1994	12/1995	12/1996	12/1997	12/1998	12/1999
Revenues	--	--	--	--	0.80	22.03
Operating Profit	--	--	-0.11	-0.45	-6.97	-54.91
Net Income	--	--	-0.11	-0.45	-6.81	-52.93
Unique Visitors (m)	--	--	--	--	--	5.29
Key Ratios:						
Gross Margin	--	--	--	--	-74.8%	36.1%
Operating Margin	--	--	--	--	-870.4%	-249.3%
Net Margin	--	--	--	--	-850.4%	-240.3%
Marketing as % of Revenues	--	--	--	--	287.5%	160.3%

AXENT Technologies, Inc.

http://www.axent.com

eSecurity

Address:

2400 Research Blvd., Ste. 200   Phone: 888.442.9368

Rockville, MD 20850   Fax: 301.330.5756

Management:

Chairman & CEO: John C. Becker

President & COO: Brett Jackson

CFO: Robert B. Edwards, Jr.

Description

AXENT secures the Internet and corporate networks. The company was spun off from Raxco Software in 1994 to provide integrated security solutions for companies doing business over private and public networks using AXENT's integrated products and services. The company's Lifecycle Security® Model, coupled with smart security architecture allows AXENT to provide security assessment, intrusion detection, remote access security, virtual private networks (VPN), web security and firewalls for a number of different computer environments. Revenues are generated from software licensing fees and consulting or services contracts. Software licensing accounts for roughly 70% of total revenues. AXENT has over 5,000 companies and government agencies, 45 of the top Fortune 50 US companies and five of the top six accounting firms, relying on it for security. Customers include MCI WorldCom, Unilever, E*Trade, the US AirForce and the US Navy.

Opportunities

- The growth in ecommerce transactions, email as a communications medium and business' growing use of the Internet in mission-critical functions will drive the growth in security solutions. IT research firm, IDC estimates that the Internet security market will grow to $7.4 billion in 2002 from an estimated $4.2 billion in 1999.
- Internet security companies were hit hard in 1999 and experienced extended sales cycles and sales slowdowns caused by corporations diverting the majority of their IT spending to preparing for Y2K. With Y2K out of the way in 2000, this is expected to reverse, leading to accelerated revenue growth.
- AXENT is the market leader in intrusion detection and assessment software.

Challenges

- Competition in the security solutions and firewall market include Check Point Software, Cisco, Network Associates, CyberGuard and Secure Computing. AXENT lags in the firewall market and is up against both Check Point and the networking giant, Cisco. Cisco has been effective in leveraging its large installed base of customers to capture market share.
- AXENT is coming out of a difficult year of slow revenue growth due to Y2K-related spending shifts from its corporate customers. If AXENT is unable to regain revenue momentum, the shares could continue to lag.

The Bottom Line

AXENT has the benefit of being one of the cheapest Internet stocks in an industry that is poised to accelerate rapidly. Increased revenue growth, a strong market position and improving margins all weigh in AXENT's favor. The competition is tough in the Internet security market, but AXENT has the benefit of having a strong integrated solutions offering. In the intrusion detection market, AXNET commands a 40% market share. If 80% of companies feel that security is the leading barrier to ecommerce, AXENT intends to change that. Bottom line? The first quarter of 2000 will be important in determining whether AXENT is successful at regaining revenue momentum.

Key Statistics	AXNT
Market Cap (4/20/00):	$482.1m
Free Float:	92.1%
IPO Date:	4/23/96
Offer Price:	$14.00
Price (4/20/00):	$16.75
52 week high:	$33.00
52 week low:	$8.50
Volatility: (avg. daily % ch)	9.2%
Price/Sales:	4.3
Price/Sales-Growth:	36.6

www.topinternetstocks.com

Annual Financial Data ($ m)	12/1994	12/1995	12/1996	12/1997	12/1998	12/1999
Revenues	8.84	18.63	36.62	69.82	101.03	112.81
Operating Profit	-7.27	-7.47	-0.56	-22.45	7.19	-10.86
Net Income	-1.45	-0.33	7.48	-18.62	6.44	-0.59
Customers	--	--	--	--	--	--
Key Ratios:						
Gross Margin	85.9%	89.0%	92.5%	90.6%	90.7%	85.8%
Operating Margin	-82.3%	-40.1%	-1.5%	-32.2%	7.1%	-9.6%
Net Margin	-16.4%	-1.8%	20.4%	-26.7%	6.4%	-0.5%
Marketing as % of Revenues	68.1%	81.4%	59.0%	45.6%	40.8%	54.3%

barnesandnoble.com, Inc.

http://www.bn.com   eTailer

Address:
76 Ninth Ave., 11th Fl.   Tel: 212.414.6000
New York, NY 10011   Fax: 212.414.6140
Management:
Chairman: Leonard Riggio
Vice-Chairman & Acting CEO: Steve Riggio
CFO: Marie Toulantis

Description

Barnesandnoble.com is the next chapter in the online retailing space. The company came late to the Web, opening its virtual store in March 1997, nearly two years after Amazon.com first appeared on the Net. Originally a division of offline giant, Barnes & Noble, the company completed its IPO in May 1999, six months after German publishing giant, Bertelsmann AG invested $200 million in barnesandnoble.com for a 50% equity stake. Since then, bn.com has been busy improving its Web site and adding new shopping categories including music, electronic greeting cards, prints and posters, software and magazines. It has also added 300,000 affiliate members that act as independent book sellers. Bn.com has over four million customers in 215 countries, and has formed partnerships with several major portals including AOL, Lycos and MSN.

Opportunities

- Bn.com came back strongly in 1999 after a slow start in 1998, quickly growing its customer base and turning those customers into repeat buyers. In the December 1999 quarter, its repeat customer rate was 66% compared to approximately 52% in the last quarter of 1998.
- International markets could be a source of strong growth for bn.com, where it can leverage its relationship with global publishing giant, Bertelsmann AG. According to Euromonitor, worldwide book sales will reach an estimated $85 billion in 2000.
- Barnesandnoble.com is experimenting with same-day delivery in Manhattan and may roll that service out in other key markets during 2000. This could be a key competitive advantage for bn.com.

Challenges

- Competition is fierce in the online retailing space. As Barnesandnoble.com enters new shopping categories, it will face increasing competition from all sides including the industry leader, Amazon.com. Amazon, with a strong first-mover advantage, still controls the online book and music category with an estimated six to one lead over bn.com.

- Both Barnes & Noble and Bertelsmann each control 48% of the voting stock of bn.com. This could lead to conflicts of interest, where the two partners could force barnesandnoble.com to pursue strategic directions that are at odds with the better interests of the online retailer. Bertelsmann also owns Web properties in Europe that could compete with barnesandnoble.com

The Bottom Line

Barnesandnoble.com may have been late to the game, but it has been learning quickly and is emerging as one of the key players in the eTailing space. Although it still lags behind industry leader, Amazon.com, two key metrics, customer growth and repeat customer rate, have seen strong improvements in 1999. In an industry that is often defined as commoditized, branding and differentiation is vital in order to attract and develop loyal customers, a fact that has not escaped bn.com. In the end, it's rather simple: loyal customers are happy customers, and happy customers spend more money.

Key Statistics	BNBN
Market Cap (4/20/00):	$259.2m
Free Float:	55.0%
IPO Date:	5/25/99
Offer Price:	$18.00
Price (4/20/00):	$8.56
52 week high:	$26.62
52 week low:	$7.50
Volatility: (avg. daily % ch)	3.4%
Price/Sales:	1.3
Price/Sales-Growth:	0.6

Barnesandnoble.com

www.topinternetstocks.com

Annual Financial Data ($ m)	12/1994	12/1995	12/1996	12/1997	12/1998	12/1999
Sales	--	--	--	11.95	61.83	202.57
Operating Profit	--	--	--	-13.55	-83.86	-122.64
Net Income	--	--	--	-13.55	-83.15	-102.41
Customers (m)	--	--	--	0.30	1.30	4.00
Key Ratios:						
Gross Margin	--	--	--	15.3%	23.1%	21.0%
Operating Margin	--	--	--	-113.4%	-135.6%	-60.5%
Net Margin	--	--	--	-113.4%	-134.5%	-50.6%
Marketing as % of Sales	--	--	--	74.1%	113.9%	55.1%

BroadVision, Inc.

http://www.broadvision.com   eBusiness

Address:
585 Broadway   Phone: 650.261.5100
Redwood City, CA 94063   Fax: 650.261.5900
Management:
Chairman, President & CEO: Dr. Pehong Chen
CFO: Randall C. Bolten

Description

BroadVision, founded in 1993, has been around longer than most Internet companies. The company develops packaged software solutions for customized marketing and ecommerce applications. The BroadVision One-to-One product suite allows businesses to tailor their Web site content to the particular interests of individual users by personalizing each visit on a real-time basis. It does this by tracking and collecting visitor profile information to a site, organizing the company's content out of a database, and then delivering the customized content to the customer.

Roughly 65% of BroadVision's revenues are derived from software licensing fees. The company also generates consulting revenues for product support and training. BroadVision has over 500 Global 2000 customers, including American Airlines, Intuit, Sears and Credit Suisse.

Opportunities

- Very few ecommerce sites offer any type of personalization, an important factor in driving sales and building customer loyalty. Forrester Research estimates that just 13 percent of Web sites deliver some type of personalization. Those sites that can provide a more personal look and feel have been the ones that have been the most successful in building loyal customers.
- BroadVision has targeted this niche with a comprehensive suite of personalized ecommerce and relationship management applications. It is also targeting larger corporations that are quickly trying to transform themselves from "brick-and-mortar" to "click-and-mortar" businesses.

Challenges

- BroadVision competes in a crowded field against both small, hungry opponents like Vignette, OpenMarket and Silknet, as well as heavyweights like IBM, Microsoft and Oracle. Competition will intensify as other Internet start-ups and traditional enterprise software vendors move into the customer relationship management space.
- Because Web site personalization requires capturing information about visitors and their preferences, it raises privacy concerns. In the US, this is less of an issue, but in Europe where BroadVision generates 23% of its revenues, on-line privacy is a serious issue and legislation has been passed that penalizes companies that violate consumer privacy laws.

The Bottom Line

BroadVision is in the business of personalizing eBusiness. It is a leading player in providing packaged software that delivers on the promise of one-to-one Web personalization, a critical factor in driving sales and building customer loyalty. However, it is not alone in the field. Although the industry is still young and fragmented, BroadVision competes under the shadow of both Microsoft and IBM. In the end, what sets BroadVision apart is its impressive roster of customers, more than 500 of the Global 2000, its strong revenue growth, which more than doubled in 1999, and its ability to generate profits, a rarity for Internet companies in general.

Key Statistics	BVSN
Market Cap (4/20/00):	$9,081m
Free Float:	60.9%
IPO Date:	6/21/96
Offer Price (adj):	$0.78
Price (4/20/00):	$36.56
52 week high:	$93.25
52 week low:	$4.31
Volatility: (avg. daily % ch)	4.7%
Price/Sales:	78.6
Price/Sales-Growth:	62.0

BroadVision

www.topinternetstocks.com

Annual Financial Data ($ m)	12/1994	12/1995	12/1996	12/1997	12/1998	12/1999
Revenues	--	0.54	10.88	27.11	50.91	115.51
Operating Profit	-1.77	-4.48	-10.70	-7.64	1.92	15.26
Net Income	-1.67	-4.32	-10.15	-7.37	4.04	18.81
Customers	--	--	--	--	--	500
Key Ratios:						
Gross Margin	--	53.9%	77.1%	78.1%	80.9%	75.1%
Operating Margin	--	-829.3%	-98.3%	-28.2%	3.8%	13.2%
Net Margin	--	-799.6%	-93.2%	-27.2%	7.9%	16.3%
Marketing as % of Revenues	--	249.6%	110.9%	67.9%	51.6%	42.3%

Charles Schwab Corporation

http://www.schwab.com   eFinancials

Address:
120 Kearny St.   Phone: 415.627.7000
San Francisco, CA 94108   Fax: 415.627.8538
Management:
Chairman & Co-CEO: Charles R. Schwab
President & Co-CEO: David S. Pottruck
CFO: Christopher V. Dodds

Description

Charles Schwab had its humble beginnings as a full-service broker-dealer back in 1971, entering the discount brokerage industry in 1974 in preparation of May Day in 1975 (when the SEC removed the fixed-rate commission structure). Since then, the company has gone on to define an industry that had quickly captured 20% of the retail brokerage industry. However, Schwab was not content with that, and in 1993 began offering online trading through its proprietary Street Smart software.

Realizing that online trading would soon revolutionize the way individual investors traded stocks and made investments, Charles Schwab, launched its Web-based online trading, *eSchwab*, in January 1998. This decision to aggressively enter the online arena helped Schwab to accelerate its asset growth and the number of its customer accounts. By year-end 1999, total customer assets reached $725 billion, up from $354 billion in early 1998, and its online division, *eSchwab* accounted for half of Charles Schwab's total trading volume.

Schwab is the largest online discount broker with over 6.6 million active accounts, 3.3 million online accounts and $725 billion in customer assets. What sets Charles Schwab apart from the other discount brokers is its "click-and-mortar" strategy. Customers can conduct trades either through the Internet, which accounts for 70% of trades, the phone or any one of more than 340 branch offices.

In addition to providing retail brokerage services, Schwab also offers mutual funds, 401(k) plans, and a host of other financial services. It will also soon provide individual investors access to IPOs and after-hours trading. In early January 2000, Schwab announced that it would acquire US Trust in a move to expand its reach into the high net worth investor market.

As Schwab expands its product and service offerings, it is positioning itself as a full-service broker with discount prices. This strategy is putting it head-to-head with the powerful traditional brokers like Merrill Lynch, Morgan Stanley and others that are starting to move online.

On the international front, Charles Schwab has built a local presence in Canada and the UK, and has entered Japan and Australia through joint ventures with local partners. The company sees itself entering five more international markets over the next few years.

Opportunities

- The online brokerage industry is quickly transforming the way investors buy and sell stocks and soon bonds. From less than a million online investors in the early 1990's, roughly 8 million individual investors traded online in 1999, and by 2003 more than 25 million US investors are expected to be trading over the Internet.
- Schwab was quick to realize that online trading would change the face of investing, and moved rapidly to establish itself as the leading online broker. The company has been successful in leveraging its strong brand name to attract new customer accounts and fuel asset growth, with the result that it is now the industry's largest online broker with 3.3 million active online accounts.
- In contrast to most of its competitors, Schwab has a compelling back up system in case of system outages and downtime – a frequent problem for eBrokers. This back up system is Schwab's network of 340 branches and 5,800 independent investment advisors. This "click and mortar" strategy is a competitive advantage that few online brokers can replicate.
- Schwab has been shifting its revenue mix away from volatile trading and commission revenues to stabler, fee-based revenue sources such as mutual fund fees, insurance and 401(k) plan administration. This reduces the risk of Schwab's business model to any potential downturns in the equity markets.
- Charles Schwab is also looking at international markets as a source of growth. It has already expanded its franchise into Canada and the UK, and has entered Japan through a joint venture with local partners.

Challenges

- The online brokerage landscape is a hyper competitive landscape, with more than 160 brokers competing for online accounts. Charles Schwab in particular is feeling the competition on two fronts: from the current crop of online brokers that are also starting to offer financial tools and research at cheaper commissions (E*Trade, TDWaterhouse and Ameritrade), and from the traditional full-service brokers that are beginning to offer online trading (Morgan Stanley, Merrill Lynch and PaineWebber) at discounted rates.
- With the increased competition comes increased margin pressure. In the battle for new customers, marketing costs are rising across the industry. At the same time, commission revenues for stock trades are trending down.
- The law of large numbers will begin to set in with Schwab. While customer and revenue growth in absolute terms has been continuing to expand strongly with 1.1 million new online accounts added in 1999 and revenues climbing 44% to $3.9 billion, growth in percentage terms will eventually begin to slow down.

The Bottom Line

As the number one online broker, Schwab is beginning to feel the squeeze, caught between the full-service traditional firms, like Merrill Lynch that are branching into online trading and the deep-discount online brokers that are starting to offer greater research and investment tools at a lower commission structure. For Schwab, the key to succeed will be differentiation.

The company is already positioning itself as a financial supermarket, offering a "one-stop shop" of financial services and advice that is more comprehensive than its deep-discount competitors such as Ameritrade or TDWaterhouse. Against the full-service firms such as Merrill Lynch and Morgan Stanley, Schwab still offers a stronger value proposition with lower trading fees and more comprehensive online financial news, content and investment tools.

Schwab has also been building its asset management and other fee-based income sources in order to reduce the earnings volatility inherent in the brokerage business model. Strategically this is a smart move and should help the company better manage the competitive pricing pressures playing out on the transaction (i.e. trading) side of the business. In addition, it also helps position the company to better weather any downturn in the equity markets. Investors may stop trading in market corrections, but assets are still being held in accounts and managed.

Over the last 20 years, Schwab wrote the book on competing successfully in the retail brokerage industry and should continue to write that book over the next 20 years.

Key Statistics	SCH
Market Cap (4/20/00):	$36,837m
Free Float:	61.0%
IPO Date:	9/22/87
Offer Price (adj):	$0.54
Price (4/20/00):	$44.00
52 week high:	$67.12
52 week low:	$26.94
Volatility: (avg. daily % ch)	3.8%
Price/Sales:	9.3
Price/Sales-Growth:	21.0

Charles Schwab

www.topinternetstocks.com

Annual Financial Data ($ m)	12/1994	12/1995	12/1996	12/1997	12/1998	12/1999
Net Revenues	1,065.00	1,420.00	1,850.92	2,298.75	2,736.22	3,944.80
Operating Profit	224.00	277.10	394.06	447.25	576.54	971.20
Net Income	135.00	173.00	234.00	270.00	348.00	588.90
Active Accounts (m)	3.00	3.40	4.00	4.80	5.60	6.60
Key Ratios:						
Gross Margin	--	--	--	--	--	--
Operating Margin	21.0%	19.5%	21.3%	19.5%	21.1%	24.6%
Net Margin	12.7%	12.2%	12.6%	11.7%	12.7%	14.9%
Marketing as % of Revenues	3.4%	3.7%	4.5%	5.6%	5.7%	6.1%

Check Point Software Technologies Ltd.

http://www.checkpoint.com   eSecurity

Address:
3A Jabotinsky St.   Phone: +972.3.753.4555
Diamond Tower   Fax: +972.3.575.9256
Ramat Gan, Israel 52520
Management:
Chairman, President & CEO: Gil Shwed
Senior VP: Marius Nacht

Description

Check Point is the security gate at the corporate border. The company was born out of the well-regarded technology lab of the Israeli military. Founded in 1993 by Gil Shwed and Marius Nacht, Check Point quickly built a reputation as the leader in firewall technology. Check Point's integrated architecture includes network security, traffic control and IP address management. Check Point's flagship product, the FireWall-1, protects company networks from unauthorized access by verifying user identity, controlling access, and detecting and responding automatically to network attacks. The company has over 40,000 customers including Nokia, France Telecom, Sprint, MCI's UUNET and Swisscom. The US accounts for 50% of revenues, Europe 33% and the rest of the world 17%.

Opportunities

- As more businesses rush to connect to the Internet, security is becoming a real concern. Now that IT budgets are freed from Y2K efforts, spending on Internet security is expected to accelerate. IDC estimates that the market for Internet security software will grow from $4.2 billion in 1999 to $7.4 billion in 2003. Firewalls will experience the fastest growth.
- Check Point has an early market leadership position in firewalls with an estimated 24% market share. It has an installed base of over 110,000 customer installations and growing.
- Check Point is positioning itself to take advantage of the broadband groundswell. Its new subsidiary, SofaWare Technologies, will protect home and small offices from security threats over cable and DSL access. This is a rapidly growing market.

Challenges

- Competition in the firewall market include Cisco, Network Associates, Axent Technologies and CyberGuard. Cisco has been effective in leveraging its giant installed base of customers to capture market share, and it is almost tied with Check Point in terms of market share.
- As an Israeli company, Check Point does not have the same disclosure requirements as a US company. Subsequently, there is less visibility to the company's operating results, which could lead to higher share volatility.

The Bottom Line

Check Point is in the sweet spot of Internet security. The firewall market is growing at twice the rate of other segments of the security industry, and Check Point is riding that growth as the market leader. But that doesn't give it the opportunity to rest on its laurels. Cisco is gunning for the number one spot, and has the advantage of a much larger customer base to sell its products. Although Cisco will give Check Point a run for its money, Check Point, as an offspring of the Israeli military, understands well how to compete against larger adversaries.

Key Statistics	CHKP
Market Cap (4/20/00):	$12,078m
Free Float:	70.0%
IPO Date:	6/28/96
Offer Price (adj):	$7.00
Price (4/20/00):	$161.69
52 week high:	$295.00
52 week low:	$15.44
Volatility: (avg. daily % ch)	3.8%
Price/Sales:	55.0
Price/Sales-Growth:	100.6

Check Point

www.topinternetstocks.com

Annual Financial Data ($ m)	12/1994	12/1995	12/1996	12/1997	12/1998	12/1999
Revenues	0.79	10.07	34.58	86.35	141.94	219.57
Operating Profit	0.08	4.95	13.98	38.03	66.84	96.92
Net Income	0.02	4.93	15.12	39.52	69.88	95.78
Customers	--	--	--	--	--	40,000
Key Ratios:						
Gross Margin	85.1%	92.3%	91.7%	92.1%	90.4%	89.8%
Operating Margin	9.7%	49.1%	40.4%	44.0%	47.1%	44.1%
Net Margin	3.0%	49.0%	43.7%	45.8%	49.2%	43.6%
Marketing as % of Revenues	--	--	28.6%	29.6%	28.2%	31.1%

CheckFree Holdings Corporation

http://www.checkfree.com   eBusiness

Address:
4411 E. Jones Bridge Rd.   Phone: 678.375.3000
Norcross, GA 30092   Fax: 678.840.1477
Management:
Chairman & CEO: Peter J. Kight
President & COO: Peter F. Sinisgalli
CFO: Allen L. Shulman

Description

CheckFree is the leading provider of electronic billing and payment services. Founded in 1981, the company originally began providing online billing through a dial-up service, then through CompuServe in 1984. CheckFree now provides electronic billing payment and presentment (EBPP) services to 3 million consumers through more than 350 financial institutions including 23 of the 25 largest US banks. In addition to allowing consumers and businesses to conduct secure online billing transactions, the company also provides investment services and financial application software for businesses and financial institutions. EBPP accounted for 68% of revenue in fiscal 1999, while software and investment services accounted for 16% each. In 1999, CheckFree partnered with Yahoo! to provide online bill payments. CheckFree acquired BlueGill in December 1999 to develop XML-based software that translates bill payments on different platforms into a common Internet format.

Opportunities

- The cost of paying bills online is roughly 40 cents compared to $1.00 to $1.50 by traditional means. Multiply that by the estimated 60 billion bills paid annually worldwide according to Killen & Associates, and the cost savings would amount to more than $36 billion each year.
- CheckFree has an estimated 70% market share of an industry that is still in its infancy. Killen & Associates estimates that only 3% of all bills are currently paid online.

- CheckFree is pursuing distribution relationships with the major portals, similar to its E-Bill service with Yahoo!. These portal agreements could help CheckFree double its customer base within a year.

Challenges

- CheckFree is facing competition from several fronts. On the EBPP front, CheckFree competes against traditional banks such as Chase Manhattan, First Union and Wells Fargo that are setting up their own solution called Spectrum. On the software and investment services side, the company competes against other portfolio accounting software providers and service bureaus.
- Although businesses see the cost savings potential of EBPP and are moving quickly online, consumers have so far been slow to adopt online billing. Overall subscriber growth was flat in the latter part of 1999, making it difficult for the company to achieve its subscriber goal of 5 million by June 2000.

The Bottom Line

Paying bills online is convenient, and CheckFree wants to see that it becomes even more convenient – and eventually mainstream. With a 70% market share, the company is the undisputed leader in an industry that is expected to grow fivefold over the next few years. Underscoring its market leadership, the Internet's largest online bank, Wells Fargo, extended its relationship with CheckFree. However, it is facing stiff competition from Spectrum and its partners as well as other major banks that no longer wish to outsource their online bill payments. Nonetheless, providing end-to-end online bill payment solutions is a technical challenge and CheckFree, with its twenty years of experience has the edge.

Key Statistics	CKFR
Market Cap (4/20/00):	$1,762m
Free Float:	59.9%
IPO Date:	9/28/95
Offer Price:	$18.00
Price (4/20/00):	$33.56
52 week high:	$125.62
52 week low:	$23.12
Volatility: (avg. daily % ch)	4.3%
Price/Sales:	6.4
Price/Sales-Growth:	45.4

CheckFree

www.topinternetstocks.com

Annual Financial Data ($ m)	12/1995	6/1996	6/1997	6/1998	6/1999	12/1999*
Revenues	49.33	76.79	176.45	233.86	250.13	141.99
Operating Profit	-1.67	-149.76	-181.40	-43.35	-8.31	-12.64
Net Income	0.22	-138.86	-161.81	-3.70	10.46	-7.91
Customers (m)	--	--	--	--	--	3.00
Key Ratios:						
Gross Margin	38.7%	33.3%	41.8%	44.4%	41.3%	38.8%
Operating Margin	-3.4%	-195.0%	-102.8%	-18.5%	-3.3%	-8.9%
Net Margin	0.4%	-180.8%	-91.7%	-1.6%	4.2%	-5.6%
Marketing as % of Revenues	14.7%	27.8%	18.5%	12.3%	12.9%	13.1%

* Six months ended 12/31/99

Chemdex (Ventro) Corporation

http://www.ventro.com   eBusiness

Address:
1500 Plymouth St.   Phone: 650.567.8900
Mountain View, CA 94043   Fax: 650.567.8950
Management:
Chairman: Brook H. Byers
President & CEO: David P. Perry
CFO: James G. Stewart

Description

Chemdex is one of the darlings of the B2B sector. The company was founded in September 1997 to provide a transparent, central marketplace for the life sciences industry. In March 1999, Chemdex partnered with the $1.5 billion distributor VWR Scientific Products. In July, Chemdex went public at $15 a share, using its new currency to buy Promedix.com and SpecialtyMD.com in order to consolidate its position as the leading marketplace for the life sciences industry.

By the end of 1999, Chemdex's marketplace offered a virtual catalog of more than 250,000 items from over 120 suppliers. Products range from biological and chemical reagents to lab supplies, instruments and equipment. Within the next year, the company anticipates having over 550,000 products available on its network. Customers include Genentech, Rhone-Polenc Rorer, SmithKline Beecham and Harvard University.

Opportunities

- The life sciences products market is an estimated $12 billion industry that is highly fragmented and inefficient. Researchers generally have to wade through dozens of paper catalogs to find specific items. The Internet allows a large, virtual catalog where scientists and researchers can easily go to search and find specific or hard-to-find products.

- Although the online life sciences market is still in its embryonic stage, Chemdex already has one of the largest selections available on its network, bringing it close to reaching critical mass.

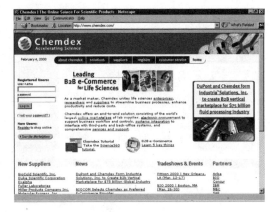

Challenges

- As with any marketplace, the challenge is to have

enough buyers and suppliers to reach critical mass, so that the network feeds itself. In other words, buyers go there because it has the most products, and suppliers go there because it has the most buyers. Chemdex is not yet at that stage.

- Gross margins are tight at 4.9% and have been trending downwards. If gross margins do not improve, Chemdex could have difficulties reaching long-term profitability. On top of such tight margins, Chemdex also bears the brunt of any product returns or uncollected accounts receivables.
- Revenue concentration risk is a challenge for Chemdex. Sales to its four largest customers accounted for roughly 74% of revenues in 1999. Roughly 35% of revenues in 1999 was to Genetech from which Chemdex receives zero gross margins (i.e. products sold at cost).

The Bottom Line

Chemdex is every investor's chemistry set. The company is one of the leading vertical marketplaces in the nascent B2B sector and already has a roster of strong blue-chip clients including Genetech, SmithKline Beecham and Rhone-Poulenc. Although there are currently few players in the life sciences market, competition is heating up, with new Internet companies like SciQuest.com and Medibuy.com, as well as traditional suppliers like Fisher Scientific that are moving their paper catalogs to the Web. For now though, Chemdex has the early lead and the largest chemistry set on the block.

Key Statistics	VNTR
Market Cap (4/20/00):	$1,328m
Free Float:	22.9%
IPO Date:	7/27/99
Offer Price:	$15.00
Price (4/20/00):	$29.69
52 week high:	$243.50
52 week low:	$15.12
Volatility: (avg. daily % ch)	7.7%
Price/Sales:	43.1
Price/Sales-Growth:	--

Ventro (Chemdex)

www.topinternetstocks.com

Annual Financial Data ($ m)	12/1994	12/1995	12/1996	12/1997	12/1998	12/1999
Revenues	--	--	--	--	0.03	30.84
Operating Profit	--	--	--	-0.40	-8.80	-51.57
Net Income	--	--	--	-0.40	-8.49	-48.57
Customers	--	--	--	--	--	--
Key Ratios:						
Gross Margin	--	--	--	--	24.1%	5.0%
Operating Margin	--	--	--	--	-30331.0%	-167.2%
Net Margin	--	--	--	--	-29269.0%	-157.5%
Marketing as % of Revenues	--	--	--	--	11196.6%	74.7%

CMGI, Inc.

http://www.cmgi.com   eServices

Address:
100 Brickstone Square   Phone: 978.684.3600
Andover, MA 01810   Fax: 978.684.3658
Management:
Chairman, President & CEO: David S. Wetherell
CFO: Andrew J. Hajducky, III

Description

CMGI brings venture capital investing to the masses. Founded originally as College Marketing Group, a direct marketing company back in 1968, the company changed its name to CMG Information Services in 1986 and later to CMGI. The company's first foray into the Internet world was in 1993 when David Wetherell funded an internal project called Booklink. Costing $900,000 to develop, CMGI sold it six months later to AOL for over $30 million. In February 1994, the company went public, and since then, CMGI has gone on to fund a number of other Internet startups, becoming in essence a large venture capital or Internet holding company. As of the end of 1999, CMGI owned or had sizeable stakes in nearly 60 Internet companies including Lycos, AltaVista, NaviSite and Silknet. Until recently, most of the company's investments have been focused on the B2C side, ranging from content providers to Internet advertising and ecommerce. Recently, CMGI launched a $1 billion venture fund focused on the emerging B2B side and is making investments in enabling technologies.

Opportunities

- CMGI has a stellar track record in its Internet investments, ranging from its first venture Booklink, to GeoCities/Yahoo and recent IPOs including Chemdex and NaviSite.
- CMGI's *keiretsu* approach focuses on leveraging synergies between the various companies in its portfolio in order to maximize their values.
- The company is aggressively expanding its footprint into the Internet marketing and advertising market which is expected to grow 45% annually to $12.5 billion by 2003.

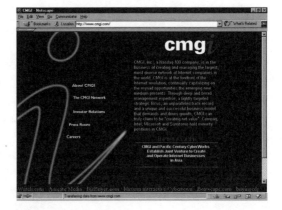

Challenges

- Because most of CMGI's earnings are from its investment portfolios and the sale of securities, revenues and operating results are irregular and less meaningful. Thus, valuation measures based on revenues or operating cash flow are virtually meaningless.
- CMGI could be classified as a mutual fund or an investment company if its operating results and non-investment assets decline in significance. If that were the case, CMGI could face greater SEC restrictions. According to the Investment Company Act of 1940, a company is deemed an investment company if its investment securities exceed 40% of the value of the total assets.
- The challenge of building a large *keiretsu* of companies is that it could be difficult integrating the various acquisitions in order to develop synergies or efficiencies between them.

The Bottom Line

For an investor who wants to own one company that represents a broad cross-section of the emerging Internet economy, CMGI is the answer. It has more companies in its portfolio than most mutual funds do. The company also has one of the best track records – as measured by its stock performance – of any Internet mutual fund. Unfortunately, in contrast to a mutual fund, CMGI's stock is a much riskier investment vehicle with higher volatility. Nevertheless, if anyone "gets the Net" CMGI's Chairman and CEO, David Wetherell does.

Key Statistics	CMGI
Market Cap (4/20/00):	$16,144m
Free Float:	70.0%
IPO Date:	1/25/94
Offer Price (adj):	$0.17
Price (4/20/00):	$57.69
52 week high:	$163.50
52 week low:	$33.12
Volatility: (avg. daily % ch)	5.3%
Price/Sales:	42.9
Price/Sales-Growth:	20.2

www.topinternetstocks.com

Annual Financial Data ($ m)	7/1995	7/1996	7/1997	7/1998	7/1999	1/2000
Revenues	11.09	17.74	60.06	81.92	175.67	277.20
Operating Profit	1.11	-18.40	-40.92	-70.26	-126.66	-686.38
Net Income	28.22	-14.32	-22.03	31.90	476.24	-302.99
Customers	--	--	--	--	--	65
Key Ratios:						
Gross Margin	34.6%	36.8%	41.9%	10.9%	3.8%	17.1%
Operating Margin	10.0%	-103.7%	-68.1%	-85.8%	-72.1%	-247.6%
Net Margin	254.4%	80.8%	-36.7%	38.9%	271.1%	-109.3%
Marketing as % of Revenues	27.3%	65.8%	55.3%	35.3%	--	66.8%

CNET, Inc.

http://www.cnet.com   eContent

Address:
150 Chestnut Street   Phone: 415.364.8525
San Francisco, CA 94111   Fax: 415.395.7815
Management:
Chairman & CEO: Halsey M. Minor
President: Richard J. Marino
CFO: Douglas Woodrum

Description

CNET is one of the leading technology-focused portal and community sites on the Web, with more than 9.6 million users visiting its property of sites each month. CNET initially gained fame with its TV shows. *CNET Central*, which appears on USA Networks and the Sci-Fi Channel is broadcast to more than 70 million households. Other television shows include *The Web*, *The New Edge* and *Cool Tech*. The company has also been successful in positioning its network of Web sites as a one-stop shopping destination for anyone searching the Web for technology news and computing information, software downloads, product reviews and shopping resources for computers and computer products. CNET was founded in 1992 and launched its first Web site in June 1995, Roughly 94% of CNET's revenues are generated through its Web properties with the other 6% generated by its TV and radio shows.

Opportunities

- The market for PC hardware and software is $82 billion, and due to the average profile of Net users (i.e. technologically savvy), more likely to buy online. Forrester Research estimates that online computer hardware and software sales will grow from $3.5 billion in 1999 to $18.1 billion in 2003.
- Computer-related advertising is one of the largest categories in the rapidly growing online advertising market. From an estimated $2.9 billion in 1999, Pegasus Research expects online advertising in the US to grow 44% compounded annually to $12.5 billion by 2003. Computer-related advertising is 20% of the total.

- CNET is the leading vertical portal focused on technology news and information. In addition to being a content aggregator, the company matches buyers and sellers for computer hardware and software for which it earns roughly $10 for each visitor that clicks through to an eTailer.

Challenges

- Competition is intense in the eContent space. In addition to competing for IT-related traffic and ad dollars against other technology-focused sites like ZDNet and EarthWeb, CNET also competes against horizontal portals such as Yahoo!, AOL and Lycos for advertising dollars.
- CNET's TV properties have been unprofitable for the company, generating negative gross margins of -12% in 1999. Despite accounting for only 6% of revenues, the division accounted for 83% or -$38.3 million of the operating loss (EBITDA) in 1999.

The Bottom Line

CNET is one of the strongest vertical players in the portal space, with its computer and technology-related news, product reviews and shopping services. CNET is launching a virtual mall for smaller merchants by offering software to easily set up and manage an online store. This is a smart move, as it helps CNET to expand its e-commerce-related revenues, further diversifying its revenue streams. Thinking of music? There's MTV. Thinking of headline news? There's CNN. Thinking of technology? There's CNET. At least, that is what the company hopes to achieve, and it is well on its way to doing just that.

Key Statistics	CNET
Market Cap (4/20/00):	$3,222m
Free Float:	37.0%
IPO Date:	7/09/96
Offer Price (adj):	$4.00
Price (4/20/00):	$38.06
52 week high:	$79.88
52 week low:	$22.50
Volatility: (avg. daily % ch)	5.7%
Price/Sales:	28.7
Price/Sales-Growth:	30.0

www.topinternetstocks.com

Annual Financial Data ($ m)	12/1994	12/1995	12/1996	12/1997	12/1998	12/1999*
Revenues	--	3.50	14.83	33.64	57.48	112.34
Operating Profit	-2.77	-8.47	-15.54	-34.14	2.96	-46.10
Net Income	-2.83	-8.61	-16.95	-24.73	3.02	416.91
Unique Visitors (m)	--	--	--	--	6.46	9.65
Key Ratios:						
Gross Margin	--	-60.9%	-3.4%	20.6%	47.3%	60.9%
Operating Margin	--	-242.0%	-104.8%	-101.5%	5.1%	-41.0%
Net Margin	--	-245.9%	-114.3%	-73.5%	5.3%	371.1%
Marketing as % of Revenues	--	67.7%	52.7%	34.5%	25.3%	81.6%

* Net income in 1999 includes gain on investment sale of $734 million

The Cobalt Group, Inc.

http://www.cobaltgroup.com   eServices

Address:
2030 First Ave., Suite 300   Phone: 206.269.6363
Seattle, WA 98121   Fax: 206.269.6350
Management:
Chairman: Howard Tullman
President & CEO: John Holt
CFO: David M. Douglas

Description

Founded in March 1995, the Cobalt Group is a Web design and marketing firm focused on bringing auto dealers onto the Web. As of year-end 1999, the company had designed and maintained Web sites for more than 5,200 car dealerships around the US. Cobalt offers Web site packages that are endorsed by the National Automobile Dealers Association (NADA). These packages provide Web site design, development and maintenance services, data collection and management services, and advertising and marketing services. In early 2000, the company extended its reach into the B2B space by launching Motorplace.com, a vertical portal aimed at aggregating auto and automotive parts data in one central place. The new B2B portal will also combine Cobalt's existing services and add the usual suspects of news, weather, sports, stock quotes, etc. in order to increase the stickiness of the site.

Opportunities

- The US automotive retailing industry is one of the largest retail sectors, representing an estimated $500 billion in new and used vehicle sales in 1998. It is also a highly fragmented market, with the top ten US dealer groups responsible for only 4.1% of total retail sales. Profitability is also an issue, with new car sales accounting for 59% of industry revenues, but only 29% of dealer profitability. In contrast, parts and service revenue accounted for 12% of sales but 47% of profitability.

- Cobalt helps bring dealers quickly online with an integrated solutions package that can improve the effectiveness of dealer marketing initiatives, which in turn drives higher sales at a lower cost.

Challenges

- In addition to the existing Web design firms such as Sapient, Scient, Razor-fish and others, Cobalt also competes with the automotive manufacturers that are developing their ecommerce initiatives. In the new B2B portal space, Cobalt will compete with Commerce One (which is partnering with GM) and other established B2B players.
- Cobalt is a specialized niche play and stands in danger of being "disintermediated". Manufacturers could begin to offer the services themselves that Cobalt currently offers to dealers (inventory data management). In addition to GM, DaimlerChrysler has also indicated that it could begin to offer similar services.

Bottom Line

Cobalt has gone "portal" – B2B portal that is. It is beginning to move its model away from the Web design and marketing area and is targeting the potentially lucrative and scalable B2B space. However, as it moves into this area, it will come up against much more established competitors such as Commerce One, VerticalNet and other B2B portals/exchanges/communities. Cobalt does have the advantage of a strong market leadership position in the automotive marketing solutions. If Cobalt can continue to leverage its first-mover advantage in order to build its B2B strategy, it could gain the needed critical mass and be the B2B auto portal to the nation's dealers.

Key Statistics	CBLT
Market Cap (4/20/00):	$170.6m
Free Float:	26.7%
IPO Date:	8/05/99
Offer Price:	$11.00
Price (4/20/00):	$10.12
52 week high:	$34.00
52 week low:	$5.50
Volatility: (avg. daily % ch)	5.4%
Price/Sales:	7.3
Price/Sales-Growth:	2.7

The Cobalt Group

www.topinternetstocks.com

Annual Financial Data ($ m)	12/1994	12/1995	12/1996	12/1997	12/1998	12/1999
Revenues	--	0.07	0.31	1.71	6.25	23.29
Operating Profit	--	-0.42	-0.83	-2.70	-5.40	-15.99
Net Income	--	-0.42	-0.83	-2.67	-5.11	-16.50
Dealer Web sites	--	--	--	--	--	5,200
Key Ratios:						
Gross Margin	--	77.1%	83.7%	83.3%	80.8%	79.3%
Operating Margin	--	-592.9%	-264.7%	-157.5%	-86.4%	-68.7%
Net Margin	--	-592.9%	-265.4%	-155.8%	-81.7%	-70.9%
Marketing as % of Revenues	--	78.6%	91.7%	101.7%	64.8%	49.8%

Commerce One, Inc.

http://www.commerceone.com   eBusiness

Address:
1600 Riviera Ave., Suite 200   Phone: 925.941.6000
Walnut Creek, CA 94596   Fax: 925.941.6060
Management:
Chairman, President & CEO: Mark B. Hoffman
CFO: Peter Pervere

Description

Commerce One is one of the leading companies at the forefront of the growing B2B sector, providing Web-based procurement software to link corporate buyers and sellers, creating giant trading exchanges. Originally founded as Distri-Vision Development Corporation in 1994, the company changed its name to Commerce One in March 1997 and launched its BuySite and MarketSite products in April 1998. The company's products span the entire procurement process from the purchase order, selection and approval, through to fulfillment. At the end of 1999, Commerce One had 66 clients including British Telecom, Siemens, SABRE and BellSouth. Its top four customers accounted for approximately 75% of revenues in 1999. In November 1999, Commerce One reached an agreement with GM to create a B2B marketplace linking GM with its 30,000 suppliers and dealers. In November, the company also acquired CommerceBid in an effort to expand into the B2B auction area.

Opportunities

- The corporate procurement process is very inefficient, accounting for 30-38% of total revenues. The cost of a corporate purchase transaction can range from $8 to $150 or more because of the manual effort, error rates and lack of economies of scale (bulk purchasing). Automating the process both within an organization and between its suppliers can lead to a 5% to 25% reduction in operating expenses.

- The GM partnership is expected to be a significant revenue generator for Commerce One. GM and its 30,000 suppliers spend over $500 billion on corporate purchases each year. GM has also stated that by 2001 all purchasing will be completed electronically.

Challenges

- Although the eProcurement market is rather young and limited to a handful of player, including Ariba, Oracle and SAP, the competition is intense and new competitors could quickly enter the arena.
- Revenues could be volatile because of long sales cycles and the small number of large orders that the company typically sees in a quarter. If one or more large sales are not closed in a particular quarter, revenue shortfalls could severely impact the company's stock price.
- Revenue concentration risk is a key concern for the company. Commerce One's top four customers accounted for roughly 75% of sales in 1999 and the company has no long-term contracts with these customers.

The Bottom Line

Commerce One succeeds because it helps organizations cut costs and increase workflows, which helps companies improve their bottom line (i.e. profits). However, the key to long-term success in the B2B space is reaching critical mass with enough buyers and sellers on its trading communities so that the network, in essence, feeds itself. The GM partnership will go a long way in helping Commerce One reach that much needed critical mass. The challenge for the company will be to manage its stellar growth effectively, lest it lose customers like it did with MCI WorldCom to Ariba. Bottom line: B2B is where the action is, and Commerce One is at the forefront.

Key Statistics	CMRC
Market Cap (4/20/00):	$8,513m
Free Float:	69.0%
IPO Date:	7/01/99
Offer Price (adj):	$7.00
Price (4/20/00):	$55.00
52 week high:	$165.50
52 week low:	$4.38
Volatility: (avg. daily % ch)	7.9%
Price/Sales:	253.7
Price/Sales-Growth:	21.0

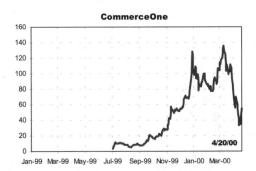

CommerceOne

www.topinternetstocks.com

Annual Financial Data ($ m)	12/1994	12/1995	12/1996	12/1997	12/1998	12/1999
Revenues	0.22	0.44	0.81	1.75	2.56	33.56
Operating Profit	-0.25	-0.31	-1.78	-11.17	-23.69	-39.61
Net Income	-0.25	-0.34	-1.81	-11.16	-24.64	-63.32
Customers	--	--	--	--	--	--
Key Ratios:						
Gross Margin	0.0%	47.2%	3.7%	-65.3%	-70.5%	52.1%
Operating Margin	-115.5%	-70.6%	-219.2%	-639.9%	-924.5%	-118.0%
Net Margin	-115.5%	-77.7%	-222.3%	-639.4%	-961.4%	-188.7%
Marketing as % of Revenues	40.5%	33.3%	106.2%	346.8%	511.4%	94.0%

Concentric Network Corp.

http://www.concentric.com   eAccess

Address:
1400 Parkmoor Ave.   Phone: 408.817.2800
San Jose, CA 95126   Fax: 408.817.2810
Management:
Chairman, President & CEO: Henry R. Nothhaft
CFO: Michael F. Anthofer

Description

Concentric was founded in 1991 as a dial-up service for bulletin board services and later offered dial-up Internet access for consumers. In 1995, the company repositioned itself to focus on providing comprehensive, value-added IP services to small and medium sized enterprises (SMEs), with the result that business services currently account for 80% of the company's revenues. Consumer dial-up access accounts for the other 20%. Internet business solutions include Web hosting and ecommerce solutions, virtual private networks (VPNs) and data center services. Concentric has also been expanding into high-speed DSL access in most major markets, and by the end of 1999, the company offered DSL access in an estimated 20 US cities.

Concentric's enterprise customers include AT&T, Bloomberg, First USA and Microsoft for which Concentric provides VPN dial-up services for WebTV customers. The WebTV relationship currently accounts for 25% of revenues for Concentric, making Microsoft one if its largest customers.

Opportunities

- The Internet services market is growing at an estimated 30% annually, with business and VPNs one of the fastest growing segments. Virtual private networks, which provide a greater level of security for companies transmitting data, is one of the fastest growing areas of the IP services market, growing at over 75% annually.

- Concentric is focusing on the business side of the ISP market, an area that is less commoditized than the consumer side. Business services generate higher margins through value-added IP services, such as Web hosting, ecommerce solutions, high-speed access and VPNs.

Challenges

- Although not as intense as on the consumer side, competition is heating up in the business IP services market. PSINet, Verio, Globix, Exodus and others are fighting aggressively to capture market share. Relative to its competitors, the company lost market share in early 1999.
- Concentric relies primarily on third-party distribution channels and other resellers to market and distribute its business IP services. Microsoft alone accounts for roughly 25% of the company's revenues. If Concentric loses these distribution channels and marketing partners, it could have a significant impact on revenue growth.

The Bottom Line

Concentric is one of the leading providers of value-added Internet services and solutions for small and medium-sized businesses. By focusing on the business-oriented, higher-margin side of the ISP market, the company has positioned itself to take advantage of the growing need of SMEs to migrate their corporate Web sites from simple brochureware to ecommerce-enabled platforms. In addition, the company's roll-out of high speed DSL services for consumers will help prepare Concentric for the coming bandwidth revolution.

Key Statistics	CNCX
Market Cap (4/20/00):	$2,112m
Free Float:	59.1%
IPO Date:	8/01/97
Offer Price (adj):	$9.00
Price (4/20/00):	$40.94
52 week high:	$61.88
52 week low:	$16.69
Volatility: (avg. daily % ch)	8.0%
Price/Sales:	14.4
Price/Sales-Growth:	18.5

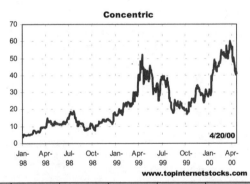

www.topinternetstocks.com

Annual Financial Data ($ m)	12/1994	12/1995	12/1996	12/1997	12/1998	12/1999
Revenues	0.44	2.48	15.65	45.46	82.81	147.06
Operating Profit	-4.23	-21.29	-63.12	-50.24	-70.80	-75.41
Net Income	-4.29	-22.01	-66.38	-55.58	-82.11	-85.09
Customers	--	--	--	--	--	--
Key Ratios:						
Gross Margin	-554.1%	-551.1%	-206.4%	-35.2%	-3.1%	8.9%
Operating Margin	-957.7%	-857.3%	-403.4%	-110.5%	-85.5%	-51.3%
Net Margin	-970.6%	-886.3%	-424.2%	-122.3%	-99.2%	-57.9%
Marketing as % of Revenues	144.6%	157.0%	106.1%	54.2%	48.1%	36.9%

Copper Mountain Networks

http://www.coppermountain.com   eBusiness

Address:
2470 Embarcadero Way   Phone: 650.687.3300
Palo Alto, CA 94303   Fax: 650.687.3372
Management:
President & CEO: Rick Gilbert
Chairman & CTO: Joe Markee
CFO: John Creelman

Description

Copper Mountain uses DSL to boost copper wires to a new level. Founded in January 1996, the company develops and markets digital subscriber line (DSL) communication products for telecommunications and Internet service providers.

The company offers an end-to-end DSL solution through three product families: CopperEdge DSL Concentrators, CopperRocket DSL Customer Premise Equipment and CopperView Network Management Tools. These products enable its customers to offer high-speed Internet connectivity over existing copper telephone lines. Customers include BTI, ICG Communications, North Point Communications, Rhythms Net Connections, Lucent and MCI's UUNET. North Point, Rhythms and Lucent account for 40%, 40% and 10% of sales respectively.

Opportunities

- As Web sites become more complex or media rich, and email is increasingly being sent with pictures or other file attachments, bandwidth is becoming a real concern. This demand for increased bandwidth will spur the growth of broadband access.
- DSL penetration is still very limited, with strong room for growth. The Yankee group estimates that the number of DSL lines will grow from only 94,000 in 1998 to more than 4.1 million in 2002, a 158% annual growth rate.
- Copper Mountain has formed strategic relationships with Lucent and 3Com to act as distribution channels to the competitive local exchange carriers (CLEC) market.

Challenges

- Technology limitations could limit wide scale DSL deployment. Currently, DSL can only operate within 17,500 feet (or about 3 miles) from a telephone central office. Any further and the signal degrades to an unusable level.
- Copper Mountain's success is dependent on the wide scale acceptance of DSL broadband access. The recent AOL/Time Warner merger could speed cable broadband penetration, making it the de facto standard, thus limiting DSL growth.
- Revenues are concentrated among a few key customers. In 1999, North Point communications, Rhythms NetConnections and Lucent accounted for 90% of total revenues. A loss of any of these customers or a delay in orders could significantly impact revenue growth and profitability.

The Bottom Line

Copper Mountain is betting on the alchemy of DSL to turn copper into gold. Having an early market share lead in the DSL equipment market, Copper Mountain stands to benefit from the rapid growth in DSL penetration. It has also forged strong distribution agreements with Lucent, 3Com and other OEM distributors. Although Copper Mountain competes with stronger telecom equipment manufacturers such as Nokia, Cisco, Alcatel, as well as one of its customers, Lucent, the greatest risk will be whether or not DSL achieves wide-scale acceptance. At least in the business world, it is shaping up to be the broadband platform of choice.

Key Statistics	CMTN
Market Cap (4/20/00):	$3,641m
Free Float:	51.9%
IPO Date:	5/13/99
Offer Price (adj):	$10.50
Price (4/20/00):	$76.06
52 week high:	$15.00
52 week low:	$25.25
Volatility: (avg. daily % ch)	6.1%
Price/Sales:	32.3
Price/Sales-Growth:	7.8

Copper Mountain

www.topinternetstocks.com

Annual Financial Data ($ m)	12/1994	12/1995	12/1996	12/1997	12/1998	12/1999
Revenues	--	--	--	0.21	21.82	112.72
Operating Profit	--	--	-2.23	-11.19	-10.52	16.61
Net Income	--	--	-2.18	-11.02	-10.33	12.22
Customers	--	--	--	--	--	--
Key Ratios:						
Gross Margin	--	--	--	-713.7%	43.2%	53.0%
Operating Margin	--	--	--	-5301.9%	-48.2%	14.7%
Net Margin	--	--	--	-5220.9%	-47.3%	10.8%
Marketing as % of Revenues	--	--	--	715.6%	24.6%	14.3%

Covad Communications

http://www.covad.com   eAccess

Address:
2330 Central Expwy.   Phone: 408.844.7500
Santa Clara, CA 95050   Fax: 408.844.7501
Management:
Chairman, President & CEO: Robert E. Knowling, Jr.
CFO: Timothy P. Laehy

Description

Covad wants to present the Internet as it should be – fast and easy to use. The company was founded in October 1996 to help businesses connect to the Internet faster than was available at the time through traditional telecommunication providers. It first began offering commercial Internet access through its TeleSpeed service in the San Francisco Bay area in December 1997. In early 1998, the company rolled out its service in other key markets including Boston, Los Angeles, New York, Seattle and Washington DC. Covad has been bus forging strategic relationships in order to help it rapidly roll out its service across the US. At the beginning of 1999, the company entered into strategic relationships with AT&T, NEXTLINK, Qwest Communications and Concentric. By March 2000, Covad offered its high-speed DSL service in nearly 63 metropolitan areas, passing 35 million homes and businesses and expanding its base of subscribers to 93,000.

Opportunities

- As Web sites become more complex or media rich, and email – with picture and file attachments – is quickly becoming the communications medium of choice, bandwidth and access speeds are becoming a concern for consumers and businesses alike.
- Increased bandwidth requirements will drive the growth in broadband Internet access, in particular DSL. The Yankee Group estimates that the number of DSL lines will grow 158% annually from 94,000 in 1998 to more than 4.1 million in 2002.

- By year-end 2000, Covad expects to bring its total metropolitan area coverage to 100 markets with 2,000 central offices. At that time, Covad's digital network will reach more than 40% of homes and 45% of businesses in the US.

Challenges

- Although still very young, the market for broadband Internet services is heating up quickly. Covad competes against cable modem, DSL, ISDN, satellite and regular dial-up access providers. Competitors include Excite@Home, Time Warner's Roadrunner, NorthPoint Communications, Rhythms NetConnections, and AOL.
- Technology limitations could limit wide-scale DSL deployment. Currently, DSL can only operate within 17,500 feet of a telephone central office.
- Covad's success is dependent on the broad acceptance of DSL as the high-speed Internet access of choice. The planned AOL/Time Warner merger could speed cable broadband penetration, making it the de facto standard, thus limiting DSL's growth.

Bottom Line

Covad is the leader in DSL Internet access with 93,000 subscribers and growing rapidly. As the number one provider of DSL access in the US, the company stands to benefit from the strong growth in broadband Internet access expected over the next few years. Covad also has strong distribution channels through strategic relationships with AT&T, Qwest Communications and Concentric. However, the path to success is not guaranteed. The planned merger of AOL and Time Warner could speed the deployment of cable access, making it the broadband access of choice for consumers. In the business world though, DSL is shaping up to be the broadband platform of choice.

Key Statistics	COVD
Market Cap (4/20/00):	$4,804m
Free Float:	26.2%
IPO Date:	1/22/99
Offer Price:	$18.00
Price (4/20/00):	$30.69
52 week high:	$66.62
52 week low:	$23.12
Volatility: (avg. daily % ch)	3.8%
Price/Sales:	72.3
Price/Sales-Growth:	6.3

Covad

www.topinternetstocks.com

Annual Financial Data ($ m)	12/1994	12/1995	12/1996	12/1997	12/1998	12/1999
Revenues	--	--	--	0.03	5.33	66.49
Operating Profit	--	--	--	-2.77	-37.68	-171.60
Net Income	--	--	--	-2.61	-48.12	-195.40
Subscribers	--	--	--	--	--	57,000
Key Ratios:						
Gross Margin	--	--	--	-107.7%	14.3%	16.8%
Operating Margin	--	--	--	nm	-707.5%	-258.1%
Net Margin	--	--	--	nm	-903.5%	-293.9%
Marketing as % of Revenues	--	--	--	--	--	--

Critical Path, Inc.

http://www.cp.net   eServices

Address:
320 First Street   Phone: 415.808.8800
San Francisco, CA 94105   Fax: 415.808.8777
Management:
Chairman: David Hayden
CEO: Douglas T. Hickey
President: David Thatcher
CFO: Mark Rubash

Description

You've got email, or at least Critical Path does. The company looks after more than 100 million email accounts both in the US and around the globe. Critical Path was launched in January 1997, but didn't begin its email outsourcing and hosting services until October 1997. The company went public in March 1999 and has grown rapidly since then, with administered mailboxes growing from 1.4 million in Q1 to 11.1 million by December 1999. Critical Path charges a monthly per mailbox fee of 15-20 cents for Web or portal email, $1 per mailbox for ISPs and $4-5 for corporate mailboxes. Customers include E*Trade, CompuServe, Network Solutions, US West and Sprint. E*Trade accounted for 23% of revenues in the first nine months of 1999. Critical Path has also been expanding into unified Internet messaging solutions, offering wireless messaging, fax, calendar and resource scheduling.

Opportunities

- Email is quickly becoming the communication method of choice for millions of consumers and businesses. Corporate email users are expected to grow from 148 million to 300 million by the end of 2000.
- International Data Corporation estimates that the volume of email messages is expected to grow from 2.5 billion per day in 1999 to 8 billion a day in 2002.
- As email increases in volume and complexity, the total cost of ownership (TCO) grows. Companies currently spend between $12 to $14 per mailbox each month for deployment and support costs. Outsourcing can reduce the costs by 50% or more.

- Portals and other Web sites are rushing to offer free email to their users in order to increase stickiness. Outsourcing is more cost-effective than adding the infrastructure and accompanying support costs.

Challenges

- Critical Path is facing growing competition from a number of sources including CommTouch Software, Mail.com and USA.net. As the company expands into unified messaging solutions, it will also expand into new competitive areas.
- Corporations are reluctant to outsource mission-critical communications to third parties due to security concerns and loss-of-control issues. A Gartner Group survey found that only 10% of companies outsourced their email, and only 1% turned over complete control.

The Bottom Line

Critical Path is offering the path of least cost to its customers, saving corporations millions of dollars each year to handle their messaging needs. The market for corporate email outsourcing and private-label email is just developing, but already growing rapidly, and Critical Path is one of the leading companies in this area. Although competition is heating up, the major challenge will be to convince corporations to outsource mission-critical and sensitive email management to third-party providers like Critical Path. However, judging by Critical Path's strong revenue and customer growth, this has not been a problem.

Key Statistics	CPTH
Market Cap (4/20/00):	$2,614m
Free Float:	70.9%
IPO Date:	3/29/99
Offer Price:	$24.00
Price (4/20/00):	$45.12
52 week high:	$123.00
52 week low:	$28.06
Volatility: (avg. daily % ch)	6.5%
Price/Sales:	161.8
Price/Sales-Growth:	9.5

Critical Path

www.topinternetstocks.com

Annual Financial Data ($ m)	12/1994	12/1995	12/1996	12/1997	12/1998	12/1999
Revenues	--	--	--	--	0.90	16.16
Operating Profit	--	--	--	-1.06	-11.45	-121.78
Net Income	--	--	--	-1.07	-11.46	-115.48
Mailboxes	--	--	--	--	1.0	11.1
Key Ratios:						
Gross Margin	--	--	--	--	-261.5%	-133.4%
Operating Margin	--	--	--	--	-1276.3%	-753.8%
Net Margin	--	--	--	--	-1277.7%	-714.7%
Marketing as % of Revenues	--	--	--	--	188.1%	85.5%

Cylink Corporation

http://www.cylink.com   eSecurity

Address:
3131 Jay Street   Phone: 408.855.6000
Santa Clara, CA 95054   Fax: 408.855.6100

Management:
Chairman: Dr. Leo A. Guthart
President & CEO: William P. Crowell
CFO: Roger A. Barnes

Description

Cylink was founded in 1983 as one of the first companies to develop and market security solutions using public key cryptography to protect computer networks. The company's security solutions protect communications across the Internet and private networks by first authenticating network access with Digital Signature Standard (DSS) supported by digital certificates, and then encrypting data transmission by issuing a "key" using public key technology. Customers include Citibank, Bankers Trust, Bank of America, Cisco, Deutsche Bank and the US Treasury Department.

Opportunities

- Security is becoming more of an issue as consumers turn to the Web for online shopping and businesses turn to the Web for mission-critical functions. This "mainstreaming" of the Internet will drive the growth in security solutions. IDC estimates that the Internet security market will expand to $7.4 billon in 2002 from an estimated $3.1 billion in 1998.
- Corporate IT budgets in 1999 were focused on solving Y2K concerns, which slowed the spending on Internet security solutions. This is expected to reverse in 2000 as businesses accelerate their IT spending on security solutions, leading to strong revenue growth for the market leaders.
- Cylink is recapturing momentum after a difficult year plagued by sales shortfalls and other factors. In the third quarter of 1999, orders and backlog had picked up substantially, pointing to accelerated revenue growth.

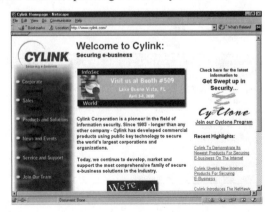

Challenges

- Cylink competes either directly or indirectly in the security solutions market with Axent Technologies, Check Point Software, RSA Security, AT&T and Northern Telecomm. In addition, it also competes indirectly with Microsoft and other software vendors that are building security solutions within their software products.
- Cylink is coming off a difficult 1999, when the company was hit by accounting concerns, disappointing earnings results and management turmoil. If the company has not been successful in putting its problems behind it, Cylink could again fall into disfavor with investors.

Bottom Line

Cylink is recapturing momentum after a difficult year plagued by sales shortfalls, account irregularities and a management exodus. It appears as if these troubles are now behind the company, and on a valuation basis, Cylink is one of the most attractive Internet stocks available. The Internet security solutions market is beginning to accelerate, with a larger percentage of corporate IT budgets being targeted towards tightening security. Cylink is a company that is well on its way to recapturing investor confidence in an accelerating market.

Key Statistics	CYLK
Market Cap (4/20/00):	$353.8m
Free Float:	41.0%
IPO Date:	2/16/96
Offer Price:	$15.00
Price (4/20/00):	$11.62
52 week high:	$22.75
52 week low:	$3.50
Volatility: (avg. daily % ch)	4.0%
Price/Sales:	5.9
Price/Sales-Growth:	15.0

www.topinternetstocks.com

Annual Financial Data ($ m)	12/1994	12/1995	12/1996	12/1997	12/1998	12/1999
Revenues	17.97	21.53	25.79	47.69	42.76	59.66
Operating Profit	-4.14	-4.13	-8.21	-67.97	-28.86	-18.79
Net Income	--	-0.06	1.20	-61.75	5.16	-14.57
Customers	--	--	--	--	--	--
Key Ratios:						
Gross Margin	--	68.0%	62.3%	70.7%	60.5%	67.9%
Operating Margin	-23.1	-19.2%	-31.8%	-142.5%	-67.5%	-31.5%
Net Margin	--	-0.3%	4.6%	-129.5%	12.1%	-24.4%
Marketing as % of Revenues	--	26.5%	36.7%	33.6%	56.4%	44.1%

Digital Island, Inc.

http://www.digisle.net   eBusiness

Address:
45 Fremont St., 12th Fl.   Tel: 415.738.4100
San Francisco, CA 94105   Fax: 415.738.4141
Management:
Chairman & CEO: Ruann F. Ernst
President: Leo S. Spiegel
CFO: Tom L. Thompson

Description

Digital Island is one of the leading providers of network services, helping multinational corporations to deliver business-critical applications for marketing, selling, servicing and distributing products over the Internet. Digital Island was founded in Hawaii in 1995 to help reduce the problem of Internet congestion or bottlenecks.

The company's services include global content delivery, hosting and application services. Digital Island's Intelligent Network operates in 21 countries throughout the US, Europe Asia and Latin America. The company has more than 169 customers including Cisco Systems, Autodesk, E*Trade, National Semiconductor and Novell. E*Trade was responsible for 35% of revenues in fiscal 1999, and the top four customers accounted for 44% of total sales.

Opportunities

- As the number of Internet users continues to grow, traffic jams or network congestion is becoming more of an issue. In addition, more businesses are using the Internet for key business applications, leading to further congestion.
- Digital Island is one of the only companies that provides an integrated solution offering everything from hosting to content delivery, application services and a high-speed private network connecting five international data centers.
- In December 1999, Digital Island acquired Sandpiper Network, adding 1,200 enterprise-class servers and extending its reach in the content delivery arena.
- Digital Island partnered with Sun and Inktomi in December 1999 to further strengthen its content delivery and network services. This alliance should help Digital Island aggres-

sively expand its server capabilities by 5,000 additional servers over the next three years.

Challenges

- As an integrated network services company, Digital Island competes on several fronts: content delivery, hosting, application services and network services. Competitors include Akamai, Adero, Exodus, AT&T and Frontier GlobalCenter. As these competitors expand their integrated services, competition will become more intense.
- Revenue concentration risk is a concern, with the top four customers accounting for 44% of revenues in fiscal (September) 1999. If Digital Island were to lose one of these customers, revenue growth would be severely impacted.

The Bottom Line

Digital Island provides an island of efficiency in a sea of network congestion and Internet traffic jams. It is one of the leading providers of integrated services, helping businesses speed up their delivery of business-critical applications and Web content through a combination of local servers and a high-speed Intelligent Network. Although Digital Island competes aggressively on several fronts including the content delivery side with Akamai and Adero, and on the hosting side with Exodus and PSINet, it is currently one of the only players to offer an integrated solution. When it comes to helping companies deliver on fast and efficient Web content and services, Digital Island has the early and important lead in the race.

Key Statistics	ISLD
Market Cap (4/20/00):	$2,089m
Free Float:	75.0%
IPO Date:	6/29/99
Offer Price:	$10.00
Price (4/20/00):	$32.38
52 week high:	$156.94
52 week low:	$8.62
Volatility: (avg. daily % ch)	8.5%
Price/Sales:	112.1
Price/Sales-Growth:	25.4

Digital Island

www.topinternetstocks.com

Annual Financial Data ($ m)	9/1994	9/1995	9/1996	9/1997	9/1998	9/1999
Revenues	--	--	--	0.22	2.34	12.43
Operating Profit	-0.03	-0.01	-0.03	-5.38	-17.12	-52.49
Net Income	-0.03	-0.01	-0.03	-5.29	-16.76	-50.94
Customers	--	--	--	--	--	130
Key Ratios:						
Gross Margin	--	--	--	-1050.5%	-285.8%	-137.3%
Operating Margin	--	--	--	-2466.1%	-730.5%	-422.2%
Net Margin	--	--	--	-2426.1%	-715.5%	-409.8%
Marketing as % of Revenues	--	--	--	552.8%	206.9%	128.8%

DLJdirect, Inc.

http://www.dljdirect.com   eFinancials

Address:
277 Park Ave.   Phone: 212.892.3000
New York, NY 10172   Fax: 212.892.7272
Management:
Chairman: John S. Chalsty (DLJ's Board)
President & CEO: Blake Darcy
CFO: Anthony F. Daddino

Description

DLJdirect puts its name on the line and succeeds. The online broker, a subsidiary of Donaldson, Lufkin & Jenrette (DLJ), first began offering online trades back in 1988 as PC Financial Network. It changed its name to DLJdirect in 1997 and relaunched its site as www.dljdirect.com. In 1999, DLJdirect had 795,000 total online customer accounts (347,000 active accounts) and $21.7 billion in customer assets. Along with brokerage services, DLJdirect is also active in equity underwriting, participating in more than 20 public offerings because of the ties to its parent company. DLJ, in a move to unlock value of its online division, issued a tracking stock of its Net brokerage operations in May 1999. A tracking stock reflects or "tracks" the performance of a particular division but holds no economic ownership. Parent company, DLJ owns roughly 82% of the outstanding shares.

Opportunities

- Online trading is quickly becoming the vehicle of choice for investors. From less than 2 million accounts in 1996, online accounts in the US are expected to grow more than 34% annually to more than 25 million by 2003.
- DLJdirect has a strong brand identity among investors, leveraging the DLJ name. The DLJ affiliation has also helped DLJdirect participate in and distribute more than 20 IPOs to its customer base in 1999.
- DLJ's association with Equitable and Alliance Capital (through AXA Financial) could help DLJdirect expand its product offering to include mutual funds, insurance and other consumer financial services.

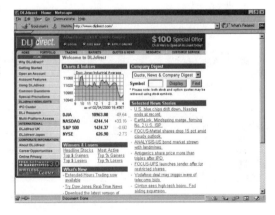

Challenges

- Over 166 online brokers and counting! The online brokerage industry is one of the most competitive sectors in the Internet economy. In addition to the scores of discount brokers competing online, the traditional financial institutions such as Merrill Lynch and Morgan Stanley, are also moving online.
- Customer acquisition costs have been trending up while trading fees have been trending down. This puts pressure on margins and profitability.
- A tracking stock merely tracks the performance of a division, it holds no equity ownership, and in DLJdirect's case, no voting rights. In addition, because DLJdirect is a unit of DLJ, conflicts of interest could arise between the parent and its subsidiary, leading to board decisions detrimental to DLJdirect.

The Bottom Line

Although DLJdirect is a veteran of online trading, with more than 10 years experience, it received little support from its parent company until recently. Now it is successfully playing catch-up and is emerging as one of the leading players in the eBrokerage industry. The company appears willing to spend heavily to acquire customers both in the US and in Japan, where it has experienced strong account growth. However, as other eBrokers spend aggressively in order to attract customers, it will become more challenging for DLJdirect to differentiate itself from the other top competitors. Having said that, DLJdirect does have the benefit of a strong brand identity, ranking as the top online broker in *Barron's* 1999 survey.

Key Statistics	DIR
Market Cap (4/20/00):	$1,072m
Free Float:	15.0%
IPO Date:	5/26/99
Offer Price:	$20.00
Price (4/20/00):	$10.44
52 week high:	$45.62
52 week low:	$9.00
Volatility: (avg. daily % ch)	3.94%
Price/Sales:	4.5
Price/Sales-Growth:	4.4

DLJdirect

www.topinternetstocks.com

Annual Financial Data ($ m)	12/1994	12/1995	12/1996	12/1997	12/1998	12/1999
Net Revenues	34.15	47.27	63.16	67.22	117.92	238.07
Operating Profit	7.66	11.62	13.28	-6.13	2.47	18.04
Net Income	4.53	6.87	7.86	-3.62	1.46	6.93
Active Accounts (m)	--	--	0.11	0.14	0.21	0.35
Key Ratios:						
Gross Margin	--	--	--	--	--	--
Operating Margin	22.4%	24.6%	21.0%	-9.1%	2.1%	7.6%
Net Margin	13.3%	14.5%	12.4%	-5.4%	1.2%	2.9%
Marketing as % of Revenues	5.8%	8.8%	14.4%	19.5%	21.3%	26.4%

DoubleClick Inc.

http://www.doubleclick.net   eServices

Address:
450 W. 33rd Street   Phone: 212.683.0001
New York, NY 10001   Fax: 212.889.0062
Management:
Chairman & CEO: Kevin J. O'Connor
President & COO: Kevin P. Ryan
CFO: Stephen Collins

Description

Advertising on the Net? Chances are, that you will end up clicking on DoubleClick. The Web's largest ad solutions company serves over one billion ads each day. The company started back in 1995 when co-founders Kevin O'Connor and Dwight Merriman developed the idea of helping companies sell, manage and track online advertising. At year-end 1999, the company sold advertising for more than 4,000 different advertisers on a network of more than 1,300 Web sites and reaching nearly 32 million unique Web users per month. In addition to selling advertising, DoubleClick also serves ads with its DART technology. DART manages all the ad serving and reporting functions for Web sites through DoubleClick's own servers. In 1999, DoubleClick acquired its competitor, NetGravity, in a move to expand its client base, as well as direct marketer, Abacus Direct, to eventually provide virtual one-to-one marketing. Eighty percent of DoubleClick's revenues are generated through ad sales commissions.

Opportunities

- Internet advertising is expected to grow from $2.9 billion in 1999 to more than $12.5 billion by 2003. Regardless of which portals may emerge as the winners in the race to capture eyeballs and generate advertising revenue, DoubleClick wins by selling the ads and supplying the technology to manage and measure performance.

- DoubleClick has a strong presence in international markets where Internet usage is growing twice as fast as in the US. International sales accounted for 20% of revenues in 1999.

- Abacus Direct is a traditional direct marketing company with a history of over 3 billion consumer transactions, including

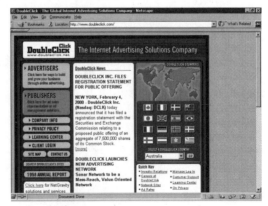

names and addresses. By integrating Abacus' offline database with Double-Click's online database, the acquisition will allow DoubleClick to better target online ads to consumer's actual purchasing histories, providing more effective ad campaigns.

Challenges

- Competition is heating up with Internet heavyweight CMGI expanding its presence in the online advertising market through its acquisition of several online ad companies and subsequent folding into Engage Technologies.
- AltaVista, which CMGI acquired in 1999, represents 25% of DoubleClick's revenues, and CMGI is unlikely to renew the contract once it expires in 2002.
- Privacy issues could pose a problem as DoubleClick strives to collect as much information as possible about consumers, then use that data to serve targeted adverting to those consumers.

The Bottom Line

McDonald's may be the leader in serving hamburgers, but DoubleClick is the leader in serving ads in cyberspace. The online ad solutions company controls the lion's share of the market. However CMGI, through a series of acquisitions, is quickly building up its presence. It remains to be seen, though, whether CMGI can smoothly integrate the six acquisitions to offer a single end-to-end solution similar to what DoubleClick offers. For now, and likely in the future, click on an ad, and you will probably be clicking on DoubleClick.

Key Statistics	DCLK
Market Cap (4/20/00):	$6,597m
Free Float:	74.2%
IPO Date:	2/20/98
Offer Price (adj):	$4.25
Price (4/20/00):	$55.44
52 week high:	$135.25
52 week low:	$30.25
Volatility: (avg. daily % ch)	5.65%
Price/Sales:	25.5
Price/Sales-Growth:	29.6

DoubleClick

www.topinternetstocks.com

Annual Financial Data ($ m)	12/1994	12/1995	12/1996	12/1997	12/1998	12/1999
Revenues	--	--	25.99	67.93	138.72	258.29
Operating Profit	--	--	-1.42	-3.83	-14.97	-58.72
Net Income	--	--	-3.95	-7.74	-18.04	-55.82
Customers	--	--	--	--	--	--
Key Ratios:						
Gross Margin	--	--	68.3%	57.1%	50.4%	58.5%
Operating Margin	--	--	-5.5%	-5.6%	-10.8%	-22.7%
Net Margin	--	--	-15.2%	-11.4%	-13.0%	-21.6%
Marketing as % of Revenues	--	--	39.3%	36.5%	37.6%	40.1%

drugstore.com, Inc.

http://www.drugstore.com   eTailer

Address:

13920 SE Eastgate Way   Phone: 425.372.3200
Ste. 300 Bellevue WA 98005   Fax: 425.372.3800

Management:

Chairman, President & CEO: Peter M. Neupert
CFO: David E. Rostov

Description

drugstore.com is the virtual pharmacy on the Web. The company was founded in April 1998 and opened its cyber-doors in February 1999. Barely five months later, in July, the cyber-drugstore completed its public offering. drugstore.com is an online retailer for health, beauty, wellness, personal care and pharmacy products. The company offers over 17,000 SKUs (different products) for sale through its site. drugstore.com acquired privately held Beauty.com in early 2000 in a move to expand its product offerings into the prestige cosmetics and fragrances market. The company also has strategic relationships with Rite Aid, General Nutrition Companies (GNC) and Amazon.com. Rite Aid owns approximately 18% and Amazon.com owns approximately 23.5% of the online retailer.

Opportunities

- Total consumer spending in the five product categories that drugstore.com is targeting was an estimated $165 billion in 1998 and could reach $220 billion by 2003. Assuming just 15% of that spending moves online by 2003, the market opportunity is close to $33 billion.
- Under the Rite Aid relationship, customers can order drugs online for same-day pickup at any Rite Aid pharmacy. This provides drugstore.com a strong distribution channel in the form of 3,800 retail outlets nationwide.
- In addition, drugstore.com entered into a strategic relationship with Rite Aid's PCS Health Systems, one of the largest pharmacy benefit managers. PCS' 56 million members can buy their prescriptions from drugstore.com using their insurance benefit.
- Drugstore.com was among the first Internet pharmacies to receive the Verified

Internet Pharmacy Practice Sites (VPPS) certification from the National Association Boards of Pharmacy (NABP).

Challenges

- Anytime a market opportunity opens up, companies quickly jump into the fray. The competitive environment has rapidly grown very intense, with Internet up-starts PlanetRX.com, MotherNature.com and Healthshop.com competing in the same markets. In addition, established giants such as Walgreens, CVS, Wal-Mart, K-Mart and Kroger also are ramping up their online strategies and could compete in the same categories that drugstore.com is active in.
- The US government is considering regulating online sales of prescription products, with the White House proposing that online drugstores receive FDA approval and be subject to a $500,000 fine if caught selling unauthorized prescriptions. These discussions could put pressure on sector valuations.

The Bottom Line

drugstore.com has claimed a strong first-mover advantage in the rapidly growing world of online prescriptions, health and beauty products. Partnerships with Rite Aid and Amazon.com, both of which have equity stakes in the company, also give drugstore.com strong distribution channels. The greater competitive challenge that the company could face would be the traditional drugstore chains and the giant retailers as they move online. However, most of these traditional companies have been slow moving to the Web, which gives drugstore.com a strong lead in the online race.

Key Statistics	DSCM
Market Cap (4/20/00):	$419.4m
Free Float:	28.1%
IPO Date:	7/28/99
Offer Price:	$18.00
Price (4/20/00):	$8.06
52 week high:	$70.00
52 week low:	$5.88
Volatility: (avg. daily % ch)	6.7%
Price/Sales:	12.0
Price/Sales-Growth:	--

drugstore.com

www.topinternetstocks.com

Annual Financial Data ($ m)	12/1994	12/1995	12/1996	12/1997	12/1998	12/1999
Sales	--	--	--	--	--	34.85
Operating Profit	--	--	--	--	-8.20	-120.74
Net Income	--	--	--	--	-8.03	-115.83
Customers	--	--	--	--	--	695,000
Key Ratios:						
Gross Margin	--	--	--	--	--	-10.3%
Operating Margin	--	--	--	--	--	-346.5%
Net Margin	--	--	--	--	--	-332.4%
Marketing as % of Sales	--	--	--	--	--	176.5%

E*TRADE Group, Inc.

http://www.etrade.com   eFinancials

Address:
4500 Bohannon Drive   Phone: 650.331.6000
Menlo Park, CA 94025   Fax: 650.842.2552
Management:
Chairman & CEO: Christos M. Cotsakos
President & COO: Kathy Levinson
EVP & CFO: Leonard C. Purkis

Description

E*TRADE, along with its other eBroker cousins, has revolutionized the way
the world invests. The company started out as a security transaction bureau under
the name of ET Execution Services back in 1982. In 1992, the company transformed itself into E*TRADE Securities and began offering online trading through
CompuServe and AOL. In February 1996, E*TRADE officially launched its
www.etrade.com Web site to offer Internet-based trading. From there, E*TRADE
went on to define an industry that brought the high-brow investment banks like
Merrill Lynch and Morgan Stanley to their knees. Six months after launching its
Web site, E*TRADE went public in August 1996. By year-end 1999, the company had amassed 1.9 million online accounts and $44 billion in customer assets.

In addition to offering discounted brokerage services, E*TRADE has also
been expanding into other areas, with the goal of becoming a comprehensive
global financial services firm. In 1999, E*TRADE acquired ClearStation, an eFi-
nance and community site, TIR Holdings, an international financial services company that offers multi-currency securities execution and settlement services and
Confluent, the developer of the Abrio calendar engine.

E*TRADE is expanding its its reach into other investment banking activities
with E*Offering, an online investment bank, as well as online banking with its
acquisition of Telebanc, one of the leading branchless banks. E*TRADE has also
been expanding aggressively overseas and now has local affiliated sites with financial news and trading in
over 20 countries including the
UK, Japan, Germany, France,
Canada, Denmark, Sweden,
Australia, New Zealand, Korea
and South Africa. The company's goal is to be the leading
online financial destination for
consumers, in essence, a financial supermarket.

Opportunities

- The brokerage industry is one area where the Internet has swept through like a firestorm, changing everything in its path. From just a handful of accounts just a few short years ago, more than 8 million investors traded online at the end of 1999. By 2003, more than 25 million people in the US are expected to be trading online.
- In contrast to online retailing, where customers can switch cyberstores at the drop of the hat, switching costs in the online brokerage industry are relatively high. This creates opportunities for those brokers that can capture the most visitors and convert them to customers.
- E*TRADE is the most recognized name in the online brokerage sector, with more than 2.2 million people visiting its site each month. In comparison, its closet competitors have less than half that number of visitors accessing their sites. The company is also the second largest Web broker with a 20% share of the estimated 8 million online accounts.
- By expanding into other financial areas, such as investment banking, online banking and possibly online bill payments, E*TRADE is diversifying its revenue base away from the volatile trading commission side and moving into higher margin financial services.

Challenges

- The online brokerage industry is a hypercompetitive environment with more than 100 brokers competing for online accounts. Competition is likely to remain fierce and could intensify with better-capitalized companies marketing aggressively to capture market share.
- Customer acquisition costs have been trending up, while trading commissions have been trending down. In other words, as eBrokers spend more on advertising, they are charging less for trades. This creates pressures on margins and profitability within the industry.
- Strong growth and popularity has its downside in the form of a Web site that is often stretched beyond capacity. Although E*TRADE has been constantly beefing up its site to manage the strong traffic and customer growth, the goal is difficult to achieve. E*TRADE's site – like many of its eBroker cousins – has been suffering from system outages many times during the year, and in some instances customers could not trade for up to two hours during busy market periods. Future outages could potentially lead to class action lawsuits and customer losses.
- Although declining as a percentage of total revenue, E*TRADE still derives substantial revenues from volatile trading commissions. This leaves the company vulnerable to any slowdown in trading volumes or stock market corrections.
- With the merger of Telebanc in January 2000, E*TRADE has increased its exposure to interest rate risk. Any changes in interest rates could have an impact on the net interest income that E*TRADE will generate from online banking activities.

The Bottom Line

The key to succeeding in the online brokerage industry is differentiation. E*TRADE has managed to do just that with its *Destination E*TRADE* campaign. The result is that E*TRADE is the top financial brokerage destination on the Web according to a survey of US Web users by Media Metrix. But the company is not stopping there. E*TRADE is also expanding aggressively into international markets with local branded Web sites throughout Europe and Asia – 20 countries in all as of early 2000.

However with margins and profitability under pressure from several fronts, E*TRADE needs to see that new accounts and new revenue streams are growing quicker than the decline in margins. Up until now, that hasn't been a problem for the company. E*TRADE's acquisition of Telebanc will also help to add new revenues for the company by giving it a broad platform of new financial products that it can leverage across its existing and new customer account base. This will also help to lessen the impact of earnings volatility that characterizes the brokerage business.

E*TRADE's mission is to be the global leader in online personal financial services well into the 21st Century. Judging by its growth and its popularity as a financial destination, E*TRADE should have no problem seeing its goal remaining a reality.

Key Statistics	EGRP
Market Cap (4/20/00):	$5,818m
Free Float:	55.0%
IPO Date:	8/16/96
Offer Price (adj):	$2.63
Price (4/20/00):	$20.12
52 week high:	$63.00
52 week low:	$16.06
Volatility: (avg. daily % ch)	5.3%
Price/Sales:	7.7
Price/Sales-Growth:	8.7

E*Trade

www.topinternetstocks.com

Annual Financial Data ($ m)	9/1994	9/1995	9/1996	9/1997	9/1998	9/1999
Net Revenues	15.41	108.96	141.80	234.13	335.76	621.40
Operating Profit	0.65	9.63	4.21	30.27	2.91	-132.40
Net Income	1.19	7.33	4.17	19.19	1.93	-54.44
Active Accounts (m)	--	.04	.09	.23	.54	1.55
Key Ratios:						
Gross Margin	--	--	--	--	--	--
Operating Margin	4.2%	8.8%	3.0%	12.9%	0.9%	-21.3%
Net Margin	7.7%	6.7%	2.9%	8.2%	0.6%	-8.8%
Marketing as % of Revenues	15.4%	41.2%	36.9%	28.7%	34.9%	48.5%

EarthLink Network, Inc.

http://www.earthlink.com

eAccess

Address:
1430 W. Peachtree NW, Ste. 400
Atlanta, GA 30309

Phone: 404.815.0770
Fax: 404.815.8805

Management:

Chairman: Charles M. Brewer
CEO: Charles G. Betty
CFO: Lee Adrean

Description

EarthLink was founded in June 1994 after its founder, Sky Dayton spent over 80 frustrating hours trying to connect to the Internet through a local ISP. In less than a year, EarthLink gained 100,000 subscribers, breaking through the one million mark by December 1998. The company is also rolling out high-speed DSL service in conjunction with Sprint, MCI's UUNet, GTE and Pacific Bell, and has partnered with Charter Communications to offer Internet access via cable modems. Joining the free PC movement, EarthLink recently entered into an exclusive agreement with FreeMac.com to be the official ISP of give away Apple Macs. EarthLink merged with rival MindSpring in early 2000, a move that should help the combined company vault ahead of Microsoft's MSN and ATT Worldnet to become the number two Internet access provider in the US.

Opportunities

- EarthLink is one of the fastest growing ISPs. The company's strategic partnership with Sprint also guarantees it an additional 750,000 subscribers from Sprint over the next five years.
- A churn rate of 3.5% per month is lower than the industry average, indicating higher-than-average consumer satisfaction with EarthLink's services. This is important in the world of consumer dial-up access, where Internet access is a commodity business and consumers regularly switch providers.
- The company is positioning itself for the coming broadband revolution. It is forming strategic partnerships with various local and long-distance telephone providers on the DSL side and Charter Communications on the cable modem side.

Challenges

- Competition is fierce and loyalty is low in the consumer ISP market. There are currently over 7,000 Internet service providers in the US, and consumers switch ISPs on a moments notice. Providing value-added services in a commodity business can be an uphill challenge.
- Free Internet access is the stealth danger for consumer-oriented ISPs. What started out taking Europe by storm has now crossed the pond and is making inroads in the US. NetZero, AltaVista and Qwest were the first companies to offer free Internet access in the US, and Microsoft may soon follow suit. If free access does catch on in the US, ISPs will need to find other revenue sources either on the advertising or ecommerce front to make up for the shortfall in subscription revenues.

The Bottom Line

EarthLink is one of the fastest growing consumer ISPs in the dial-up access market. However, subscription-based business models for dial-up Internet access stand in danger of going the way of the dinosaur, with free Internet access being the norm in one to two years. EarthLink is at risk here and will need to find other revenue opportunities either by bundling free PCs with Internet access, a move which will lock in subscribers for three years, or by developing advertising, ecommerce, or other value-added revenues sources. The merger with MindSpring will help create the second largest ISP behind America Online.

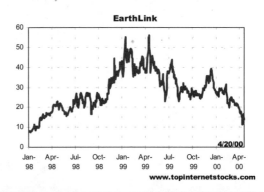

Key Statistics	ELNK
Market Cap (4/20/00):	$1,662m
Free Float:	50.9%
IPO Date:	1/22/97
Offer Price (adj):	$6.50
Price (4/20/00):	$14.06
52 week high:	$76.69
52 week low:	$10.56
Volatility: (avg. daily % ch)	5.3%
Price/Sales:	2.5
Price/Sales-Growth:	1.9

www.topinternetstocks.com

Annual Financial Data ($ m)	12/1994	12/1995	12/1996	12/1997	12/1998	12/1999
Revenues	0.21	5.26	51.36	133.45	290.61	670.43
Operating Profit	-0.23	-7.25	-37.78	-32.20	-4.77	-47.41
Net Income	-0.23	-8.08	-38.76	-34.00	-53.18	-173.69
Subscribers (m)	--	--	--	.70	1.69	3.12
Key Ratios:						
Gross Margin	67.8%	55.9%	45.5%	58.9%	60.2%	62.9%
Operating Margin	-108.1%	-137.8%	-73.6%	-24.1%	-1.6%	-7.1%
Net Margin	-108.1%	-153.7%	-75.5%	-25.5%	-18.3%	-25.9%
Marketing as % of Revenues	17.5%	82.6%	41.8%	25.8%	22.4%	32.7%

EarthWeb Inc.

http://www.earthweb.com   eServices

Address:
3 Park Avenue   Phone: 212.725.6550
New York, NY 10016   Fax: 212.725.6559
Management:
Chairman:
President & CEO: Jack D. Hidary
SVP of Finance: Irene Math

Description

   EarthWeb is the information technology (IT) portal to the world. EarthWeb started out as a Web design and development shop in October 1994 but shifted its strategy in late 1995 toward providing IT-related resources including Java developer kits, technical manuals and other content to the developer community. Today, EarthWeb offers over 150,000 technical resources including online technical books, articles, news, discussion forums and a retail store for development software. EarthWeb is also one of the leading career sites for IT professionals with over 200,000 job listings on its dice.com job board. Revenues are generated through paid job listings (51%), banner and sponsorship advertising (32%) and premium products (17%) which include subscriptions and ecommerce revenues. Barter or non-cash revenues account for roughly 10% of total revenue.

Opportunities

- International Data Corporation (IDC) estimates that the worldwide market for IT products and services is expected to grow from an estimated $800 billion in 1998 to more than $1.1 trillion by 2002. This strong spending growth will be accompanied by a rapid growth in IT professionals, which is the market that EarthWeb is targeting.
- Internet advertising, although a new medium, has already surpassed outdoor advertising in revenues. By 2003, Pegasus Research estimates that Internet advertising in the US will grow to more than $12.5 billion.

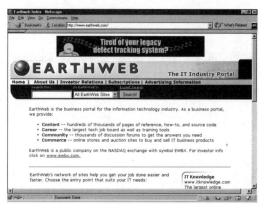

- EarthWeb has successfully distinguished itself from some of its competitors, through the breadth of services aimed at the IT professional community.

Challenges

- Barriers to entry are virtually nonexistent in the hyper competitive portal space. EarthWeb competes against CNET, ZDNet, CMP and Internet.com for IT-related traffic and advertising dollars. In addition, it also competes with the larger horizontal portals such as Yahoo!, AOL and Lycos for advertising revenues. EarthWeb's dice.com competes against career Web sites such as HotJobs.com, Monster.com and CareerPath for traffic and paid job listings.
- Since changing its focus in 1996, EarthWeb has been growing quickly through a series of acquisitions and is likely to continue its growth through further acquisitions. The challenge with this strategy is that EarthWeb may have difficulties smoothly integrating the various properties it targets, which could lead to higher turnover and slower revenue growth.

Bottom Line

EarthWeb is solidly grounded in its portal strategy to IT professionals. Although it faces competition from a number of sites including CNET, ZDNet and Internet.com, its content offering is much more technically-oriented, a fact that has helped it become the leading community to IT professionals. The breadth of its services also include one of the leading IT job boards (dice.com) as well as training and certification services. If EarthWeb can continue to maintain its quality and depth of IT technical content and service (i.e. successfully differentiate itself), it stands a very good chance of being the Yahoo! to the techno crowd.

Key Statistics	EWBX
Market Cap (4/20/00):	$106.0m
Free Float:	51.2%
IPO Date:	11/11/98
Offer Price:	$14.00
Price (4/20/00):	$10.50
52 week high:	$62.75
52 week low:	$8.12
Volatility: (avg. daily % ch)	4.4%
Price/Sales:	3.4
Price/Sales-Growth:	0.4

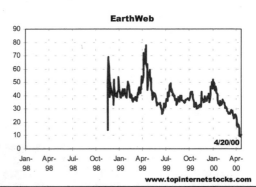

EarthWeb

www.topinternetstocks.com

Annual Financial Data ($ m)	12/1994	12/1995	12/1996	12/1997	12/1998	12/1999
Revenues	--	--	0.47	1.14	3.35	31.05
Operating Profit	--	-0.70	-2.07	-5.70	-9.28	-35.52
Net Income	--	-0.64	-2.05	-7.82	-8.97	-34.71
Unique Visitors	--	--	--	--	--	--
Key Ratios:						
Gross Margin	--	--	33.5%	-19.6%	36.4%	64.7%
Operating Margin	--	--	-437.5%	-502.6%	-277.0%	-114.4%
Net Margin	--	--	-433.5%	-689.1%	-267.8%	-111.8%
Sales+Marketing as % of Revenues	--	--	53.4%	89.7%	135.8%	89.3%

eBay Inc.

http://www.ebay.com   eTailer

Address:
2125 Hamilton Ave.   Phone: 408.558.7400
San Jose, CA 95125   Fax: 408.369.4855
Management:
Founder & Chairman: Pierre M. Omidyar
President & CEO: Margaret C. Whitman
CFO & VP: Gary F. Bengier

Description

Going once, going twice, sold! That is the mantra that is playing out over 450,000 times a day on eBay, the Internet's largest virtual auction house. eBay was initially launched in September 1995 as Auction Web when founder, Pierre Omidyar helped his wife use the Internet to collect Pez candy dispensers. The company changed its name to eBay in September 1997, and by the end of that year, it had amassed 340,000 registered users. From those beginnings, eBay grew to be the largest person-to-person trading community on the Internet, offering auctions, chat rooms and bulletin boards. Along the way, eBay completed its own auction with a initial public offering in September 1998. Shares were bid up 163% on its first day.

As of the end of 1999, the company had an estimated 10 million registered users on its site who were buying and selling over 3.5 million items in more than 3,000 different categories including collectibles, antiques, sports memorabilia, Beanie Babies, dolls, coins and much more.

eBay has been busy on the acquisition trail in a bid to broaden its product offerings. In 1999, it acquired the tony auction house, Butterfield & Butterfield, classic car auction and appraisal service, Kruse International, and alando, a German online auction site. eBay is also targeting the global Internet trading community, expanding its presence with country-specific services for Canada, the UK, Australia, Germany and Japan. The company estimates that its user base are at home in over 200 different countries. eBay Germany is already the second largest trading community in the world with sales of $600,000 per day.

In early 2000, eBay teamed up with Wells Fargo to roll out Billpoint, an online person-to-person bill payment service, for consumers. Billpoint will allow consumers the ability to accept credit cards for payment.

Opportunities

- eBay generates revenues by a taking a percentage of any transactions completed over its site and for placement fees. Because eBay does not actually sell the item itself, but merely acts as the middleman, it has virtually no cost of goods sold which leads to some of the highest gross margins in the Internet sector.
- The eBay or auction model is one of the most scalable models on the Web, with the majority of expenses focused on relatively fixed personnel and technology expenses. Advertising and marketing expenses are the major variable expenses. Now that eBay has reached critical mass (a self-feeding state where buyers go to the site because that is where the greatest selection is, and sellers use the site because it reaches the most buyers), it can begin scaling back advertising and marketing expenses.
- Next to Amazon.com, eBay is the Internet's second most visited ecommerce site, with more than 10.5 million unique visitors visiting its site each month. eBay is also one of the "stickiest" sites on the Web, with some users spending hours browsing through different auctions on each visit.
- In March 1999, eBay entered into a four-year agreement with America Online to run a cobranded auction site and also to be prominently featured on a number of AOL's other sites including AOL.com, CompuServe and Netscape. This gives the company access to AOL's large footprint of 23 million members and 54 million visitors.
- In order to combat fraud, the company has instituted a feedback policy where buyers can rate registered sellers. eBay users can also review the feedback form to check on another user's reputation. This has been very successful at keeping fraudulent trading activities at a minimum and gaining consumers' trust in online commerce.

Challenges

- eBay has been a victim of strong growth, with its Web site often strained to capacity. In June 1999, the company's site was down over 22 hours, which cost eBay nearly $4 million in lost revenues and $3.9 million in credits to its users. These technical challenges could continue to plague eBay in the future, both in terms of higher infrastructure spending and lost revenues.
- With switching costs low in the online auction sector (its just as easy for a shopper to go to Amazon.com's auction site), any system outages could quickly send buyers to either of its major competitor's sites, including Yahoo! Auctions, Go.com, Fairmarket, Onsale and others.
- Fraud is a major concern online, and in particular for person-to-person auction sites. There is no guarantee that either the buyer or seller is legitimate, and any perception of heightened fraud could damage eBay's reputation, leading to lost customers.
- Collectible auctions are highly dependent on particular trends. For example, Beanie Babies accounted for 7% of all transactions in the December 1998 quarter. Other trends, including the Pokeman craze, could lead to volatile

revenue growth. A decline in popularity in these trends could lead to lower transaction volumes and revenue.

The Bottom Line

eBay pioneered the online auction concept and now has the distinction of being one of the most visited ecommerce sites on the Web. But more than just an ecommerce site, it is also an addictive pastime for millions of Web surfers. Just ask any eBay user! Already one of the stickiest sites on the Web, the company is also taking steps to keep registered users on its site longer by adding personalized home pages and other features.

eBay is quickly becoming the ubiquitous global trading community for consumers as it expands into overseas markets, including Europe and Japan. Japan, a nation that is fascinated with collectibles and memorabilia, could provide a strong source of growth for the company on top of its already strong growth in the US and Europe.

Despite eBay's phenomenal success to date, the competition is nipping closely at its heels. Both Amazon.com and Yahoo! have entered the online auction arena, and each boasts more visitors to their sites than eBay (although less customers). In addition, new entrant, Fairmarket, has put together an auction network with MSN, Excite@Home, Lycos, ZDNet and more than 100 other sites. However, eBay still has the lead in terms of the number of items on its cyberauctions. In the end, people are still asking, "Did you get it on eBay?" That's the power of branding.

Key Statistics	EBAY
Market Cap (4/20/00):	$19,560m
Free Float:	27.0%
IPO Date:	10/24/98
Offer Price (adj):	$6.00
Price (4/20/00):	$150.25
52 week high:	$255.00
52 week low:	$70.25
Volatility: (avg. daily % ch)	4.9%
Price/Sales:	87.0
Price/Sales-Growth:	54.1

eBay

www.topinternetstocks.com

Annual Financial Data ($ m)	12/1994	12/1995	12/1996	12/1997	12/1998	12/1999
Sales	--	--	0.37	5.74	86.13	224.72
Operating Profit	--	--	0.25	1.49	12.77	-1.16
Net Income	--	--	0.15	0.87	7.27	10.83
Customers (m)	--	--	.04	.34	2.18	10.00
Key Ratios:						
Gross Margin	--	--	96.2%	87.0%	81.3%	74.4%
Operating Margin	--	--	68.0%	25.9%	14.8%	-0.5%
Net Margin	--	--	39.8%	15.2%	8.4%	4.8%
Marketing as % of Sales	--	--	8.6%	30.1%	41.8%	42.7%

Engage Technologies

http://www.engage.com   eServices

Address:
100 Brickstone Square, 1ˢᵗ Fl.   Phone: 978.684.3884
Andover, MA 01810   Fax: 978.684.3636
Management:
Chairman: David S. Wetherell
CEO & President: Paul L. Schaut
CFO: Stephen A. Royal

Description

Engage has the help of big brother CMGI in becoming one of the leading Internet marketers in its bid to take on industry giant, DoubleClick. The company was born from the incubator lab of CMGI in July 1995 when co-founders David Wetherell and Daniel Jaye decided to combine CMGI's roots in database marketing with its growing knowledge of the Internet. Engage completed its initial public offering in July 1999. The company provides a wide range of software and services that offers profile-driven Internet marketing solutions. This includes Engage AudienceNet, a profile-driven advertising and marketing network, Engage Knowledge, a demographic database of 42 million consumer profiles, AdKnowledge, a Web marketing management service with strong analytic and measurement capabilities, Accipiter AdManager, an ad management system that automates the scheduling, targeting and delivery of ads on Web sites, and I/PRO which provides traffic verification, measurement and analysis software.

Opportunities

- Internet advertising is expected to continue its rapid growth trend, expanding from an estimated $2.9 billion in 1999 to more than $12.5 billion in 2003 according to estimates by Pegasus Research. Despite its short history, Internet advertising revenues have already exceeded the revenues spent on outdoor advertising.
- In January 2000, CMGI announced that it will fold two other Internet ad properties, Adsmart and Flycast Communications into Engage in a $2.6 billion deal. This creates a strong single entity that can provide end-to-end advertising solutions for companies, rivaling industry giant, DoubleClick.

Challenges

- Competition in the online advertising and marketing arena is strong. On the demographic profiling side, Engage competes directly or indirectly with a number of companies including Personify, NetGravity, MyPoints, and DoubleClick. On the online ad serving side, Engage competes directly with DoubleClick, NetGravity and RealMedia.
- Privacy is a key issue on the Net, and there is a growing concern regarding companies that are collecting browsing habits and demographic information on the Web. A backlash from consumers could potentially lead to regulation in the US similar to the strict guidelines in Europe.

Bottom Line

Engage Technologies is gunning for the top spot as the Internet advertising and marketing leader. With CMGI behind it, the company is putting together a strong group of companies to define the online ad space, giving top competitor, DoubleClick, a run for its money. However, DoubleClick is still the undisputed market leader in this space and is unlikely to give up easily. Although privacy is an issue on the Web, Engage's profiles contain no personally identifiable information. The bottom line? The planned addition of Adsmart and Flycast on top of the recent acquisitions of AdKnowledge and I/PRO will considerably strengthen Engage's position as one of the leading advertising and marketing powerhouses on the Web.

Key Statistics	ENGA
Market Cap (4/20/00):	$2,601m
Free Float:	6.1%
IPO Date:	7/20/99
Offer Price (adj):	$7.50
Price (4/20/00):	$24.00
52 week high:	$94.50
52 week low:	$11.56
Volatility: (avg. daily % ch)	7.2%
Price/Sales:	79.2
Price/Sales-Growth:	19.5

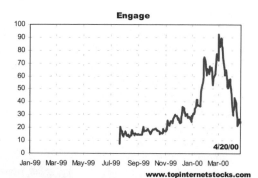

Engage

www.topinternetstocks.com

Annual Financial Data ($ m)	7/1995	7/1996	7/1997	7/1998	7/1999	1/2000
Revenues	--	--	0.03	2.22	16.02	21.07
Operating Profit	--	-2.38	-10.26	-22.91	-30.80	-39.77
Net Income	--	-2.38	-10.26	-13.84	-32.00	-37.90
Customers	--	--	--	--	--	556
Key Ratios:						
Gross Margin	--	--	24.0%	2.1%	41.0%	35.8%
Operating Margin	--	--	-41048.0%	-1033.2%	-192.2%	-188.8%
Net Margin	--	--	-41048.0%	-624.1%	-199.7%	-179.9%
Marketing as % of Revenues	--	--	6264.0%	181.1%	79.7%	85.8%

Entrust Technologies

http://www.entrust.com   eSecurity

Address:
4975 Preston Park Blvd., Ste. 400   Phone: 972.943.7300
Plano, TX 75093   Fax: 972.943.7305
Management:
Chairman: F. William Conner
President & CEO: John A. Ryan
CFO: Michele L. Axelson

Description

The entrusted partner in Internet security. At least, that is what Entrust would like to be for the world. Spun off from Canadian telecommunications giant, Northern Telecom in January 1997, Entrust specializes in digital certificates and public key infrastructure (PKI) for corporate intranets and the Internet. Digital certificates or IDs are the dog tags of the virtual world, identifying the parties in a transaction, while PKI manages the life cycle of those certificates. Entrust has more than 1,300 customers including J.P. Morgan, Salomon Smith Barney, FedEx, ScotiaBank, the Government of Canada and several US government agencies. Revenues are derived from product licensing (70%) and maintenance and services (30%). The US accounts for 70% of total revenues and Canada for 16%.

Opportunities

- The rapid growth in the Internet as a communications medium and transactional tool is driving business to the Web. This, in turn, is fueling the increased concerns over security on a public network like the Internet. International Data Corporation estimates that the Internet security market will grow from an estimated $4.2 billion in 1999 to $7.4 billion by 2003.
- Revenue growth is expected to accelerate in 2000 due to post-Y2K spending shifts. In 1999, corporate IT budgets were focused primarily on preparing for the Y2K rollover, slowing spending on security solutions.
- Entrust has one of the broadest portfolios of PKI solutions in the sector, providing security over a wide range of platforms including VPNs, the Web and even wireless.

Challenges

- Entrust competes in the digital certificates and security solutions space with VeriSign, RSA Security, Cybertrust Solutions, Baltimore Technologies and Network Associates. In addition, Netscape, Microsoft and IBM are also beginning to incorporate security solutions in their products and services.
- The adoption of digital certificates could be slowed by the lack of standards and different technologies used. In other words, different certificate providers do not normally support certificates from other vendors. If Entrust cannot firmly establish its position as one of the leading digital certificate providers, it will lose market share, and revenue growth could slow considerably.

Bottom Line

Entrust brings trust to eBusiness and looks to do the same for investors. The company operates in the sweet spot of the Internet economy. The rush of organizations to "webify" their businesses and to trust more of their mission-critical functions to a public network like the Internet will drive the accelerated growth in Internet security solutions. Although Entrust is well-positioned for this growth, it is up against tough competition such as from industry leader, VeriSign. Nevertheless, Entrust has the advantage of being able to offer a more comprehensive suite of security solutions across a wider range of platforms than many of its competitors.

Key Statistics	ENTU
Market Cap (4/20/00):	$2,480m
Free Float:	19.1%
IPO Date:	8/18/98
Offer Price:	$16.00
Price (4/20/00):	$42.62
52 week high:	$150.00
52 week low:	$16.88
Volatility: (avg. daily % ch)	4.5%
Price/Sales:	29.1
Price/Sales-Growth:	39.3

Entrust

www.topinternetstocks.com

Annual Financial Data ($ m)	12/1994	12/1995	12/1996	12/1997	12/1998	12/1999
Revenues	3.88	3.97	12.80	25.01	48.99	85.21
Operating Profit	0.03	-2.42	0.06	-0.49	-25.80	3.94
Net Income	0.14	-2.12	0.39	0.51	-23.83	5.92
Customers	--	--	--	--	770	1,300
Key Ratios:						
Gross Margin	69.5%	75.2%	72.3%	80.3%	80.5%	82.0%
Operating Margin	0.7%	-61.0%	0.4%	-2.0%	-52.7%	4.6%
Net Margin	3.6%	-53.4%	3.0%	2.1%	-48.6%	6.9%
Marketing as % of Revenues	27.9%	48.2%	30.1%	44.8%	54.7%	48.0%

E.piphany, Inc.

http://www.epiphany.com   eBusiness

Address:
1900 South Norfolk St., Ste. 310   Phone: 650.356.3800
San Mateo, CA 94403   Fax: 650.356.3801
Management:
Chairman, President & CEO: Roger S. Siboni
CFO: Kevin Yeaman

Description

E.piphany was founded in November 1996 to help companies build stronger relationships with their customers. E.piphany's E.4 product suite of Web-based customer relationship management (CRM) software solutions enables companies to create a single enterprise-wide view of each customer, enabling insight and action across all points of interaction in real-time. E.piphany's software solutions are grouped into three product families: reporting and analysis, distributing database marketing and ecommerce. The company also provides implementation, consulting, training and support services. In August 1998, E.piphany hired KPMG's former COO, Roger Siboni as CEO, bringing strong management experience to the company. Since then, the company has grown quickly, with revenues increasing nearly sixfold in 1999. Software licensing fees account for 53% of revenues, while professional service fees account for 47%. Customers include Sallie Mae, KPMG and Charles Schwab. E.piphany's top five customers accounted for an estimated 50% of sales in 1999.

Opportunities

- Managing customer relationships is a key strategic issue for companies where customer acquisition costs are typically six times the cost of retaining existing customers. By focusing on increasing sales to existing customers and efficiently targeting new customers, companies can drive higher revenue growth while improving margins.
- E.piphany is the leading company in the Web-based customer relationship management (CRM) area. The Aberdeen Group estimates that this industry will grow from $2.5 billion in 1998 to more than $9 billion in 2002.

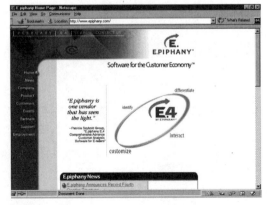

Challenges

- The CRM market is quickly becoming very competitive, with Oracle, Siebel and SAP extending their reach into the customer relationship management area. In addition, the company also competes with other fast-growing eBusiness companies including BroadVision, Informatica and Vignette.
- E.piphany's professional services (i.e. consulting) revenues are not profitable, with the cost of providing those services greater than the revenues it generates, at 113% of service revenues. In other words, for every dollar the company receives on the professional services side, it costs them $1.13 to provide that service. If E.piphany is to achieve profitability, it will need to better manage this side of the business.

Bottom Line

E.piphany provides software for the customer economy. As businesses begin to focus on front-end Web applications to drive sales and cut costs, the growth of the CRM market will accelerate. Although E.piphany faces formidable competitors in the form of Oracle, Siebel and SAP, it has an early lead over these software giants. It also helps that E.piphany has strong partner relationships with KPMG, Ernst & Young and Hewlett Packard. The main challenges facing E.piphany will be to stay ahead of the technology curve and improve its revenue mix to higher-margin software licensing fees. If it can manage that and continue its stellar growth, the company has a bright future.

Key Statistics	EPNY
Market Cap (4/20/00):	$2,334m
Free Float:	43.0%
IPO Date:	9/22/99
Offer Price:	$16.00
Price (4/20/00):	$72.25
52 week high:	$324.88
52 week low:	$38.00
Volatility: (avg. daily % ch)	10.0%
Price/Sales:	121.7
Price/Sales-Growth:	26.0

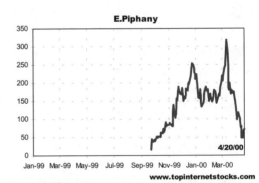

E.Piphany

www.topinternetstocks.com

Annual Financial Data ($ m)	12/1994	12/1995	12/1996	12/1997	12/1998	12/1999
Revenues	--	--	--	--	3.38	19.18
Operating Profit	--	--	--	-3.22	-10.61	-23.47
Net Income	--	--	--	-3.15	-10.33	-22.39
Customers	--	--	--	--	--	75
Key Ratios:						
Gross Margin	--	--	--	--	58.5%	51.3%
Operating Margin	--	--	--	--	-314.3%	-122.4%
Net Margin	--	--	--	--	-305.9%	-116.7%
Marketing as % of Revenues	--	--	--	--	193.0%	97.6%

eToys Inc.

http://www.etoys.com   eTailer

Address:
3100 Ocean Park Blvd., Ste. 300   Phone: 310.664.8100
Santa Monica, CA 90405   Fax: 310.664.8101
Management:
Chairman, President & CEO: Edward C. Lenk
CFO: Steven J. Schoch

Description

Tired of fighting the madness of scrambling children and harried mothers in toy stores? eToys is the answer. The virtual toy store offers over 100,000 items from more than 750 brands on its cybershelves, more than the industry giant, Toys 'R' Us offers in its offline aisles. The company was founded in November 1996 by former Disney director, Edward Lenk to be the Amazon of the toy world. Since then, the company has grown in typical Internet fashion, going from $687,000 in revenues in fiscal 1998 to $30 million the next. In the nine months of fiscal 2000 (ended December 31, 1999), revenues jumped to $128 million. Approximately 80% of eToys' revenues are generated in the Christmas quarter.

The company has focused on expanding its product line and reducing its seasonality. In June 1999, eToys acquired BabyCenter in order to offer baby items including apparel, cribs, and infant-related news and information.

Opportunities

- According to the International Council of Toy Industries, retail toy sales including video games is roughly $68 billion worldwide and $28 billion in North America. Online toy sales could capture 5% or $1.7 billion of the estimated $35 billion US market by 2004.
- eToys is expanding overseas, with a UK site that was launched in late 1999. Although the adoption rates are likely to be slower in Europe than in the US, the European toy and video game market is a $17 billion industry.
- eToys has a strong first-mover advantage, enabling it to virtually dominate the online toy selling market.

Challenges

- The competitive environment in the online toy market is intense, with new players entering from all sides. These include Net upstarts like SmarterKids.com, Toysmart.com, iBaby, and BabyCatalog.com, as well as traditional retailers including Toys "R" Us, FAO Schwarz, BabyGap and Wal-Mart. In addition, eToys also competes with online giant, Amazon.com in several product areas.
- As the company continues to grow, it will need to add distribution facilities in key areas around the country. These anticipated capital expenditures will weigh on the company's profitability goals over the next few years.

The Bottom Line

eToys is the undisputed leader in the online toy market and has a significant advantage over its traditional counterpart, Toysrus.com. It was particularly interesting comparing the two sites this past Christmas. Whereas eToys' site had a wide selection and was easy and intuitive to navigate, Toysrus.com's site still looked only partially complete with several navigation tabs marked "coming soon". In a virtual world where customer service is key, eToys comes out ahead.

However, the path to riches is not a guaranteed walk in the park for the online toy retailer. The competition is heating up, and competing against an Amazon.com could be a far greater challenge than competing against an industry giant like Toys R Us. In addition, sleeping giants have also been known to wake up occasionally.

Key Statistics	ETYS
Market Cap (4/20/00):	$723.5m
Free Float:	35.0%
IPO Date:	5/20/99
Offer Price:	$20.00
Price (4/20/00):	$6.00
52 week high:	$86.00
52 week low:	$4.50
Volatility: (avg. daily % ch)	7.0%
Price/Sales:	5.4
Price/Sales-Growth:	1.2

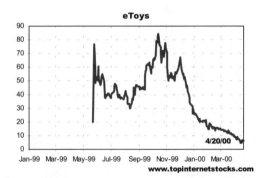

eToys

www.topinternetstocks.com

Annual Financial Data ($ m)	3/1995	3/1996	3/1997	3/1998	3/1999	12/1999*
Sales	--	--	--	0.69	30.0	128.03
Operating Profit	--	--	--	-2.27	-29.1	-144.87
Net Income	--	--	--	-2.27	-28.6	-141.21
Customers (m)	--	--	--	--	.37	1.70
Key Ratios:						
Gross Margin	--	--	--	17.3%	19.1%	19.0%
Operating Margin	--	--	--	-330.4%	-97.1%	-113.2%
Net Margin	--	--	--	-330.1%	-95.3%	-110.3%
Marketing as % of Sales	--	--	--	187.8%	69.2%	76.2%

* Nine months ended December 31, 1999

Excite@Home

http://www.excite.com   http://www.excitehome.net   eContent

Address:
450 Broadway   Phone: 650.556.5000
Redwood City, CA 94063   Fax: 650.556.5100
Management:
Chairman: Thomas A. Jermoluk
President & CEO: George Bell
CFO: Kenneth A. Goldman

Description

Excite@Home is the next generation media company, combining high-speed Internet access and content under one roof. The company is a result of the May 1999 merger of Web portal, Excite, and @Home, a high-speed Internet access provider. Excite was launched in October 1995, while @Home was founded in March 1995. Excite is the fifth largest portal on the Web, offering a search engine, news, 18 channels of content, personalized pages, chat rooms, instant messaging, and other features. @Home provides high-speed Internet access over cable lines to 1.15 million subscribers. In addition, through its relationships with 22 cable companies including AT&T and Cox, the company has access to over 72 million homes in North America, Europe, Japan and Australia. Excite@Home also provides broadband Inter- and Intranet connectivity for businesses through its @Work division. Revenues are generated through advertising fees (60%) and subscription revenues (40%). The company plans on issuing a separate tracking stock on Excite and its eContent properties later this year.

Opportunities

- As the Web becomes more complex and media rich, consumers will increasingly expect the same access speeds as television (i.e. real-time audio/video transmission). This will drive the growth in broadband access, which is expected to reach 15 million households by 2003.

- Excite also stands to benefit from the growth in Internet advertising, which is quickly shaping up to be a $12.5 billion market in 2003 from less than $3 billion in 1999.
- Excite has quickly become a major destination

on the Web, growing its visitor base by 80% during the fourth quarter of 1999 and breaking into the top five list with 27 million unique visitors.

- The company has a strong competitive lead in the broadband access space, spending five years and $500 million building the architecture to link the Internet with existing cable systems, creating its own fiber-optic backbone.

Challenges

- Excite competes on two fronts, fighting against the other major portals including Yahoo!, AOL and MSN for its share of ad revenues, and against other broadband Internet access providers including Covad, NorthPoint and Rhythms NetConnect for Internet access fees.
- Excite@Home's future direction is still unclear because of the controlling interest of AT&T and AT&T's lack of interest in the content side of the company. In addition, the board is split between the telco giant, which control's 57% of the voting shares, and several cable companies which do not always share the same strategic goals.

The Bottom Line

Excite@Home is excited about being the broadband Internet provider to the home. Although wide-scale broadband access is likely still several years out, Excite has an early and significant lead with a potential reach of nearly 72 million homes worldwide. Its recent acquisition of Bluemountain.com has also propelled the company into the top five list of hot Web properties. Excite's greatest challenge is likely to come from its own board and the different directions that Excite@Home and AT&T want to head.

Key Statistics	ATHM
Market Cap (4/20/00):	$6,902m
Free Float:	26.0%
IPO Date:	7/11/97
Offer Price (adj):	$5.25
Price (4/20/00):	$17.94
52 week high:	$84.81
52 week low:	$17.06
Volatility: (avg. daily % ch)	4.6%
Price/Sales:	20.5
Price/Sales-Growth:	3.4

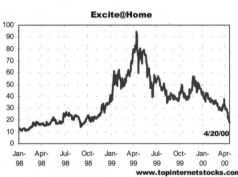

Excite@Home

www.topinternetstocks.com

Annual Financial Data ($ m)	12/1994	12/1995	12/1996	12/1997	12/1998	12/1999
Revenues	--	--	0.68	7.44	48.05	336.96
Operating Profit	--	-2.89	-25.03	-49.50	-46.45	-21.91
Net Income	--	-2.76	-24.51	-55.72	-144.18	-1,457.64
Unique Visitors (m)	--	--	--	--	16.57	27.67
Key Ratios:						
Gross Margin	--	--	-930.9%	-202.0%	2.2%	57.5%
Operating Margin	--	--	-3702.2%	-665.6%	-96.7%	-6.5%
Net Margin	--	--	-3626.2%	-749.2%	-300.1%	-432.6%
Marketing as % of Revenues	--	--	942.0%	159.5%	37.7%	38.8%

Exodus Communications Inc.

http://www.exodus.net   eAccess

Address:
2831 Mission College Blvd.   Phone: 408.346.2200
Santa Clara, CA 95054   Fax: 408.346.2201
Management:
Chairman: K.B. Chandrasekhar
President & CEO: Ellen M. Hancock
CFO: R. Marshall Case

Description

   Exodus Communications is the Bulgari of Web hosting, catering to the high-end Web hosting and Internet services market. Founded originally as a computer consulting company in 1992, the company repositioned itself as an Internet access provider in 1995, but made the transition to Web hosting and other high-margin Internet services in late 1996. The company's 20 Internet Data Centers provide outsourcing of mission-critical Internet operations including network management, Web hosting and system security to large and medium sized enterprises (LMEs). In addition, the company also provides professional services such as strategy, planning, design and implementation services. Among Exodus' clients are Yahoo, eBay, Lycos, DoubleClick and Sun Microsystems.

Opportunities

- Web hosting is big business, or at least soon will be. Forrester predicts that the Web hosting and services market will grow over sevenfold in the next four years to an estimated $15 billion in 2003. Driving this growth is businesses' rush to embrace the Internet within their corporate strategy, and lacking the in-house capability, the need to outsource much of their network management and Internet operations.
- Exodus is one of the leading brand names in high-end Web hosting with experience managing high traffic sites like eBay and Yahoo!. Many of its competitors do not have the experience managing large-scale sites, where downtimes are critical and can cost companies millions of dollars per day.
- Exodus is planning to add 17 new Internet Data Centers in 2000, thus greatly expanding its capacity.

Challenges

- Once the domain of just a few companies, Web hosting is quickly becoming a crowded field. Verio, PSINet, and major telcos like MCI Worldcom, Qwest, and AT&T are all attempting to muscle in on this area.
- Strong growth brings with it further demands on the infrastructure requirements, leading to potential bandwidth bottlenecks and system crashes. It is one thing to see this happen on the consumer side with brochureware sites, but it is another matter entirely when handling a company's mission-critical operations.
- Exodus' customer service has been spotty at times, which has led to a somewhat tarnished reputation. High-profile system outages, like what happened to eBay in 1999, do not help. If Exodus is not successful in improving its customer service image, it could begin to lose market share.

Bottom Line

Exodus Communications is one of the leading Web hosting companies with experience handling mission-critical operations for major Web companies. Revenue growth has been stellar, growing at twice the rate of many of its competitors. Unfortunately, this growth has come at a price, with customer dissatisfaction increasing somewhat. High-profile system outages like what happened to eBay (down 22 hours in June 1999) also do not help. If Exodus can solve both its technical hosting challenges and its bandwidth limitations, it has the potential to become the undisputed leader in the Web hosting market.

Key Statistics	EXDS
Market Cap (4/20/00):	$19,853m
Free Float:	86.0%
IPO Date:	3/19/98
Offer Price (adj):	$1.88
Price (4/20/00):	$107.69
52 week high:	$179.62
52 week low:	$15.00
Volatility: (avg. daily % ch)	5.3%
Price/Sales:	82.0
Price/Sales-Growth:	22.8

Exodus

www.topinternetstocks.com

Annual Financial Data ($ m)	12/1994	12/1995	12/1996	12/1997	12/1998	12/1999
Revenues	--	1.41	3.13	12.41	52.74	242.14
Operating Profit	--	-1.27	-4.09	-24.79	-57.57	-97.22
Net Income	--	-1.31	-4.13	-25.30	-67.32	-130.32
Subscribers	--	--	--	200	800	2,240
Key Ratios:						
Gross Margin	--	19.9%	4.5%	-35.9%	-16.8%	18.5%
Operating Margin	--	-90.4%	-130.8%	-199.8%	-109.2%	-40.1%
Net Margin	--	-93.1%	-132.0%	-203.9%	-127.6%	-53.8%
Marketing as % of Revenues	--	75.0%	87.3%	102.4%	55.1%	31.3%

Expedia, Inc.

http://www.expedia.com   eTailer

Address:
4200 150th Ave. NE   Phone: 425.705.5161
Redmond WA 98052   Fax: 425.707.2722
Management:
Chairman: Gregory Maffei
President & CEO: Richard Barton
CFO: Gregory Stanger

Description

Expedia offers one-stop travel shopping and reservation services on the Web. Founded by Richard Barton at Microsoft in July 1994, the company didn't launch its online travel services until October 1996. Today, it is one of the leading online branded travel services targeting the consumer and small business market. Consumers can make travel reservations, check pricing, schedules and availability in real-time for over 450 airlines, 40,000 hotels and all the major car rental companies. Since launching its service in 1996, more than 7.5 million individuals have registered on its website, with roughly 1.16 million actually buying airline tickets or making hotel or car reservations. Revenues are generated through commissions (69%), advertising (18%) and licensing fees (13%).

Opportunities

- The travel industry is growing solidly, with spending on travel and tourism expected to grow from $3.7 trillion in 1999 to $7.5 trillion by 2010 according to the World Travel and Tourism Council. Roughly 72% of the revenues in this market will be due to personal travel and tourism (i.e. non business travel).
- According to Forrester Research, travel is the largest online retail category, with an estimated $7.8 billion in revenues in 1999. By 2004, online travel transactions are expected to grow to $32 billion.
- Expedia is one of the leaders in the online travel area. According to Media Metrix, 3.32 million Web users visited Expedia's website in December 1999, compared to 2.95 million for Travelocity and 2.15 million for Preview Travel.

Challenges

- Expedia competes in the online travel space against Priceline.com, Preview Travel – which is set to merge with Sabre's Travelocity, CheapTickets.com and LowestFare.com. It also competes against the myriad of brick-and-mortar travel agencies as well as against the airlines who are also beginning to sell tickets directly to consumers online.
- Similar to the offline travel industry, Expedia generates revenues primarily through commissions that are determined by the airlines. These rates have been declining steadily in recent years, falling from 10% to 5%. In 1998, most airlines implemented a fixed rate commission of $10 for domestic online round-trip ticket sales. If commission rates continue to fall, revenue growth could slow.

Bottom Line

Expedia is one of the leaders in the online travel and reservation space, and ranks as one of the top travel destination sites on the Web. It has been successful in creating a strong brand identity and community on the Web, thanks in large part to its exclusive relationship with Microsoft's MSN. However, the competitive landscape is changing rapidly. In addition to Priceline.com, airlines are increasingly turning to the Web in order to sell directly to the traveler. What gives Expedia an advantage is its strategy of offering news, travel tips and other resources to visitors, then making it easy for them to buy their vacation or travel package right on the site.

Key Statistics	EXPE
Market Cap (4/20/00):	$653.0m
Free Float:	13.6%
IPO Date:	11/10/99
Offer Price:	$14.00
Price (4/20/00):	$16.75
52 week high:	$65.88
52 week low:	$13.88
Volatility: (avg. daily % ch)	11.8%
Price/Sales:	11.3
Price/Sales-Growth:	9.4

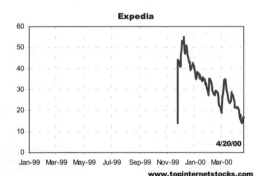

Expedia

www.topinternetstocks.com

Annual Financial Data ($ m)	6/1995	6/1996	6/1997	6/1998	6/1999	12/1999*
Sales	--	--	2.74	13.83	38.70	33.09
Operating Profit	-0.96	-7.80	-28.92	-29.48	-19.60	-28.68
Net Income	-0.96	-7.80	-28.92	-29.48	-19.60	-28.13
Customers	--	--	--	--	--	1.16
Key Ratios:						
Gross Margin	--	--	--	--	58.8%	61.7%
Operating Margin	--	--	-1054.7%	-213.2%	-50.7%	-86.7%
Net Margin	--	--	-1054.7%	-213.2%	-50.7%	-85.0%
Marketing as % of Sales	--	--	321.7%	78.3%	38.5%	52.3%

* Six months ended December 31, 1999

F5 Networks Inc.

http://www.F5.com   eBusiness

Address:
200 First Ave. West, Ste. 500   Phone: 206.505.0800
Seattle, WA 98119   Fax: 206.505.0801
Management:
Chairman, President & CEO: Jeffrey S. Hussey
CFO: Robert J. Chamberlain

Description

F5 Networks was launched in February 1996 to provide Internet traffic management (ITM) solutions for corporations. F5 wants the Internet to be as reliable as picking up the phone and hearing a dial tone. Its products are designed to improve the reliability and speed of the Internet through load-balancing controllers that monitor servers in various locations, rerouting traffic if performance is slow or if servers are down. F5's hardware/software product suite monitors and optimizes Internet sites through four control points: servers (BIG/ip), the network (3DNS), content (global/SITE) and network management (see/IT). Revenues are derived from product sales (84%) and professional services (16%).

By year end 1999, F5 Networks had over 1,000 customers including Alaska Airlines, MCI, WorldCom, PSINet and Exodus Communications. Exodus accounted for 24% of net revenues in the quarter ended December 31, 1999.

Opportunities

- The rapid growth in Internet usage – from less than 50 million users just a few years ago to more than 430 million by 2003 – in addition to the increased complexity of Web sites, is leading to often sluggish or poor performance of many corporate sites.
- The rapid growth in Net usage and increased bandwidth requirements is expected to drive the need for ITM solutions. According to Collaborative Research, the ITM market is expected to grow at more than 65% annually through 2002.
- F5's technology helps companies improve the performance of their Web sites, which can help drive revenue growth and reduce costs.

Challenges

- F5 competes in the Internet traffic management space against several competitors including Radware, Alteon WebSystems, ArrowPoint Communications and industry giant Cisco. With the industry rapidly evolving and the cost of developing new technologies falling, new competitors can quickly enter the playing field, increasing the pricing pressure in this marketplace.
- Roughly 72% of F5's revenues are derived from one product, the BIG/ip controller. As a "one product" company, F5 Networks is particularly susceptible to any competitive pricing pressure in this particular area. Also, if this product (introduced in July 1997) is no longer considered state-of-the-art and is technologically surpassed by a competitive product, sales could quickly fall.

Bottom Line

F5 is considered one of the rising stars in the Internet sector. This is reflected in the rapid growth in customers, from 217 customers in December 1998 to more than 1,000 by December 1999. F5 Networks has a strong suite of products that is being quickly adopted by the leading portals, ecommerce, financial and application service providers (ASP) businesses. Although Cisco presents a formidable competitor in this space, F5 has in typical nimble Internet fashion been able to capture market share from the technology giant through a David-like strategy. F5 attacks the market on two fronts: driving appliances through third party resellers and distribution partners such as Exodus Communications, PSINet and Frontier GlobalCenter, and providing a platform for OEMs such as Hewlett-Packard and Dell.

Key Statistics	FFIV
Market Cap (4/20/00):	$1,115m
Free Float:	41.9%
IPO Date:	6/04/99
Offer Price:	$10.00
Price (4/20/00):	$52.75
52 week high:	$160.50
52 week low:	$10.12
Volatility: (avg. daily % ch)	7.1%
Price/Sales:	25.2
Price/Sales-Growth:	4.5

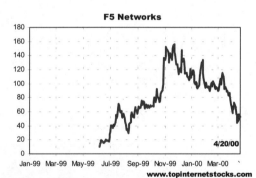

F5 Networks

www.topinternetstocks.com

Annual Financial Data ($ m)	9/1994	9/1995	9/1996	9/1997	9/1998	9/1999
Revenues	--	--	0.002	0.23	4.89	27.83
Operating Profit	--	--	-0.35	-1.43	-3.67	-4.88
Net Income	--	--	-0.33	-1.46	-3.67	-4.34
Customers	--	--	--	--	--	750
Key Ratios:						
Gross Margin	--	--	50.0%	69.0%	71.3%	74.1%
Operating Margin	--	--	--	-623.6%	-75.0%	-17.5%
Net Margin	--	--	--	-635.8%	-75.1%	-15.6%
Marketing as % of Revenues	--	--	3100.0%	246.7%	79.4%	48.5%

FreeMarkets, Inc.

http://www.freemarkets.com   eBusiness

Address:
210 Sixth Ave., 22nd Fl.   Phone: 412.434.0500
Pittsburgh, PA 15222   Fax: 412.297.8700
Management:
Chairman, President & CEO: Glen T. Meakem
CFO: Joan S Hooper

Description

FreeMarkets builds and operates online business-to-business auctions for industrial parts, raw materials, commodities and services. Since 1995, the company has auctioned goods and services in more than 70 categories, including injection molded plastic parts, commercial machining, metal fabrications, chemicals, printed circuit boards, coal and corrugated packaging. FreeMarkets estimates that it has saved buyers an estimated 2% to 25% by making their procurement processes cheaper and more efficient. The company's BidWare technology links buyers and sellers in a reverse-auction environment. Revenues are generated through a combination of fixed monthly service fees and commissions for successfully completed auctions. Customers include United Technologies, Emerson Electric and Quaker Oats.

Opportunities

- Manufacturers spend an estimated $5 trillion annually on the purchase of direct materials, the industrial resources used to manufacture finished products. This is a highly fragmented market with little visibility in the purchasing process. Adding transparency to the purchase process through online marketplaces can save manufacturers an estimated 2% to 25%.
- FreeMarkets takes a buyer-centric approach, commonly referred to as a reverse, or downward-price auction. Buyers solicit a bid from suppliers in a real-time, interactive competition. This type of approach tends to generate the largest cost savings for purchasers – a strong incentive for buyers to participate.

- Customer growth has been strong, with the company doubling its customer base to 34 between the third and fourth quarter of 1999.

Challenges

- Competition in the online B2B marketplace is intense. FreeMarkets competes with Commerce One, Ariba, VerticalNet, Chemdex (Ventro) and others that provide B2B marketplaces and eProcurement solutions.
- As with any marketplace, the challenge is to have enough buyers and sellers to reach critical mass, so that the network feeds itself. In other words, buyers go there because they can attract the most sellers, and sellers go there because they can target the most buyers. FreeMarkets is not yet at that stage.
- Revenue concentration, i.e. a few customers accounting for the bulk of sales, is a constant challenge. In 1999, two customers, United Technologies and General Motors, accounted for 49% of revenues. In January 2000, GM announced that it was switching to rival Commerce One. If FreeMarkets were to lose either United Technologies or another large customer, revenue growth could be severely impacted.

Bottom Line

FreeMarkets wants to make the $5 trillion direct materials market transparent and cost-effective by bringing it online. Despite the major setback of losing GM as a customer in early 2000, FreeMarkets has been successful in aggressively growing its customer base, doubling it in the fourth quarter of 1999 alone. But the road ahead is likely to be a rough-and-tumble competitive arena, with Commerce One and others fighting for the same Global 1000 customers. Quickly gaining critical mass is the long-term key to survival in the B2B marketplace. If FreeMarkets can achieve that, it just might be a free ride for investors.

Key Statistics	FMKT
Market Cap (4/20/00):	$2,122m
Free Float:	10.6%
IPO Date:	12/10/99
Offer Price:	$48.00
Price (4/20/00):	$59.81
52 week high:	$370.00
52 week low:	$39.50
Volatility: (avg. daily % ch)	39.2%
Price/Sales:	101.6
Price/Sales-Growth:	60.6

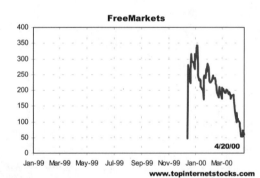

FreeMarkets

www.topinternetstocks.com

Annual Financial Data ($ m)	12/1994	12/1995	12/1996	12/1997	12/1998	12/1999
Revenues	--	0.02	0.44	1.78	7.80	20.88
Operating Profit	--	-0.93	-1.44	-1.08	0.02	-22.65
Net Income	--	-0.92	-1.43	-1.06	0.23	-21.82
Customers	--	--	8	13	12	35
Key Ratios:						
Gross Margin	--	-47.1%	-23.7%	35.6%	45.4%	41.7%
Operating Margin	--	-5447.1%	-352.6%	-60.6%	0.2%	-108.5%
Net Margin	--	-5423.5%	-349.9%	-59.5%	3.0%	-104.5%
Marketing as % of Revenues	--	347.1%	78.5%	32.9%	8.4%	57.2%

Go2Net, Inc.

http://www.go2net.com   eContent

Address:
999 Third Ave., Ste. 4700   Phone: 206.447.1595
Seattle, WA 98104   Fax: 206.447.1625
Management:
Chairman, CEO & CFO: Russell C. Horowitz
President: John Keister

Description

Go2Net is a network of branded Web sites focused on four categories: personal finance, search and directory, ecommerce and multiplayer games. The company was launched by co-founders Russell Horowitz and John Keister in February 1996, initially offering news and information on sports, business and the Internet. After going public in April 1997, Go2Net went on an acquisition spree, buying up a number of niche Web properties including Silicon Investor, MetaCrawler, Dogpile, HyperMart and PlaySite. Go2Net has grown quickly in popularity, rising to the 13th most visited site on the Web in December 1999 with 11.2 million unique visitors a month. Revenues are generated through a combination of advertising, subscription and ecommerce fees. Advertising revenues accounted for 73% of total revenues in fiscal 1999, with subscription fees and ecommerce revenues accounting for the rest. Vulcan Ventures owns 31% of Go2Net.

Opportunities

- Go2Net has been one of the fastest growing properties on the Web, rising from the 25th spot and 4.6 million visitors in January 1998 to 11.2 million unique visitors in December 1999, vaulting Go2Net into 13th place on the all-important Media Metrix Web rankings.
- Internet advertising is ramping up quickly in the US, growing from an estimated $2.9 billion in 1999 to more than $12.5 billion by 2003. The top ten Web properties, of which Go2Net had briefly achieved, account for the lion's share of ad dollars, or 75% according to IAB and PWC estimates.
- Vulcan Ventures and Go2Net recently formed a joint venture to deliver broadband Internet services. This positions the company for the coming broadband revolution.

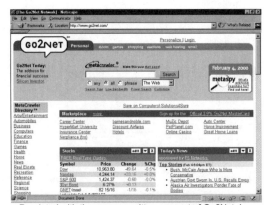

Reprinted with the express written consent of Go2Net, Inc.

Challenges

- The eContent sector is a fiercely competitive industry where barriers to entry are virtually nonexistent. Only the top 10 portal sites receive the lion's share of ad dollars. If Go2Net cannot sustain its place near the top 10 Media Metrix list, revenue growth could slow.
- Go2Net's strategy of growth through a large number of small acquisitions is a risky strategy. The company typically acquires, upgrades, and then relaunches these acquired sites. A rapid acquisition strategy could put considerable strain on resources leading to a decline in traffic and revenues.

Bottom Line

Go2Net has been on a winning streak, with both traffic and revenues growing strongly. The company has vaulted up the Web rankings, breaking into the top 10 list briefly in November 1999, proving its ability to capture market share. However, the competition is intense in the eContent space, and if Go2Net loses focus and stumbles, it can just as quickly lose market share. The company's piece-meal growth strategy is also a riskier acquisition strategy than acquiring larger sites. Nevertheless, judging by the results, Go2Net's strategy has paid off handsomely. Its recent broadband joint venture with Microsoft's co-founder Paul Allen is a major step in preparing for the coming broadband revolution.

Key Statistics	GNET
Market Cap (4/20/00):	$1,582m
Free Float:	70.8%
IPO Date:	4/23/97
Offer Price (adj):	$2.00
Price (4/20/00):	$51.75
52 week high:	$111.75
52 week low:	$44.06
Volatility: (avg. daily % ch)	5.5%
Price/Sales:	46.7
Price/Sales-Growth:	15.9

www.topinternetstocks.com

Annual Financial Data ($ m)	9/1994	9/1995	9/1996	9/1997	9/1998	9/1999
Revenues	--	0.05	0.30	1.63	7.11	22.44
Operating Profit	--	0.00	-0.44	-1.86	-2.71	-18.37
Net Income	--	0.00	-0.43	-1.67	-2.27	-10.84
Unique Visitors (m)	--	--	--	--	--	11.24
Key Ratios:						
Gross Margin	--	68.9%	93.7%	77.2%	67.7%	79.5%
Operating Margin	--	-5.3%	-146.6%	-114.0%	-38.1%	-81.9%
Net Margin	--	-7.0%	-142.6%	-102.8%	-31.9%	-48.3%
Marketing as % of Revenues	--	0.6%	5.2%	32.7%	28.8%	28.3%

GoTo.com, Inc.

http://www.goto.com   eContent

Address:
14 West Union Street   Phone: 626.685.5600
Pasadena, CA 91103   Fax: 626.685.5601
Management:
Chairman: Robert M. Kavner
CEO: Jeffrey S. Brewer
President: Ted Meisel
CFO: Todd Tappin

Description

    GoTo.com is a search engine with a twist. Companies pay GoTo to be listed
in its search queries. The more advertisers pay, the higher they appear in the
search results. The company was founded by Internet incubator, Idealab! in September 1997 and officially launched its site in June 1998. GoTo earns revenues
from advertisers who pay a priority placement fee based on keyword searches.
Advertisers bid on the price and the placement of their search result, paying GoTo
for each click-through to their Web site. GoTo.com had more than 21,000 advertisers in December 1999, paying on average 17 cents per click for consumers who
clicked on a search result listing that particular advertiser. Advertisers include
Amazon.com, eBay and FTD. GoTo is acquiring Cadabra to expand its service
using Catabra's online comparison-shopping tools.

Opportunities

- Internet advertising is a nascent industry that is growing quickly. Barely four
  years old, Internet advertising has already surpassed outdoor advertising in total revenues and is expected to grow to more than $12.5 billion by 2003.
- GoTo provides a novel twist on the Internet advertising and search-engine
  concept. It is a pay-for-placement approach that favors the better capitalized
  companies willing to bid
  the highest dollar for a
  higher ranking.
- This approach has the advantage of aligning consumer and advertiser interests. Advertisers have a
  vehicle for generating
  strong leads from highly
  targeted consumers, and
  consumers have a search
  engine that tends to filter
  out nonrelevant, or garbage

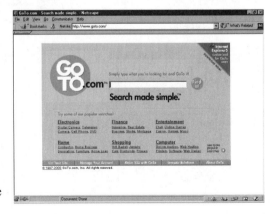

sites. The site has been popular enough with consumers that it ranked as the 19th most popular Web site in December 1999 according to Media Metrix.

Challenges

- Barriers to entry in the hyper-competitive directory and search-engine space are nonexistent. Competitors include Yahoo!, AOL, AltaVista, Lycos, Ask Jeeves and Walt Disney's Go Network.
- Twenty percent of GoTo's traffic has been through premier placing in Microsoft Explorer's search function. That contract expired in late 1999 and has not been renewed. If Microsoft no longer features GoTo in its MS Explorer search function, and GoTo cannot replace that traffic, revenue growth could slow significantly.

Bottom Line

GoTo.com has carved out a nice niche for itself, gaining a strong lead in the pay-for-placement space. Rather than competing directly against larger Web directories and portals like Yahoo! or Lycos for banner advertising, GoTo provides a service that can deliver higher quality leads. One concern is the possibility that GoTo.com will lose its premier status with Microsoft, leading to a large shortfall in traffic. To counter these concerns, the company recently closed deals with recently merged EarthLink and MindSpring to be the default search engine. This gives the company valuable real estate on what is soon to be the second largest ISP in the US. This should help solidify GoTo as one of the top search engine services on the Web.

Key Statistics	GOTO
Market Cap (4/20/00):	$1,758m
Free Float:	34.1%
IPO Date:	6/18/99
Offer Price (adj):	$15.00
Price (4/20/00):	$35.88
52 week high:	$114.50
52 week low:	$20.00
Volatility: (avg. daily % ch)	6.7%
Price/Sales:	65.6
Price/Sales-Growth:	2.1

GoTo.com

www.topinternetstocks.com

Annual Financial Data ($ m)	12/1994	12/1995	12/1996	12/1997	12/1998	12/1999
Revenues	--	--	--	0.02	0.82	26.81
Operating Profit	--	--	--	-0.12	-14.34	-33.60
Net Income	--	--	--	-0.12	-14.02	-29.26
Unique Visitors (m)	--	--	--	--	--	7.06
Key Ratios:						
Gross Margin	--	--	--	72.7%	-73.8%	76.8%
Operating Margin	--	--	--	-540.9%	-1744.3%	-125.3%
Net Margin	--	--	--	-545.5%	-1706.0%	-109.1%
Marketing as % of Revenues	--	--	--	295.5%	1173.4%	128.5%

Healtheon/WebMD Corporation

http://www.webmd.com   eBusiness

Address:

400 The Lenox Bldg.   Phone: 404.495.7600
3399 Peachtree Rd. NE   Fax: 404.495.7822
Atlanta, GA 30326

Management:

Chairman and COO: W. Michael Long
CEO: Jeffrey Arnold
CFO & Treasurer: John L. Westermann

Description

Healtheon/WebMD is the health center on the Web. The company was born out of the 1999 four-way merger of Healtheon, a service founded by former Netscape Chairman, Jim Clark in 1995 to connect doctors, insurers and pharmacies online; WebMD, an online healthcare information portal targeted towards consumers and doctors; MEDE America; and Medcast. Combined, the company provides end-to-end healthcare services connecting patients to doctors to hospitals to insurers and other healthcare organizations. This includes automated administrative functions (i.e. HMO enrollment, referrals, insurance, prescription writing), communications (i.e. personalized Web sites, email, discussion areas) and research services (i.e. breaking medical news, online database, clinical reports). Healtheon/WebMD has over 280,000 physicians, 11,000 dentists, 1,100 hospitals and 46,000 pharmacies using its services.

Opportunities

- The healthcare industry is one area that is widely known for being inefficient (next to the defense sector), with an estimated $250 billion being wasted in administrative inefficiencies. This is 25% of the estimated $1 trillion being spent on healthcare annually in the US.
- Healtheon/WebMD has a strong first-mover advantage in the online healthcare industry and has established itself as the most comprehensive end-to-end services provider available online.
- Healtheon/MD also has strong relationships with Microsoft, Softbank, Excite@Home, CNN and News Corp. As many of

these partners are also strategic investors, it gives Healtheon deep pockets to continue its aggressive growth strategy while strengthening its branding, marketing and distribution efforts.

Challenges

- Competition is strong in the online healthcare industry, with a number of Internet startups and established players offering healthcare content and connectivity over the Web. These include drkoop.com, adam.com, CareInsite.com, Medscape and McKesson HBOC.
- One of the major challenges is the issue of privacy and confidentiality. In other words, for patient/doctor/insurer interaction, how much patient information should be available on the Web where security concerns remain high? These concerns could limit the adoption of Healtheon's services.

Bottom Line

Health has a home page on the Web, and it is Healtheon/WebMD. The company is also aggressively bringing doctors online and into its fold by offering inexpensive PCs already pre-installed with its software. Although competition is strong in the online healthcare market, with a number of companies offering similar services, the greatest challenge could be privacy concerns and the threat of regulation within the industry. Notwithstanding, Healtheon/WebMD has a solid first-mover advantage in an industry that by all accounts is growing rapidly and should continue to grow.

Key Statistics	HLTH
Market Cap (4/20/00):	$3,416m
Free Float:	66.0%
IPO Date:	2/11/99
Offer Price:	$8.00
Price (4/20/00):	$18.94
52 week high:	$126.19
52 week low:	$15.62
Volatility: (avg. daily % ch)	5.0%
Price/Sales:	33.4
Price/Sales-Growth:	30.6

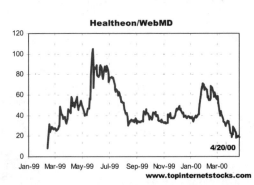

Healtheon/WebMD

www.topinternetstocks.com

Annual Financial Data ($ m)	12/1994	12/1995	12/1996	12/1997	12/1998	12/1999
Revenues	--	--	--	--	48.84	102.15
Operating Profit	--	--	--	--	-53.95	-291.48
Net Income	--	--	--	--	-54.05	-287.99
Customers	--	--	--	--	--	--
Key Ratios:						
Gross Margin	--	--	--	--	11.9%	13.3%
Operating Margin	--	--	--	--	-110.5%	-285.3%
Net Margin	--	--	--	--	-110.7%	-281.9%
Marketing as % of Revenues	--	--	--	--	18.9	53.4

Homestore.com, Inc.

http://www.homestore.com   eContent

Address:
225 West Hillcrest Dr., Ste. 100   Phone: 805.557.2300
Thousand Oaks, CA 91360   Fax: 805.557.2680
Management:
Chairman & CEO: Stuart H. Wolff, Ph.D.
President & COO: Michael A. Buckman
CFO: John M. Giesecke

Description

Homestore.com is the home finder on the Web. The company was founded originally as InfoTouch in 1993 to develop interactive kiosks that consumers could search for home listings. It began developing real estate sites on the Web in December 1996 and changed its name to Homestore.com in August 1999 just prior to going public. Homestore.com's family of Web sites are a comprehensive source of real estate listings and related content. Consumers can view over 1.37 million homes on REALTOR.com, choose from over 130,000 models of new homes on HomeBuilder.com, find apartment listings for 45,000 properties in 6,000 cities on SpringStreet.com and more. Homestore.com has distribution arrangements with America Online, Excite@Home and Go Networks. Revenues are generated through advertising fees and professional subscription fees.

Opportunities

- The real estate industry accounts for roughly 15% of the US's GDP, with the residential sector, which includes the purchase, sale, rental, remodeling and new construction of homes, representing a $1 trillion a year market.
- Homestore's REALTOR.com is the official Web site of the National Association of Realtors (NAR), the largest trade association in the US representing roughly 720,000 real estate professionals. The company also has an exclusive arrangement with the National Association of Home Builders (NAHB), giving Homestore two strong distribution channels that are locked out to its competition.
- The company is the leader in home listings, with over 1.37 million home listings in its database out of an estimated 1.47 million homes listed for sale in the US.

Challenges

- Homestore competes with several players in the online real estate listing, home builders and apartment finder area. In addition to smaller players like Rent.net, Apartments.com, HomeSeekers.com and CyberHomes.com, the company competes against Microsoft's HomeAdvisor as well as traditional real estate brokers, such as Century 21 and Coldwell Banker, which are extending their presence on the Internet.
- The REALTOR.com Web domain and trademark is owned by the National Association of Realtors (NAR), not Homestore. The NAR has the right to terminate the lifetime agreement under certain conditions. If Homestore were to lose those rights, traffic and revenue growth could be severely impacted.

Bottom Line

Homestore.com has an early first-mover advantage when it comes to buying and selling houses on the Web. It lists 93% of all homes being sold in the US, far outdistancing its competition. Homestore's greatest competitive challenge is likely to come from Cendant (Century 21, Coldwell Banker, Rent.net). But in the competitive online world, Homestore has an edge. Its exclusive relationships with NAR and NAHB give it a strong competitive position, effectively raising the barriers to entry for its competitors. Homestore also has strong distribution agreements with a number of major portals including AOL, Go Network, Excite@Home and Lycos.

Key Statistics	HOMS
Market Cap (4/20/00):	$1,847m
Free Float:	56.8%
IPO Date:	8/05/99
Offer Price:	$20.00
Price (4/20/00):	$24.62
52 week high:	$138.00
52 week low:	$19.75
Volatility: (avg. daily % ch)	6.6%
Price/Sales:	29.5
Price/Sales-Growth:	3.0

HomeStore.com

www.topinternetstocks.com

Annual Financial Data ($ m)	12/1994	12/1995	12/1996	12/1997	12/1998	12/1999
Revenues	0.42	0.86	1.36	0.04	--	62.58
Operating Profit	-1.55	-0.88	-0.23	-0.02	--	-95.37
Net Income	-1.57	-0.91	-0.25	-0.02	--	-93.01
Unique Visitors (m)	--	--	--	--	--	2.10
Key Ratios:						
Gross Margin	84.9%	93.2%	96.9%	85.7%	--	66.4%
Operating Margin	-372.8%	-103.0%	-17.0%	-38.1%	--	-152.4%
Net Margin	-376.9%	-106.5%	-18.5%	-40.5%	--	-148.6%
Marketing as % of Revenues	229.8%	65.2%	35.2%	33.3%	--	112.5%

InfoSpace.com, Inc.

http://www.infospace.com   eContent

Address:
15375 N.E. 90th Street   Phone: 425.882.1602
Redmond, WA 98052   Fax: 425.882.0988
Management:
Chairman & CEO: Naveen Jain
President & COO: Bernee D.L. Strom
CFO: Tammy Halstead

Description

InfoSpace.com is the content behind eContent. The company was founded in March 1996 with the idea of delivering real world information on the Internet – anytime, anywhere and on any device. Rather than becoming "just-another-portal", the company adopted the strategy of being the behind-the-scenes content provider, supplying yellow pages, city guides, sports, news, calendars, and shopping directories to more than 2,500 Web sites including 4 of the top 5 most trafficked Web sties on the Net. Its private label solutions are divided into three categories: consumer, merchant and wireless services. Consumer services, which includes news, classifieds and personal home pages, is responsible for an estimated 75% of revenues, merchant services includes Store Builder and shopping directories and is roughly 23% of revenues. Wireless services include Internet content for cellular phones, pagers and handheld computers. Major customers include AOL, MSN, NBCi and Disney's Go Network.

Opportunities

- InfoSpace has been shifting its revenue mix, expanding aggressively into other revenue channels. Merchant licensing and transaction revenues are expected to account for 20-25% of revenues in 2000, and wireless services are estimated to represent 5-10% of total revenues in 2000.
- By diversifying its revenue mix, the company is broadening its market potential to an estimated $178 billion in 2003 (Internet advertising: $12.5 billion; B2C ecommerce: $165 billion).
- In addition to extending its market opportunity, diversifying the revenue mix also helps it to develop stabler revenue growth.

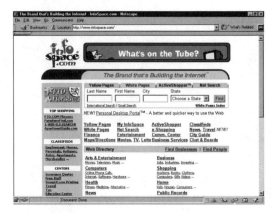

Challenges

- Although the company has no meaningful competition on the private label content side, it does compete in a number of areas for advertising dollars. These include Yahoo! and infoUSA in the directory space, AOL and Excite in the community area, and other content providers that offer classifieds, horoscopes and stock quotes. In the commerce area, InfoSpace competes with Inktomi, Amazon.com's Junglee and Excite's Jango.
- Revenues are concentrated among a few key customers. The top ten customers account for more than 50% of revenues, and one customer, 800-US Search, is responsible for 26% of revenues. If InfoSpace loses these customers, revenue growth could be sharply curtailed.

Bottom Line

InfoSpace's mission is simple: InfoSpace in every space. As the leading provider of private label content and a blue-chip roster of customers – AOL, MSN, AT&T and Disney, the company may well achieve that. The company is also betting on wireless devices to be the next major development in Internet access and ecommerce services. Although InfoSpace's customer list reads like a Who's Who of the portal space, this also presents one of the largest risks for the company. Customers could quickly turn into competitors, leading to lost revenues and more intense competition. Bottom line? Its ubiquitous private label strategy is a compelling competitive advantage and a shifting revenue mix should lead to stronger market opportunities.

Key Statistics	INSP
Market Cap (4/20/00):	$12,467m
Free Float:	51.0%
IPO Date:	12/15/98
Offer Price (adj):	$1.88
Price (4/20/00):	$57.56
52 week high:	$138.50
52 week low:	$8.81
Volatility: (avg. daily % ch)	5.6%
Price/Sales:	338.4
Price/Sales-Growth:	119.7

www.topinternetstocks.com

Annual Financial Data ($ m)	12/1994	12/1995	12/1996	12/1997	12/1998	12/1999
Revenues	--	--	0.20	1.69	9.62	36.84
Operating Profit	--	--	-0.40	-0.45	-12.13	-21.32
Net Income	--	--	-0.38	-0.43	-11.82	-10.31
Unique Visitors (m)	--	--	--	--	5.66	6.92
Key Ratios:						
Gross Margin	--	--	51.3%	76.3%	83.0%	85.7%
Operating Margin	--	--	-202.0%	-26.7%	-126.0%	-57.9%
Net Margin	--	--	-191.5%	-25.5%	-122.8%	-28.0%
Marketing as % of Revenues	--	--	116.1%	49.9%	65.3%	65.0%

Inktomi Corporation

http://www.inktomi.com   eBusiness

Address:
4100 East Third Ave.   Phone: 650.653.2800
Foster City, CA 94404   Fax: 650.653.2801
Management:
Chairman, President & CEO: David C. Peterschmidt
CFO: Jerry M. Kennelly

Description

Inktomi is the little engine that could. The little search engine that is, and the little shopping engine, and the little directory engine, and the network caching engine. Founded in February 1996 by two professors at UC of Berkeley, the company, named after a Lakota Indian spider known for its wit and cunning, is the behind-the-scenes workhorse of such popular sites as Yahoo!, AOL, CNET, British Telecommunications, CNN and others.

Inktomi's products are divided into two broad categories encompassing four different services. The first category, network products, includes Traffic Server network cache, which helps to reduce network congestion over the Internet by caching frequently requested content close to the users. The second category is portal services, which includes the search-and-directory engines and the shopping engine. For the search-and-directory engines, Inktomi receives revenues on a per-query basis, for search service hosting, advertising and licensing and maintenance fees. The company is still refining the business model for the shopping engine.

Opportunities

- As traffic and network congestion grows, there will be a greater demand for Inktomi's network product software, which accounted for roughly 61% of total revenues. The evolution of the Web into a richer media with video and music content will place greater demands on bandwidth over the Internet, increasing the need for software that can effectively manage the congestion and improve network efficiency.

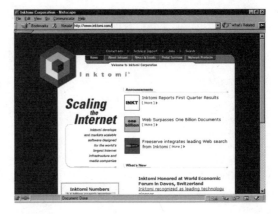

- The rapid growth in Web pages, over 1 billion at last count, will drive the demand for search engines.
- As ecommerce expands, and more consumers and merchants jump onto the Internet, shopping comparison engines will be-

come more popular. Ecommerce, not advertising, is where the real revenues will be on the Net, and Inktomi with its shopping engine technology is positioning itself to benefit from this growth.

Challenges

- Inktomi competes on several fronts. On the networking caching side, the company competes with Cisco, Microsoft, Netscape, Novell and others. On the search-and-directory engine side, Inktomi competes with Alta Vista, Ask Jeeves, Excite@Home, Lycos and Infoseek. On the shopping engine side, the company competes with Excite@Home's Jango.com, Amazon.com's Junglee, mySimon.com, CNET's KillApp and others.

The Bottom Line

Inktomi is the neutral Switzerland of the portal wars. Rather than competing head to head with Yahoo!, AOL and others, the company has opted to help the portals in their efforts to grab market share by supplying them with the underlying search technology. Less visible, but more important, is Inktomi's network caching services. In this area, Inktomi stands to win as the Web becomes more complex and bandwidth limitations start to slow Web performance. It's no secret that most visitors to a site bail out or leave if the page they are trying to access fails to load within 30 seconds or less. Inktomi is there to solve this mission-critical problem.

Key Statistics	INKT
Market Cap (4/20/00):	$14,039m
Free Float:	74.4%
IPO Date:	6/10/98
Offer Price (adj):	$4.50
Price (4/20/00):	$129.12
52 week high:	$241.50
52 week low:	$42.00
Volatility: (avg. daily % ch)	5.6%
Price/Sales:	142.1
Price/Sales-Growth:	61.1

Inktomi

www.topinternetstocks.com

Annual Financial Data* ($ m)	9/1994	9/1995	9/1996	9/1997	9/1998	9/1999
Revenues	--	--	0.53	5.79	21.34	73.50
Operating Profit	--	--	-3.43	-11.52	-30.24	-35.68
Net Income	--	--	-3.53	-11.71	-29.73	-31.13
Customers	--	--	--	--	--	--
Key Ratios:						
Gross Margin	--	--	55.0%	73.9%	76.4%	82.1%
Operating Margin	--	--	-647.1%	-199.2%	-141.7%	-48.5%
Net Margin	--	--	-666.7%	-202.5%	-139.4%	-42.4%
Sales+Marketing as % of Revenues	--	--	169.4%	144.5%	115.7%	77.1%

* Reflecting acquisition of WebSpective

Interliant, Inc.

http://www.interliant.com   eServices

Address:
Two Manhattanville Rd.   Phone: 914.640.9000
Purchase, NY 10577   Fax: 914.694.1190
Management:
Co-Chairmen: Bradley A. Feld, Leonard J. Fassler
CEO: Herb Hribar
President: James M Lidestri
CFO: William A Wilson

Description

Interliant is a Web hosting and application services provider targeted towards small and mid-sized businesses. Since its inception in December 1997, the company has grown quickly through a series of acquisitions, buying 19 Web hosting and related companies from inception through September. Interliant's services are divided into three areas: Web hosting, which includes virtual, dedicated and co-located hosting; application hosting, which includes groupware and application outsourcing (customers rent the application as they need it); and consulting services. Web hosting accounts for 35% of revenues, application hosting 40%, and consulting services 25%. Interliant has more than 37,000 Web hosting customers and 1,300 application hosting customers.

Opportunities

- The market for application service providers (ASP) is a relatively new market and is expected to grow rapidly. Dataquest Research estimates that the ASP market will grow from $889 million in 1998 to $22.7 billion in 2003.
- Driving the growth is the lack of in-house IT talent for many corporations and the tight labor markets in the technology sector. Businesses also realize it is more cost-effective to outsource functions when they do not have the expertise, thus allowing them to focus on their core competencies.
- Interliant has strategic relationships with IBM, Microsoft, UUNET and Whittman-Hart. These partners act as resellers and referral partners, enabling Interliant to extend its distribution channel.

Challenges

- Interliant competes on several fronts in an aggressive competitive environment. On the Web hosting and Internet services side, the company competes with Verio, PSINet, AboveNet Communications and others. On the ASP side, Interliant competes with Usinternetworking, IBM Global Services and Silknet.
- Interliant has been growing quickly through a series of acquisitions. This presents substantial integration risk. If Interliant cannot smoothly integrate the operations (accounting and billing, server relocation, etc.), service disruptions could occur, which would lead to customer turnover.
- The ASP market is still an immature market, and it is not yet known whether the concept of rented applications will be widely accepted by corporate America.

Bottom Line

Interliant is the leader in Lotus Notes/domino hosting solutions and intends to be the leader in other rentable software packages. Interliant also has the benefit of being positioned in a niche market whose growth is doubling every year. However, as the market grows larger, more established Web hosting companies such as Verio and Concentric could also begin offering bundled Web/application hosting services. Interliant does have the edge with a market leadership position in an industry that is growing rapidly. Not to mention a strong customer base and partners.

Key Statistics	INIT
Market Cap (4/20/00):	$922.4m
Free Float:	19.0%
IPO Date:	7/8/99
Offer Price:	$10.00
Price (4/20/00):	$19.50
52 week high:	$55.50
52 week low:	$9.25
Volatility: (avg. daily % ch)	5.9%
Price/Sales:	19.6
Price/Sales-Growth:	2.3

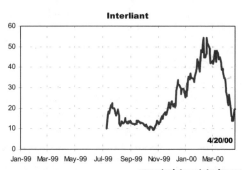

Interliant

www.topinternetstocks.com

Annual Financial Data ($ m)	12/1994	12/1995	12/1996	12/1997	12/1998	12/1999
Revenues	--	--	--	--	4.91	47.11
Operating Profit	--	--	--	-0.16	-10.87	-54.82
Net Income	--	--	--	-0.16	-10.73	-53.93
Customers	--	--	--	--	--	1,300
Key Ratios:						
Gross Margin	--	--	--	--	34.0%	41.6%
Operating Margin	--	--	--	--	-221.6%	-116.4%
Net Margin	--	--	--	--	-218.8%	-114.5%
Marketing as % of Revenues	--	--	--	--	52.1%	36.6%

InterNAP Network Services Corporation

http://www.internap.com   eBusiness

Address:
Two Union Square   Phone: 206.441.8800
601 Union St., Suite 1000   Fax: 206.264.1833
Seattle, WA 98101
Management:
Chairman: Eugene Eidenberg
President & CEO: Anthony C. Naughtin
VP of Finance & CFO: Paul E. McBride

Description

InterNAP was founded in May 1996 to help businesses improve their Internet performance. During Internet rush hour, traffic can slow and back up at intersections, also known as Internet connectivity points or public network access points (NAP). InterNAP solves Internet congestion by setting up Private-Network Access Point (P-NAP) facilities – a combination of a network infrastructure and proprietary routing technology – which bypass the public NAPs, sending data along the shortest, most direct path. The company's P-NAP facilities are connected directly to the various Internet backbones and transmit customer data directly over the correct backbone rather than a randomly chosen NAP. InterNAP has over 247 customers including Amazon.com, Nasdaq, Fidelity and Go2Net. Revenues are generated by charging for Internet connectivity, which it buys from backbone providers (i.e. UUNet, AT&T, PSINet) then resells to customers with a 5% to 8% premium.

Opportunities

- The Internet was not originally designed to handle the rapid growth and increasing bandwidth needs that it is experiencing today. Industry estimates indicate that the demand for increased bandwidth will grow from 310 Gigabits per second in 1999 to 2,990 Gigabits/second in 2003.
- This high level of traffic flow results in slow and often unreliable Internet performance. Data loss of only 1% can double the time it takes to download files. During peak traffic times, packet loss at bottlenecks such as public NAPs can exceed 20%. InterNAP's P-NAP technology significantly reduces data loss for businesses.

Challenges

- Competition in the Internet connectivity area is intense. InterNAP competes with Internet backbone providers that also provide connectivity services as well as other high-speed data services. These include AT&T, GTE Internet-working, PSINet, Verio, UUNET and Sprint.
- InterNAP could face pricing pressure if telecommunication companies reduce communication costs for Internet services. This could force InterNAP to re-duce its prices, leading to shrinking margins and widening losses.
- The time to deploy new P-NAPs takes on average four to six months, and the company had only thirteen deployed by January 1999. There is a risk that In-terNAP may not be able to roll out new P-NAPs on schedule, which could lead to revenue shortfalls and higher costs.

Bottom Line

On the Internet, it is all about speed and performance, and InterNAP is at the front lines. Its P-NAP technology acts like a private toll road for businesses, improving performance and reducing data or packet loss. InterNAP also has an aggressive roll-out strategy and anticipates doubling the number of P-NAPs to 24 by the end of 2000. The major concern is whether InterNAP's technology will become re-dundant when a more robust Internet comes onto the scene or when it becomes technologically obsolete. For now though, InterNAP has a strong technological edge and looks to be maintaining that lead.

Key Statistics	INAP
Market Cap (4/20/00):	$4,751m
Free Float:	32.0%
IPO Date:	9/29/99
Offer Price (adj):	$10.00
Price (4/20/00):	$34.94
52 week high:	$111.00
52 week low:	$19.50
Volatility: (avg. daily % ch)	8.4%
Price/Sales:	379.5
Price/Sales-Growth:	70.3

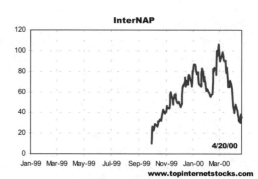

InterNAP

www.topinternetstocks.com

Annual Financial Data ($ m)	12/1994	12/1995	12/1996	12/1997	12/1998	12/1999
Revenues	--	--	0.04	1.05	1.96	12.52
Operating Profit	--	--	-0.92	-1.41	-6.95	-52.23
Net Income	--	--	-0.96	-1.61	-6.97	-49.92
Customers	--	--	--	--	--	247
Key Ratios:						
Gross Margin	--	--	-629.5%	-4.5%	-64.3%	-118.9%
Operating Margin	--	--	-2084.1%	-134.9%	-355.1%	-417.2%
Net Margin	--	--	-2179.5%	-154.0%	-356.3%	-398.7%
Marketing as % of Revenues	--	--	177.3%	25.0%	144.2%	84.3%

Internet Capital Group

http://www.internetcapital.com   eServices

Address:
425 Devon Park Drive, Bld. 800   Phone: 610.989.0111
Wayne, PA 19087   Fax: 610.989.0112
Management:
Chairman: Robert Keith, Jr.
President & CEO: Walter Buckley III
CFO & Treasurer: David Gathman

Description

Internet Capital Group was founded in March 1996 by Walter Buckley and
Ken Fox to capitalize on emerging opportunities in the budding B2B industry. The
company grew quickly, taking early investments in VerticalNet, MatchLogic and
13 other companies in 1997. As of the end of 1999, ICG had 49 companies in its
portfolio. The company's investments are focused on two B2B segments: market
makers, which act as intermediaries between buyers and sellers, and infrastructure
service providers or ecommerce enablers. Some of ICG's holdings include Com-
puterJobs.com, CommerceQuest, Deja.com, e-Chemicals, Purchasing Solutions
and Traffic.com. In December 1999, both Ford and AT&T invested $50 million
each in Internet Capital Group.

Opportunities

- B2B ecommerce is a nascent industry and expected to be worth well over a
  trillion dollars within a few years, rivaling the GDP of England. ICG is moving in early, taking key stakes in what could turn out to be the next eBays and
  Yahoos of the B2B world. ICG's stake in VerticalNet, which went public in
  early 1999, was worth $2 billion at the end of 1999.
- The company's growth strategy is focused primarily on the vertical market
  makers or B2B marketplace sector. This is one of the faster growing areas in
  the emerging B2B sector.
  It has investments in over
  25 major industries including chemicals, legal, metal,
  telecom and auto parts.
- Part of ICG's strategy is to
  make key investments in a
  network of partner companies and to leverage synergies between the various
  investments before taking
  them public.

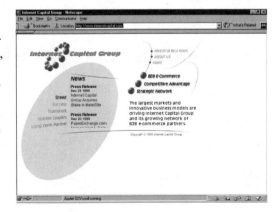

Challenges

- ICG is a new, publicly traded Internet holding company focused strictly on one sector of the Internet space. As such, its business model is extremely risky, and the company does not have a long track record. As of the end of 1999, ICG had brought only three companies public out of the 49 it has stakes in.
- At a market value of over $44 billion as of the end of 1999, ICG is one of the richest valued companies in the Internet arena. Internet Capital Group's holdings are worth roughly one-sixth of its market value. If ICG cannot realize substantial returns on its portfolio of investments, the stock has significant downside risk.

Bottom Line

Heading forward, B2B is where the real action is, and ICG aims to be in the thick of it with investments spread throughout the B2B sector. ICG has investments in 49 B2B companies at various stages of harvest. However, the company is also one of the riskiest in the Internet arena, with an unproven track record and a sky-high valuation. Nevertheless, if the company can realize substantial gains from its portfolio of properties (which is not unusual in this sector), then the shares may well have plenty of room to run. So far-reaching was England in the 19th century, that it was said the sun never set on the British Empire. In the 21st century, with its far-reaching B2B properties, the sun may never sit on ICG.

Key Statistics	ICGE
Market Cap (4/20/00):	$11,562m
Free Float:	8.0%
IPO Date:	8/05/99
Offer Price (adj):	$6.00
Price (4/20/00):	$43.75
52 week high:	$212.00
52 week low:	$7.00
Volatility: (avg. daily % ch)	7.9%
Price/Sales:	699.2
Price/Sales-Growth:	163.6

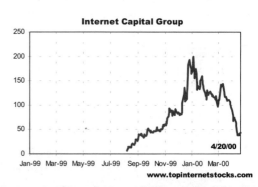

Internet Capital Group

www.topinternetstocks.com

Annual Financial Data ($ m)	12/1994	12/1995	12/1996	12/1997	12/1998	12/1999
Revenues	--	--	0.29	0.79	3.13	16.54
Operating Profit	--	--	-1.98	-6.58	-17.02	-40.54
Net Income	--	--	-2.06	-6.58	13.90	-29.78
Companies	--	--	--	--	--	49
Key Ratios:						
Gross Margin	--	--	-723.9%	-848.2%	-48.1%	-50.7%
Operating Margin	--	--	-693.0%	-830.8%	543.0%	-245.2%
Net Margin	--	--	-723.5%	-830.8%	-443.4%	-180.1%
Marketing as % of Revenues	--	--	--	--	--	--

InterTrust Technologies Corporation

http://www.intertrust.com   eSecurity

Address:
4750 Patrick Henry Blvd.   Phone: 408.855.0100
Santa Clara, CA 94086   Fax: 408.855.0144
Management:
Chairman & CEO: Victor Shear
Director, President & COO: Peter Van Cuylenburg
CFO: Erwin N. Lenowitz

Description

InterTrust was founded in 1990 to develop a method to protect and manage the rights and interests in digital content for artists, authors, publishers and distributors. In December 1998, the company shipped its first commercial product and went public in October 1999. Its Digital Rights Management (DRM) technology encrypts songs and other content for distribution, tracks the distribution, and provides access to the content in a way that the distributor can control. As an example, this could include the number of times that a song can be listened to or how often the song can be copied and passed along. InterTrust's customers include Universal Music Group, BMG Entertainment, Diamond Multimedia and Mitsubishi. Revenues are currently generated through licensing fees. Within the next several years, InterTrust intends to generate the majority of its revenues through transaction or ecommerce fees, taking a percentage, for example, of any pay-per-view digital videos and movies.

Opportunities

- The Internet is the next stage in media distribution, with anything that can be digitized, rapidly being digitized and distributed over the Internet. This includes music, books, magazines and newspapers. As a result, there is a strong demand from artists, recording companies and other media publishers to protect their royalty streams from piracy.

- Pegasus Research estimates that the market for digitized media products will grow from an estimated $1.4 billion in 1999 to more than $68 billion in 2003.

- InterTrust's business model is highly scalable and based on receiving a percentage of transaction revenues generated through the use of its technology.

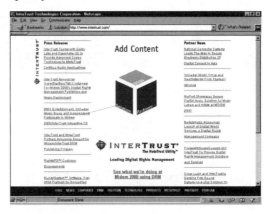

Challenges

- It is unclear if there is any interest from consumers for InterTrust's DRM technology. The concept of pay-per-view or pay-per-listen has been tried before and failed. One example of this failed concept was the DIVX video disk, which consumers could rent but had to watch within 48 hours or the disk would no longer work. DIVX lasted only one year before dying a quiet death.
- Revenues are concentrated among a few customers, with the top three customers accounting for an estimated 70% of revenues in 1999. If InterTrust were to lose any of these customers, revenues would be severely impacted.

Bottom Line

InterTrust intends to be the digital answer to music and software piracy. Protecting intellectual property rights on the Net is a great market opportunity that InterTrust is well positioned to benefit from. It is still unclear though, whether consumers will adopt the technology that InterTrust is offering, or whether the company can scale the technology to manage strong demand. Bottom line? InterTrust is a great concept stock in an untested market. Just watch out for the volatility.

Key Statistics	ITRU
Market Cap (4/20/00):	$2,691m
Free Float:	16.5%
IPO Date:	10/27/99
Offer Price (adj):	$9.00
Price (4/20/00):	$32.88
52 week high:	$99.75
52 week low:	$18.94
Volatility: (avg. daily % ch)	11.5%
Price/Sales:	1,746.4
Price/Sales-Growth:	191.1

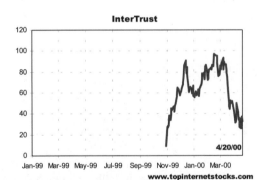

InterTrust

www.topinternetstocks.com

Annual Financial Data ($ m)	12/1994	12/1995	12/1996	12/1997	12/1998	12/1999
Revenues	0.85	--	0.03	1.10	0.15	1.54
Operating Profit	-1.55	-3.42	-8.14	-11.94	-19.67	-30.16
Net Income	-1.59	-3.58	-7.96	-11.71	-19.66	-28.61
Customers	--	--	--	--	--	--
Key Ratios:						
Gross Margin	100.0%	--	80.0%	90.7%	-25.7%	32.1%
Operating Margin	-182.2%	--	-32560.0%	-1085.3%	-12938.8%	-1956.9%
Net Margin	-186.8%	--	-31840.0%	-1064.5%	-12935.5%	-1856.3%
Marketing as % of Revenues	--	--	5092.0%	247.0%	2546.1%	446.9%

iXL Enterprises, Inc.

http://www.ixl.com   eServices

Address:
1900 Emery St. NW   Phone: 404.267.3800
Atlanta, GA 30318   Fax: 404.267.3801
Management:
Chairman & CEO: Bert Ellis, Jr.
President & COO (iXL, Inc.):   William Nussey
CFO: actively seeking

Description

iXL wants to excel at Web consulting and integration. The company was founded in March 1996 through the merger of three media properties. Between 1996 and September 1998, iXL grew quickly through a series of 34 acquisitions. These acquisitions ranged from Web design shops to online publishers and ISPs. Since then, the company has focused on growing organically, scaling back its acquisitions to one in January 2000. iXL Enterprises is the parent company of iXL, Inc, and Consumer Financial Network (CFN), an online financial insurance vendor, which also provides an ecommerce platform for financial services and employee benefits. iXL, Inc. provides Internet strategy consulting and Internet based solutions to Fortune 1000 companies. Its customers include GE, Chase Manhattan Bank, Delta Airlines, Merrill Lynch and FedEx. General Electric accounted for an estimated 13% of revenues in 1999. GE also owns 23% of Consumer Financial Network.

Opportunities

- According to IDC, the Internet professional services market will grow tenfold over the next few years to an estimated $78 billion in 2003. Leading this growth is corporate America's rush to "webify" their businesses.
- IXL is one of the fastest growing companies in the iBuilders arena, with its revenues growing 237% in 1999.
- iXL is extending its solutions offerings into the customer relationship management (CRM) area with the recent acquisition of Tessera. CRM allows companies to mine data collected from Web visitors and customers in order to cross-sell other products and services.

Challenges

- The Internet consulting, or iBuilders, industry is an intensely competitive market with hundreds of "me-too" firms all promoting virtually the same core competencies. Competitors include smaller, nimbler firms like Razorfish, Scient and AppNet, and the large consulting firms like Andersen Consulting, McKinsey, and PricewaterhouseCoopers.
- Although the iBuilders industry is growing rapidly, the business model is not as scalable as other Internet business models. Revenue growth is largely a function of billable employee growth.
- iXL has been focusing recently on growing organically (vs. growing through acquisitions). The challenge with this strategy is the ability to hire enough billiable employees in a tight labor market to continue the strong revenue momentum.

Bottom Line

iXL is moving at Internet speed to be one of the leading architects of the Internet economy. It has grown quickly through an aggressive acquisition strategy, 36 companies in four years. This is a necessary strategy in an area where in a few years only the larger iBuilders will survive. Like Godzilla, size does matter. However, its competitors all have the same strategy in mind, leading to a fiercely competitive environment. The good news though, is that the demand for iBuilders is so strong that it is likely to outstrip the supply over the next couple of years, with the market expected to grow tenfold by 2003.

Key Statistics	IIXL
Market Cap (4/20/00):	$1,437m
Free Float:	30.1%
IPO Date:	6/3/99
Offer Price:	$12.00
Price (4/20/00):	$20.00
52 week high:	$58.75
52 week low:	$13.75
Volatility: (avg. daily % ch)	5.3%
Price/Sales:	6.6
Price/Sales-Growth:	2.8

iXL Enterprises

www.topinternetstocks.com

Annual Financial Data ($ m)*	12/1994	12/1995	12/1996	12/1997	12/1998	12/1999
Revenues	--	--	5.38	18.99	64.77	218.34
Operating Profit	--	--	-1.56	-16.79	-47.18	-72.58
Net Income	--	--	-1.45	-15.44	-48.87	-70.21
Customers	--	--	--	--	--	--
Key Ratios:						
Gross Margin	--	--	33.5%	40.3%	31.7%	42.4%
Operating Margin	--	--	-28.9%	-88.4%	-72.8%	-33.2%
Net Margin	--	--	-27.0%	-81.3%	-75.4%	-32.2%
Marketing as % of Revenues	--	--	15.1%	20.6%	26.7%	25.5%

* Consolidated data for iXL Enterprises which includes CFN

ITXC Corporation

http://www.itxc.com   eServices

Address:
600 College Rd. East   Phone: 609.419.1500
Princeton, NJ 08540   Fax: 609.419.1511
Management:
Chairman & CEO: Tom Evslin
COO: John G. Musci
CFO: Ed Jordan

Description

With ITXC, the phone is just an Internet away. The company was founded by former AT&T executive, Tom Evslin, in July 1997 to provide telephone and fax service over the Internet. ITXC.net is a global, actively managed network that is overlaid on the public Internet. The network has 118 points of presence (PoPs) in 35 countries around the globe. The company's WWeXchangeSM Service provides wholesale international calling over the Internet for originating carriers and resellers, allowing them to offer Internet telephony services from anywhere in the world without needing their own facilities. ITXC's customers are traditional national phone carriers, PTTs, call-back companies, resellers and ISPs. Major customers and affiliates include China Telecom, Japan Telecom, Ameritech and Bell Atlantic. Revenues are generated by fees that it receives for terminating calls that have originated on the Internet.

Opportunities

- The market for international long-distance traffic is expected to grow from 94 billion minutes in 1998 to a projected 143 billion minutes in 2001. International Data Corporation estimates that Internet protocol telephony revenue will grow rapidly to over $23.4 billion by 2003.
- Calling long-distance over the Internet is substantially cheaper than through a traditional telephone network, as the cost of using the Internet is not determined by the distance calls need to travel.
- IXTC uses technology to improve the quality of sound transmission on the Internet (one of the chief complaints of Internet telephony), bringing it close to a normal telephone conversation.

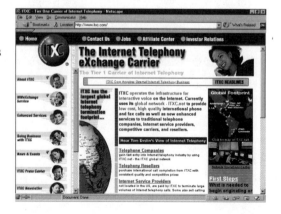

Challenges

- Competition is heating up in the Internet telephony market. In addition to the smaller Internet players like iBasis, established telecommunication companies are also entering the fray, offering competitive pricing. These include AT&T, Deutsche Telekom, MCI WorldCom and Qwest Communications.
- One of the major challenges with Internet telephony is the poor sound quality, often compared to talking through walkie-talkies. This is because of the way that data is sent over the Internet. Voice is converted to data, sent in packets, and later reassembled and converted back to voice. This process can lead to lost or delayed data if Internet traffic is congested, resulting in poor quality and/or delays of up to half a second.

Bottom Line

ITXC is the Internet Telephony eXchange Carrier and one of the leading companies offering wholesale Internet telephony services in a market that is just beginning to develop. Although many of the larger, more established telecommunications companies are beginning to move into the IP telephony market, it is doubtful that they will aggressively promote it for fear of cannibalizing their existing long-distance services. A larger threat could be if regulation is passed in the US, forcing IP telephony companies to pay the same access charges as traditional telcos. Bottom line? Internet phone services is a great concept with strong potential if it gains popularity, but it is still an unproven model.

Key Statistics	ITXC
Market Cap (4/20/00):	$1,310m
Free Float:	34.0%
IPO Date:	9/28/99
Offer Price:	$12.00
Price (4/20/00):	$34.50
52 week high:	$124.75
52 week low:	$18.38
Volatility: (avg. daily % ch)	6.1%
Price/Sales:	51.6
Price/Sales-Growth:	4.1

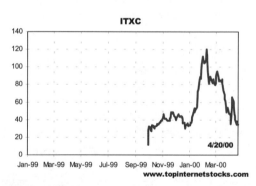

ITXC

4/20/00

www.topinternetstocks.com

Annual Financial Data ($ m)	12/1994	12/1995	12/1996	12/1997	12/1998	12/1999
Revenues	--	--	--	0.06	1.89	25.41
Operating Profit	--	--	--	-0.65	-7.30	-20.95
Net Income	--	--	--	-0.65	-7.21	-19.66
Customers	--	--	--	--	--	--
Key Ratios:						
Gross Margin	--	--	--	100.0%	-86.7%	-3.6%
Operating Margin	--	--	--	-1096.6%	-385.9%	-82.5%
Net Margin	--	--	--	-1094.9%	-381.1%	-77.4%
Marketing as % of Revenues	--	--	--	591.5%	133.2%	--

Kana Communications, Inc.

http://www.kana.com   eBusiness

Address:
740 Bay Road   Phone: 650.298.9282
Redwood City, CA 94063   Fax: 650.474.8501
Management:
Chairman & President: Mark Gainey
CEO: Michael McCloskey
VP Finance: Joseph D. McCarthy

Description

Kana believes good communications is at the heart of customer service. Kana was founded in July 1996 to develop software that manages and sort the huge volume of email that companies were receiving. Today, its customer communication software allows businesses to manage the entire customer life cycle from customer acquisition to the transaction and afterwards to after-sales support . This includes inbound and outbound email, Web-based customer service, real-time messaging and voice communications over the Internet. Kana's software focuses on three areas: Kana Connect (marketing), Kana Notify (ecommerce transactions) and Kana Response (service). Kana had more than 350 customers at the end of 1999 including eBay, Chase Manhattan Bank, Ford and Priceline.com. Revenues are generated through software licensing fees (75%) and services including installation and maintenance fees (25%).

Opportunities

- As Internet usage continues to grow, both consumers and businesses are turning to the Web as a communications medium. The Gartner Group estimates that by 2001, businesses will receive 25% of all customer contacts and inquiries over email or the Web.
- A survey by Jupiter Communications found that 42% of the surveyed companies' Web sites took longer than 5 days to reply to email inquiries, never replied or could not be contacted by email.
- Kana provides one of the most comprehensive packages available for managing customer communications.

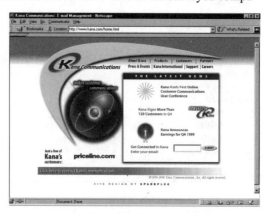

Challenges

- Competition is strong within the space that Kana operates and includes stand-alone solutions providers such as Brightware, eGain and Mustang Software; customer relationship management companies such as Clarify, Oracle, Siebel and Silknet; and in-house and third-party development efforts.
- Kana is operating with heavy losses as it continues to grow aggressively and attempts to quickly reach scale (in 1999, it had losses of $117 million on sales of $14 million). This will result in negative free cash flows for the foreseeable future, which in turn will require the company to come back to the public markets in order to raise cash. If it is unable to raise cash in the equity markets, Kana could run into financial difficulties.

Bottom Line

Kana is about online customer communications. It has established itself as one of the leaders in the area, with a comprehensive suite of software applications that can manage the entire customer life cycle from acquisition through the sale and to retention. However, as companies refocus on the customer retention side of the equation to drive additional sales at a lower cost, other companies are rushing to join the competitive fray. Kana at least, has the early lead. Recent acquisitions have also helped it to strengthen its product offerings. In late 1999, Kana acquired BEI to provide real-time Internet voice chat and support.

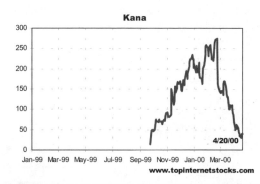

www.topinternetstocks.com

Key Statistics	KANA
Market Cap (4/20/00):	$2,432m
Free Float:	11.4%
IPO Date:	9/22/99
Offer Price (adj):	$7.50
Price (4/20/00):	$40.00
52 week high:	$175.50
52 week low:	$22.75
Volatility: (avg. daily % ch)	9.8%
Price/Sales:	173.0
Price/Sales-Growth:	34.6

Annual Financial Data ($ m)	12/1994	12/1995	12/1996	12/1997	12/1998	12/1999
Revenues	--	--	--	--	2.35	14.06
Operating Profit	--	--	--	-1.44	-12.83	-118.00
Net Income	--	--	--	-1.38	-12.60	-117.16
Customers	--	--	--	--	--	350
Key Ratios:						
Gross Margin	--	--	--	--	69.3%	51.2%
Operating Margin	--	--	--	--	-546.8%	-839.1%
Net Margin	--	--	--	--	-537.1%	-833.1%
Marketing as % of Revenues	--	--	--	--	234.6%	150.7%

LookSmart, Ltd.

http://www.looksmart.com   eContent

Address:
487 Bryant St.   Phone: 415.597.4850
San Francisco, CA 94107   Fax: 415.597.4860
Management:
Chairman & CEO: Evan Thornley
President: Tracey Ellery
CFO: Patricia Cole

Description

LookSmart helps Web surfers look for information "smarter". The company was originally founded by Evan Thornley and Tracey Ellery as NetGet in July 1996 with the help of funding from *Reader's Digest*. In October 1996, it changed its name to LookSmart and in 1997, moved its headquarters from Australia to San Francisco. Today, it is one of the leading search and navigation sites on the Internet, reaching over 45 million people a month through its own site as well as its partner sites. LookSmart has a directory database of over 1.5 million different Web sites (URLs) organized into more than 100,000 different categories. LookSmart also provides navigation and content products to more than 600,000 other Web sites and 280 ISPs. Customers include The Microsoft Network, Netscape, Time Warner, Excite@Home, US West, NetZero and AltaVista. Revenues are generated through advertising and syndication fees (45%), licensing and navigation (39%) and ecommerce and distribution (15%).

Opportunities

- The money spent on Internet advertising is expected to grow significantly in the next few years to more than $12.5 billion in 2003 according to estimates by Pegasus Research. Internet advertising has grown so quickly that it has already surpassed outdoor advertising in total ad dollars generated.
- LookSmart has been one of the fastest growing Web properties, with its base of users growing 73% in 1999, putting it on the list of top 10 search-engine sites according to Media Metrix.
- The company has extended its reach by licensing its navigation database and content to more than 600,000 other Web sites.

- In November 1999, LookSmart partnered with British Telecom to provide navigation and news to BT's 31 million Internet and wireless customers in 17 countries.

Challenges

- LookSmart is often perceived as "just another search engine" operating in a hyper-competitive arena where differentiation is difficult. Although it licenses its navigation database to the major portals, including MSN and AltaVista, it also competes with these portals for advertising dollars.
- Microsoft accounted for 46% of total revenues in the first nine months of 1999. After June 2000, Microsoft can cancel its contract with LookSmart for any reason on six-months notice. If LookSmart were to lose MSN as a customer, revenue growth would be severely impacted.

Bottom Line

LookSmart has positioned itself well in the hyper-competitive portal wars. By providing navigation and other services to the major Web sites, it has been able to diversify its revenue stream with licensing and ecommerce revenues, lessening its reliance on advertising fees. (which accounted for 98% of revenues in 1997). Traffic has also been growing strongly on LookSmart's Web site, indicating that the company has been successfully capturing market share. If LookSmart can continue to capture market share despite the intensely competitive environment, the company will look a lot smarter for investors.

Key Statistics	LOOK
Market Cap (4/20/00):	$1,538m
Free Float:	23.0%
IPO Date:	8/20/99
Offer Price:	$12.00
Price (4/20/00):	$17.50
52 week high:	$72.00
52 week low:	$15.00
Volatility: (avg. daily % ch)	6.2%
Price/Sales:	31.5
Price/Sales-Growth:	6.9

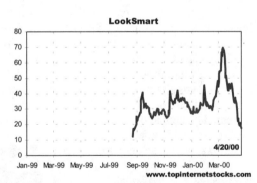

LookSmart

www.topinternetstocks.com

Annual Financial Data ($ m)	12/1994	12/1995	12/1996	12/1997	12/1998	12/1999
Revenues	--	--	0.00	0.95	8.79	48.87
Operating Profit	--	--	-2.83	-7.33	-11.90	-67.12
Net Income	--	--	-2.90	-7.51	-12.86	-64.66
Unique Visitors (m)	--	--	--	--	--	9.41
Key Ratios:						
Gross Margin	--	--	-2900.0%	54.7%	81.9%	85.8%
Operating Margin	--	--	-94200.0%	-772.3%	-135.4%	-137.4%
Net Margin	--	--	-96666.7%	-791.8%	-146.4%	-132.3%
Marketing as % of Revenues	--	--	37166.7%	386.5%	123.5%	120.9%

Lycos, Inc.

http://www.lycos.com   eContent

Address:
400-2 Totten Pond Road   Phone: 781.370.2700
Waltham, MA 02451   Fax: 781.370.2600
Management:
President & CEO: Robert J. Davis
COO & CFO: Edward M. Philip

Description

Lycos was founded in June 1995 as a search and navigation engine to help cybersurfers find their way around the World Wide Web. Named after the wolf spider, *Lycosidae*, the company has since focused on developing a community of Web properties offering the usual suspects of search and navigation tools, home-page building and community services, chat rooms, e-mail, personalized news and other services. Lycos' properties include community sites, Tripod and AngelFire, search engine, Hotbot, directory service, WhoWhere, and news and content sites, Hotwired and Wired News through the Wired Digital acquisition.

Lycos went public in April 1996 and has since grown to be the fourth most visited site on the Web with 30 million visitors a month. Roughly 70% of Lycos' revenues are advertising-based, with the remaining derived from ecommerce and licensing revenues.

Early in 1999, Lycos went through a very public battle in a failed attempt to merge with Barry Diller's USA Networks. In July 1999, Lycos teamed up with WingspanBank.com to strengthen its ecommerce capabilities by adding online banking and other financial products. The deal could bring in $135 million in additional revenues for Lycos over the next few years. Hoping to copy CMGI's successes, Lycos also announced the formation of a $70 million investment fund along with Microsoft co-founder Paul Allen. The fund will act as an incubator for potential content and ecommerce companies that Lycos could add to its network of Web sites. In September 1999, Lycos acquired Quote.com, a provider of finan-

cial news, quotes and other financial data. The company has also recently added online auctions to its list of services on its site.

The company is also expanding its presence in international markets, offering its services in 24 countries in Europe, Asia and Latin America through joint ventures and partnerships.

Opportunities

- Lycos has been growing quickly, thanks in large part to a series of acquisitions including Wired Digital, Tripod, AngelFire and others. In terms of revenue growth, the company is the one of the fastest growing major portal players, up 126% versus 134% for Yahoo!, and 115% for Infoseek and 47% for AOL.
- As consolidation picks up in the portal space, Lycos could become much more active on the acquisition side. Lycos' strategy is twofold: acquire eyeballs or visitors to its site in order to sell advertising and use the rapidly growing traffic to drive ecommerce revenues.
- Lycos is expanding its presence as an online financial center. In addition to its equity stake in online investment bank, Wit Capital, and its deal with WingspanBank.com, Lycos recently acquired financial quote and news provider, Quote.com. Online financial news is an attractive demographic, and advertisers typically pay top dollar on those sites. In addition, registered users of financial sites are typically more loyal, enabling Lycos to capture valuable marketing data and custom tailor financial products on an almost individual basis. This could help Lycos to generate significant ecommerce revenues in this area.

Challenges

- The company is at the top of the list of mid-tier portal players, ahead of Disney's Go Network, Excite@Home, and NBCi, yet trailing AOL, Yahoo! and Microsoft's MSN. With the majority of advertising dollars going to the top Web sites, Lycos could potentially fall behind if smaller portal sites merge to eclipse the independent company. As companies drop in the all important Web rankings, advertising revenues drop exponentially. The top 10 portals account for roughly 75% of all Internet ad revenue, and the next 40 media properties account for the next 20%.
- Internet advertising is still an unproven business, and lacking reliable ROI metrics, mainstream companies are still hesitant to commit to the medium. In addition, advertising rates have been trending down in the online world. Over 70% of Lycos' revenues are advertising generated.
- Ecommerce dollars may be difficult to generate. Many online retailers have been disappointed with the lack of revenues coming from placement agreements with the portals. If this disappointment were to continue, eTailers could pull or not renew what have otherwise been lucrative contracts for the portal companies.
- If Lycos were to acquire or merge with a non-Internet company, investors will likely not react favorably. Although this could make Lycos a stronger company financially speaking, Internet investors are concerned when a company dilutes its revenue growth with a slower growing partner.

The Bottom Line

Lycos is a solid player in the portal or content aggregator space and is gunning for the number two position, hoping to move ahead of Microsoft's MSN and nip at the heels of Yahoo!. However, as number four in the portal wars, Lycos is at a crossroads – remain either a mid-tier portal site or become a top-tier player. If it intends to continue its stellar growth and break into the top three list, it will need to either acquire eyeballs or be acquired. Consolidation will only increase in the eContent sector.

On the consolidation front, Lycos will need to tread carefully. As the failed USA Networks merger showed, Lycos' investors do not think well of an Internet company that merges with a non-Internet company. The reason? Fast growth company + slow growth company = medium growth company. Never mind that such a merger could potentially strengthen long-term margins and profits for Lycos.

As one of the last remaining independents, Lycos has three directions it could go: be acquired, continue acquiring and move up in the rankings, or remain in the mid-tier group as a lonely and fading independent portal. Given Lycos' commitment to be a major player, the third option is the least likely. More likely is that Lycos could be an acquisition target for a major Internet or traditional media company. In the meantime, expect to see strong revenue and visitor growth as Lycos continues to gobble up smaller players.

Key Statistics	LCOS
Market Cap (4/20/00):	$3,957m
Free Float:	73.0%
IPO Date:	4/01/96
Offer Price (adj):	$4.00
Price (4/20/00):	$36.00
52 week high:	$93.62
52 week low:	$28.56
Volatility: (avg. daily % ch)	6.2%
Price/Sales:	19.5
Price/Sales-Growth:	15.5

www.topinternetstocks.com

Annual Financial Data ($ m)	7/1995	7/1996	7/1997	7/1998	7/1999	1/2000*
Revenues	0.01	5.26	22.27	56.06	135.52	124.43
Operating Profit	-0.11	-5.80	-8.75	-31.49	-66.97	-65.46
Net Income	-0.11	-5.09	-6.62	28.44	-52.04	-61.92
Unique Visitors (m)	--	--	--	--	--	30.35
Key Ratios:						
Gross Margin	-451.5%	44.8%	80.5%	77.7%	78.8%	80.0%
Operating Margin	-2107.6%	-110.4%	-39.3%	-56.2%	-49.4%	-52.6%
Net Margin	-2107.6%	-96.8%	-29.7%	50.7%	-38.4%	-49.8%
Marketing as % of Revenues	590.0%	90.3%	85.9%	62.5%	58.2%	54.6%

* Six months ended January 30, 2000

MarketWatch.com, Inc.

http://www.cbs.marketwatch.com   eContent

Address:
825 Battery St.   Phone: 415.733.0500
San Francisco, CA 94111   Fax: 415.392.1972
Management:
Chairman, President & CEO: Larry S. Kramer
CFO: Joan Platt

Description

CBS MarketWatch has its eye on the financial markets. The company was founded in October 1997 as a 50/50 joint venture by CBS and Data Broadcasting Corp to provide real-time financial news, information, and personal finance tools to individual investors over the Internet. CBS MarketWatch is the leading financial news service on the Web, with more than 4.3 million people visiting its site each month. Since completing its IPO in January 1999, the company has been actively expanding its reach through a number of distribution arrangements with AOL, Yahoo!, Fidelity and the Financial Times. In June 1999, it acquired Big-Charts, the leading provider of stock charts on the Internet. Parent companies CBS and DBC each own 32% of the public company. MarketWatch generates revenues through advertising fees (74%), news delivery services (13%), licensing fees (8%) and subscription revenues (4%).

Opportunities

- The Internet advertising industry is growing rapidly and has exceeded TV ad spending in its first three years, in comparable dollars. Internet ad spending in the US is expected to grow to $12.5 billion in 2003, from an estimated $2.9 billion in 1999.
- CBS MarketWatch is the leading financial news portal with over 4.3 million unique visitors each month. Recent agreements with AOL and the Financial Times, as well as stronger ties with Yahoo!, should help CBS MarketWatch remain the top financial portal, helping to drive traffic and revenue growth.
- The company is extending its relationship with CBS in order to enhance the value of its brand and drive additional traffic to its site. In late 1999, it launched its first TV program *CBS*

MarketWatch Weekend, and began providing daily financial reports on *CBS' Early Show*. It also provides content for more than 90 CBS radio stations.

Challenges

- CBS MarketWatch is facing tough competition for advertising dollars in the eContent space. With virtually no barriers to entry and many sites offering financial news and information, differentiation is difficult. If MarketWatch fails to distinguish itself from other finance-oriented portals, traffic and revenue growth could slow substantially.
- MarketWatch has an agreement to pay CBS between 6 to 8% of gross revenues through 2005. This agreement will limit profitability over the next five years. Higher marketing expenses associated with the AOL and Yahoo! distribution deals will also weigh on profitability.

The Bottom Line

CBS MarketWatch delivers the financial news to millions of people every day. The company has seen the strongest revenue growth in the financial portal area: 254% in 1999, compared to 210% for theStreet.com and 86% for Multex.com. It has also been experiencing the strongest traffic growth and currently ranks as the number one vertical financial portal with 4.3 million unique visitors according to Media Metrix. In the race for ad dollars, the competition is not sitting still. MarketWatch also competes aggressively with Yahoo!, MSN and a host of others for eyeballs. But CBS MarketWatch has a significant competitive advantage over the other financial-oriented sites – CBS Broadcasting as a partner.

Key Statistics	MKTW
Market Cap (4/20/00):	$232.8m
Free Float:	24.8%
IPO Date:	1/15/99
Offer Price:	$17.00
Price (4/20/00):	$16.50
52 week high:	$83.38
52 week low:	$15.62
Volatility: (avg. daily % ch)	6.2%
Price/Sales:	9.3
Price/Sales-Growth:	3.7

MarketWatch

www.topinternetstocks.com

Annual Financial Data ($ m)	12/1994	12/1995	12/1996	12/1997	12/1998	12/1999
Revenues	--	--	0.61	1.80	7.03	24.94
Operating Profit	--	--	-1.87	-1.46	-12.25	-32.31
Net Income	--	--	-1.17	-1.02	-12.41	-38.88
Unique Visitors (m)	--	--	--	--	--	4.32
Key Ratios:						
Gross Margin	--	--	25.7%	55.2%	59.6%	60.3%
Operating Margin	--	--	-307.6%	-81.2%	-174.4%	-129.6%
Net Margin	--	--	-193.1%	-56.8%	-176.6%	-155.9%
Marketing as % of Revenues	--	--	21.7%	10.9%	64.0%	77.9%

MyPoints.com, Inc.

www.mypoints.com   eServices

Address:
100 California   Phone: 415.676.3700
San Francisco, CA 94111   Fax: 415.676.2054
Management:
Chairman & CEO: Steven M. Markowitz
President & COO: Robert C. Hoyler
CFO: Thomas Caldwell

Description

MyPoints.com enables Web users to earn rewards points by interacting with advertisers in a variety of settings, such as reading email, visiting Web sites and shopping online. The company originally started out as Intellipost, a direct marketer, in November 1996, and began offering email direct marketing in May 1997. It acquired MotivationNet and other Internet assets from Experian, including the Web-based loyalty program MyPoints in December 1998, changing its name to MyPoints.com in March 1999 in preparation for its August 1999 IPO.

MyPoints.com operates online loyalty programs with more than than 7 million members (as of February 2000), and provides its advertising clients and partners with an integrated set of Internet direct marketing and loyalty products. Members in its database earn rewards by responding to targeted email offers. Revenues are earned from corporate advertisers either through the number of offers delivered to members, the number of qualified responses generated or the number of qualified purchases generated. Customers include Barnes & Noble, eBay, Ford, Macy's, Microsoft, NextCard, Sprint and Wells Fargo.

Opportunities

- Internet advertising in the US – of which online direct marketing is part – is expected to grow from an estimated $2.9 billion in 1999 to more than $12.5 billion by 2003. According to Forrester Research, Internet direct marketing is one of the fastest growing areas in Internet advertising due to the declining response rates of banner advertising.
- While banner ads generate response rates of only 0.5%, opt-in programs similar to MyPoints can generate response rates in excess of 15%.

- MyPoints' growth has been explosive. In 1999, revenues grew to over $24 million from less than $1.3 million in 1998. The company also doubled its member base in less than six months to 7 million members.

Challenges

- MyPoints.com competes in the incentive-based online marketing area against CyberGold, Netcentives and other Internet start-ups. In addition, it also competes against opt-in or permission-based email marketers such as CMGI's Yesmail.com.
- Privacy is a key issue on the Net, and there is a growing concern regarding companies that are collecting browsing habits and demographic information on the Web. A backlash from consumers could potentially lead to consumers being less willing to divulge personal information to companies. If this were to happen, membership growth could slow in the US.

Bottom Line

Judging by the stellar growth in both members and revenues, MyPoints has been scoring points with Web surfers and advertisers. Revenues climbed over eighteenfold in 1999, and membership growth has been stunning, doubling in less than six months. Competition is intensifying with a host of Web start-ups and Internet giant CMGI moving into the email marketing space. However, the market is growing fast enough for several players, and MyPoints.com is at the front.

Key Statistics	MYPT
Market Cap (4/20/00):	$480.9m
Free Float:	19.8%
IPO Date:	8/20/99
Offer Price:	$8.00
Price (4/20/00):	$16.75
52 week high:	$97.69
52 week low:	$10.50
Volatility: (avg. daily % ch)	8.0%
Price/Sales:	19.9
Price/Sales-Growth:	1.1

MyPoints.com

www.topinternetstocks.com

Annual Financial Data ($ m)	12/1994	12/1995	12/1996	12/1997	12/1998	12/1999
Revenues	--	--	--	0.15	1.29	24.14
Operating Profit	--	--	-0.07	-2.95	-8.33	37.95
Net Income	--	--	-0.07	-2.89	-8.27	37.46
Members (m)	--	--	--	0.10	1.70	5.90
Key Ratios:						
Gross Margin	--	--	--	48.3%	12.8%	69.3%
Operating Margin	--	--	--	-1950.3%	-647.7%	157.2%
Net Margin	--	--	--	-1913.2%	-642.8%	155.2%
Marketing as % of Revenues	--	--	--	970.2%	350.9%	125.3%

NaviSite, Inc.

http://www.navisite.com   eServices

Address:
100 Brickstone Square   Phone: 978.684.3500
Andover, MA 01810   Fax: 978.684.3599
Management:
CEO: Joel Rosen
President: Robert Eisenberg
CFO: Ken Hale

Description

NaviSite is one of the leading providers of outsourced Web hosting and application services for businesses using the Internet for mission-critical functions. The company was originally organized by CMGI in 1996 to host the Web site of CMGI and its affiliates. In late 1997, the company began supporting non-CMGI companies. CMGI and its related companies account for roughly 58% of total revenues. NaviSite offers businesses the ability to outsource the deployment, configuration, hosting and management of their Web sites and Internet applications. Customers also have access to NaviSite's data centers through private Internet connections. Navisite has over 158 customers including AltaVista, Engage Technologies, Send.com and Raging Bull.

Opportunities

- The Web hosting and applications services market is driven by the trend towards outsourcing as corporations are increasingly faced with a shortage of skilled in-house IT expertise. Corporations are also realizing that it is more cost-effective to outsource business functions where they lack the expertise, allowing them to focus on their core competencies.
- The applications service providers (ASP) market is a nascent market that is expected to grow rapidly. Forrester Research estimates that the ASP market will grow to $21 billion in 2001 from less than $1 billion in 1997.

- NaviSite has a strong competitive advantage in with CMGI, which controls a wide number of Internet properties. This gives NaviSite the ability to leverage CMGI's extended *keiretsu* family as a marketing and distribution channel.

Challenges

* NaviSite competes on several fronts including against other Web hosting and application providers such as AboveNet, Exodus and Interliant, Internet application software vendors including Open Market, DoubleClick and Broad-Vision, and large system integrators and IT outsourcing firms such as EDS and IBM.
* CMGI still controls roughly 70% of NaviSite's ownership interests. As majority shareholder, CMGI could force NaviSite to pursue strategic initiatives that are not in the best interests of NaviSite itself.
* The ASP market is still a nascent industry, and as such, it is still unknown whether the concept of rented or leased applications will be widely accepted by corporations. There is also still a hesitancy among corporations to outsource business-critical functions and applications.

Bottom Line

NaviSite is on sight to deliver mission-critical applications for businesses over the Internet. It is one of the leaders in this nascent, but rapidly growing market. NaviSite also has the benefit of being able to leverage its strong relationship with CMGI, to help it grow its customer base and increase its product offering. The concept of outsourcing mission-critical business applications to a third party is still a hurdle for many companies. However, with the shortage of experienced in-house IT talent, outsourcing offers a strong benefit in the form of rapid, cost-effective deployment. In other words, plug and play.

Key Statistics	NAVI
Market Cap (4/20/00):	$2,240m
Free Float:	19.6%
IPO Date:	10/22/99
Offer Price (adj):	$7.00
Price (4/20/00):	$39.88
52 week high:	$164.94
52 week low:	$14.06
Volatility: (avg. daily % ch)	8.6%
Price/Sales:	103.1
Price/Sales-Growth:	40.1

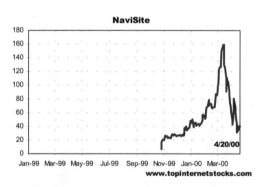

NaviSite

www.topinternetstocks.com

Annual Financial Data ($ m)	7/1995	7/1996	7/1997	7/1998	7/1999	1/2000
Revenues	--	--	3.36	4.03	10.52	15.04
Operating Profit	--	-0.03	-0.95	-9.08	-24.15	-22.64
Net Income	--	-0.03	-0.95	-9.17	-24.53	-21.99
Customers	--	--	--	--	--	196
Key Ratios:						
Gross Margin	--	--	-4.0%	-120.3%	-93.3%	-42.3%
Operating Margin	--	--	-28.2%	-225.3%	-229.6%	-150.5%
Net Margin	--	--	-28.2%	-227.6%	-233.2%	-146.3%
Marketing as % of Revenues	--	--	10.3%	62.8%	65.5%	--

NBC Internet, Inc.

http://www.nbci.com   eContent

Address:
225 Bush Street   Phone: 415.375.5000
San Francisco, CA 94104   Fax: 415.989.1365
Management:
Chairman: Bob Wright
CEO: Chris Kitze
President & COO: Edmond P. Sanctis
CFO: John Harbottle

Description

NBCi was born in November 1999 out of the merger of online media company, XOOM.com, several Web properties of offline media company, NBC and Snap.com. The new NBCi represents the growing trend towards convergence between new and old media, combining broadcasting, cable TV and radio with the Internet. Snap.com and XOOM.com are the Internet portals with the standard array of content, search and directory services, homepage building, chat rooms, etc. NBC and Interactive Neighborhood features programming from NBC and its affiliate stations throughout the US. Videoseeker.com offers video on demand as well as a video directory and search capabilities. AccessHollywood.com is the online site for the popular entertainment program. Revenues are generated primarily through advertising and to a lesser extent, ecommerce transactions.

Opportunities

- Internet advertising is quickly becoming mainstream, already surpassing outdoor advertising in total revenues and exceeding TV advertising if compared to the first three years for each (in equivalent dollars).
- Pegasus Research estimates that US Internet advertising revenues will grow from an estimated $2.9 billion in 1999 to more than $12.5 billion in 2003. The Internet Advertising Bureau estimates that the top 10 eContent sites account for 75% of total industry sales.
- NBCi is one of the most popular branded Web properties, ranking as the eighth most visited collection of Web properties with 14.9 million unique visitors, according to Media Metrix.

Challenges

- Competition is fierce in the online portal or eContent space, with hundreds of content-related sites vying for Web surfers' attention and businesses' advertising dollars. In an industry where the top 10 portal sites receive the lion's share of ad dollars, NBCi is in a position that could take it quickly in either direction. If NBCi fails to maintain its audience reach, revenue growth could slow substantially.
- NBCi's expansion into ecommerce is a promising strategy, but it is unclear how successful NBCi will be in generating meaningful ecommerce revenues. If it is not successful in diversifying its revenue stream, it will be dependent on volatile ad revenues.

Bottom Line

NBCi has put together a strong collection of branded Internet properties, which has helped it gain a strong following on the Web with nearly 15 million visitors. As is usually the case, where the Web surfers go, so go the advertising dollars. NBCi is also looking at expanding its ecommerce offerings by leveraging NBC's offline daytime programs with special online promotions. The key issue for NBCi going forward is how successful it will be at differentiating its content from the rest of the portal pack. Having said that, convergence is quickly becoming a reality, and NBCi is at the front of the trend. On the Internet, content is still king.

Key Statistics	NBCI
Market Cap (4/20/00):	$1,137m
Free Float:	32.2%
IPO Date (XMCM):	12/09/98
Offer Price:	$14.00
Price (4/20/00):	$20.19
52 week high:	$106.12
52 week low:	$16.88
Volatility: (avg. daily % ch)	5.0%
Price/Sales:	32.0
Price/Sales-Growth:	9.8

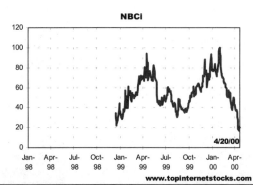

www.topinternetstocks.com

Annual Financial Data ($ m)	12/1994	12/1995	12/1996	12/1997	12/1998	12/1999
Revenues	--	--	--	--	8.32	35.58
Operating Profit	--	--	--	--	-9.36	-96.37
Net Income	--	--	--	--	-10.80	-86.83
Unique Visitors (m)	--	--	--	--	10.72	14.93
Key Ratios:						
Gross Margin	--	--	--	--	40.8%	52.8%
Operating Margin	--	--	--	--	-112.5%	-270.9%
Net Margin	--	--	--	--	-129.8%	-244.0%
Marketing as % of Revenues	--	--	--	--	28.8%	61.7%

Network Solutions, Inc.

http://www.nsol.com   eServices

Address:
505 Huntmar Park Dr.   Phone: 703.742.0400
Herndon, VA 20170   Fax: 703.742.3386
Management:
Chairman: Michael A. Daniels
President & CEO: James P. Rutt
CFO: Robert J. Korzeniewski

Description

Network Solutions is the dot-com people™ to the World Wide Web. The company had its beginning back in 1979, but it didn't begin registering domain names until 1993, when it was granted a contract by the US government to manage the domain name registration business for all the *.com, *.net, *.org, *.edu and *.gov names. It took four years to register its first one million Web addresses; the next one million were registered within 15 months. With the phase out of its monopoly, Network Solutions will continue to act as the central registry (depository) for .com, .net and .org, but now faces competition as a registrar in granting domain names. However, the company will receive $6 per address per year from all registrars, including it registrar, to maintain the master registry. Network Solutions also provides Internet Technology services focused on network engineering, security and management solutions.

Opportunities

- As the Web continues to grow exponentially, domain name registration is becoming big business. Network Solutions is aggressively targeting small businesses in the US and in international markets where the number of businesses having Web sites is still relatively small.
- Network Solutions has a strong brand identity, benefiting from its seven-year-old monopoly. It is still recognized as the place to go to register domain names and is leveraging that brand identity to develop value-added services such as e-mail, the dot-com™ directory and ImageCafe.
- More flexibility in new domain names (i.e. longer domains, new endings, etc.)

could generate additional revenue streams as businesses and cybersquatters rush to register the new names.

Challenges

- As the market to register domain names opens up, the competition is heating up. At the end of 1999, 70 companies were approved by ICANN to register domains and over 20 had already begun to register domain names. With the intense competition, the $35 annual fee to register names could come under pressure, leading to declining profit margins.
- Network Solutions will act as the registry of domain names until November 2003 (this can be extended to November 2007 if ownership of its registry and registrar operations is separated by May 2000), after which it is unclear whether the company will continue to receive the $6 annual registry fee from its competitors for acting as the central registry.

Bottom Line

Al Gore may have invented the Internet, but Network Solutions manages the Internet – at least the addresses. However, that is changing with the opening up of the registration business. Already, heavyweights such as AOL and France Telecom are registering domain names, and more are poised to enter the space. Network Solutions still owns the master registry and stands to earn $6 per year per address from the explosive growth in Net names expected from the new competition. The company could also split off its registry business into a separate company, which would guarantee it maintenance fees as the master registry until 2007.

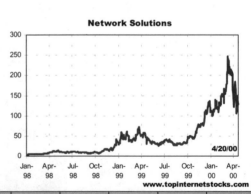

Key Statistics	NSOL
Market Cap (4/20/00):	$9,277m
Free Float:	47.0%
IPO Date:	9/26/97
Offer Price (adj):	$2.75
Price (4/20/00):	$128.19
52 week high:	$255.62
52 week low:	$24.50
Volatility: (avg. daily % ch)	5.5%
Price/Sales:	42.0
Price/Sales-Growth:	30.9

Network Solutions

www.topinternetstocks.com

Annual Financial Data ($ m)	12/1994	12/1995	12/1996	12/1997	12/1998	12/1999
Revenues	5.03	6.49	18.86	45.33	93.65	220.81
Operating Profit	0.30	-1.67	-2.27	7.70	19.34	45.58
Net Income	-0.98	-2.84	-1.63	4.23	11.24	26.89
New Registrants (000s)	--	--	--	--	--	5,000
Key Ratios:						
Gross Margin	38.9%	12.1%	22.2%	43.1%	58.9%	63.0%
Operating Margin	6.0%	-25.8%	-12.0%	17.0%	20.7%	20.6%
Net Margin	-19.5%	-43.7%	-8.6%	9.3%	12.0%	12.2%
Marketing as % of Revenues	--	--	--	--	--	--

NetZero

http://www.netzero.com   eAccess

Address:
2555 Townsgate Rd.   Phone: 805.418.2000
Westlake Village, CA 91361   Fax: 805.418.2001
Management:
Chairman & CEO: Mark R. Goldston
President: Ronald T. Burr
CFO: Charles S. Hilliard

Description

Surf the Net for free is the promise NetZero makes to consumers. The company was founded in July 1997 and launched its free Internet access service in October 1998. Since then, subscriber growth has blossomed, with more than 3 million users registering for its service at the end of 1999. Active subscribers are roughly half the total number of registered subscribers. NetZero offers consumers unlimited Internet access, e-mail and navigational tools, all for free. The catch? Consumers who register must provide detailed demographic data including their hobbies and interests. In addition, Web surfers who access the Internet through NetZero have a small permanent box of advertising, the ZeroPort, floating on their screen.

Opportunities

- Falling PC prices, and email developing as a common communications medium will continue to drive the growth in Internet usage. Pegasus Research estimates that the number of Net users in the US will grow from an estimated 85 million in 1999 to 160 million in 2003 (431 million worldwide by 2003).
- Internet advertising is growing rapidly, from an estimated $2.9 billion in 1999 to more than $12.5 billion by 2003. NetZero's ability to capture detailed demographic data and combine that with usage patterns is a compelling value proposition for Internet advertisers.

- NetZero, with 3 million registered subscribers or 1.5 million active subscribers, is the fastest growing Internet service provider in the US, surpassing Microsoft and AT&T to be the third largest ISP in the US.

Challenges

- The ISP market is an extremely competitive industry, with over 7,500 ISPs operating in the US. A number of companies are beginning to offer free Internet access including AltaVista, Qwest, and others. In addition, customer loyalty is low, with consumers switching ISPs at the drop of a hat.
- NetZero competes in the Internet advertising space for revenues, another hyper-competitive industry. The companies that capture the most eyeballs are the ones generating the bulk of the revenues. According to the Internet Advertising Bureau, the top 10 Web properties receive 75% of all Web ad dollars.
- NetZero is currently a money-losing proposition. Unless it can generate more ad dollars ($3.30/month per user) than its cost of providing Net access (between $4-$5/user per month), it will not succeed.

Bottom Line

NetZero is betting that free is better when it comes to Internet access. Judging by the explosive growth in users, it may be right. Having defined the space, it is the undisputed market leader in providing free Internet access in the US, despite a number of competitors, including CMGI's AltaVista, moving into the area. The greatest challenge going forward for NetZero is to gain enough critical mass (in users and advertisers) to eventually be able to generate profits. With ad revenues per active subscriber at only $3.30/month, it has a long way to go. Bottom line? Great concept and explosive subscriber growth but high risk.

Key Statistics	NZRO
Market Cap (4/20/00):	$867.8m
Free Float:	9.6%
IPO Date:	9/23/99
Offer Price:	$16.00
Price (4/20/00):	$8.28
52 week high:	$40.00
52 week low:	$5.00
Volatility: (avg. daily % ch)	6.6%
Price/Sales:	35.5
Price/Sales-Growth:	0.2

NetZero

www.topinternetstocks.com

Annual Financial Data ($ m)	6/1995	6/1996	6/1997	6/1998	6/1999	12/1999*
Revenues	--	--	--	--	4.63	19.96
Operating Profit	--	--	--	-0.02	-15.42	-41.50
Net Income	--	--	--	-0.03	-15.30	-39.50
Subscribers (m)	--	--	--	--	.89	1.45
Key Ratios:						
Gross Margin	--	--	--	--	-168.1%	-36.5%
Operating Margin	--	--	--	--	-332.6%	-207.9%
Net Margin	--	--	--	--	-330.2%	-197.9%
Marketing as % of Revenues	--	--	--	--	18.9%	101.6%

* Six months ended December 31, 1999

NextCard, Inc.

http://www.nextcard.com   eFinancials

Address:
595 Market St. Suite 1800   Phone: 415.836.9700
San Francisco, CA 94105   Fax: 415.836.9701
Management:
Chairman, President &CEO: Jeremy Lent
COO: Timothy J. Coltrell
CFO: John V. Hashman

Description

NextCard is the next model for online financial services, offering credit cards via the Internet in less than a minute. NextCard was founded by former Providian CFO, Jeremy Lent, in June 1996, and launched its NextCard Visa in December 1997. In September 1999, the company formed NextBank, an FDIC-insured online bank. NextBank accepts deposits as a source of funding for its credit card operations. NextCard also offers special online sales promotions through its GoShopping service, a shopping search engine that helps customers search for the lowest prices on specific products as well as being a report card on Internet merchants based on customer reviews and ratings.

Opportunities

- Business-to-consumer (B2C) Internet commerce is expected to grow from an estimated $23.4 billion in 1999 to $165 million by 2003. The vast majority of these purchase will be through credit cards. The Nilson Report estimates that the total charges on Visa and MasterCard will grow form $750 billion in 1998 to $929 billion in 2000.
- As a credit card issuer over the Internet, NextCard is able to collect valuable demographic information on consumers and their online shopping habits, and in turn use that data to effectively target value-added services to its customer base.
- NextCard has forged a number of strong partnerships in a move to broaden its distribution channel. In late 1999 and early 2000, the company began offering cobranded credit cards with industry leaders, Amazon.com and Priceline.com. In addition, it has over 30,000 members in its affiliate program.

Challenges

- Competition in the credit card market is intense, with over 6,600 financial institutions, including Banc One, Citibank and American Express, offering consumer credit cards. NextCard also competes with other Internet companies, including Yahoo! (through Banc One), that also offer credit cards.
- Pricing and surf balancing is a concern as consumers become inundated with credit card offers and low interest introductory teaser rates, hopping from one to the next. If NextCard is unable to retain customer balances after the introductory period is over, and if its competitors offer better rates, account and revenue growth would slow.
- Managing credit quality is one of the challenges in the credit card industry. In the last quarter of 1999, NextCard's delinquency rate (30+ days) increased to 1.5% from 1.2% in the prior quarter. If NextCard is unable to effectively manage the credit quality of its accounts, profitability could be negatively impacted.

Bottom Line

NextCard is the market leader in approving and issuing credit cards online. Customer accounts are growing at over 60% each quarter, and net interest income (net revenues) nearly doubled in the December 1999 quarter from September. As NextCard continues to grow aggressively, it will need to carefully monitor the credit quality of accounts, all the while fighting off competition from Banc One, Citibank, and others. NextCard does have the advantage however, of a strong affiliate network and strong partners in the form of Amazon.com and Priceline.com.

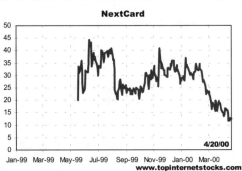

Key Statistics	NXCD
Market Cap (4/20/00):	$650.7m
Free Float:	46.0%
IPO Date:	5/14/99
Offer Price:	$20.00
Price (4/20/00):	$12.62
52 week high:	$53.12
52 week low:	$9.25
Volatility: (avg. daily % ch)	6.2%
Price/Sales:	24.5
Price/Sales-Growth:	1.2

NextCard

4/20/00

Jan-99 Mar-99 May-99 Jul-99 Sep-99 Nov-99 Jan-00 Mar-00
www.topinternetstocks.com

Annual Financial Data ($ m)	12/1994	12/1995	12/1996	12/1997	12/1998	12/1999
Net Revenues	--	--	--	0.09	1.20	26.56
Operating Profit	--	--	--	-1.89	-16.06	-77.20
Net Income	--	--	--	-1.89	-16.06	-77.20
Accounts	--	--	--	--	40,000	220,000
Key Ratios:						
Gross Margin	--	--	--	--	--	--
Operating Margin	--	--	--	-2026.9%	-1339.6%	-290.6%
Net Margin	--	--	--	-2028.0%	-1339.8%	-290.6%
Marketing as % of Revenues	--	--	--	53.8%	360.6%	--

NorthPoint Communications Group

http://www.northpoint.net   eAccess

Address:
303 2nd Street, South Tower   Phone: 415.403.4003
San Francisco, CA 94107   Fax: 415.403.4004
Management:
Chairman & CEO: Michael Malaga
President & COO: Elizbeth Fetter
CFO: Henry Huff

Description

NorthPoint is leading the way in high-speed DSL access. The company was founded in May 1997 to provide high-speed Internet access using DSL or digital subscriber lines. It first began offering commercial service in the San Francisco Bay area in March 1998 and has grown quickly since then, expanding its base of subscribers across the US to more than 23,500 by the end of 1999.

At the end of 1999, NorthPoint offered DSL service in nearly 2,000 cities and towns including 33 major metropolitan areas, through 1,560 central offices. To help expand its footprint, NorthPoint has signed distribution agreements with Intel, Verio, and in November 1999 with Microsoft and Tandy. The company markets its DSL services to ISPs, broadband data service providers and local telephone companies.

Opportunities

- As Web sites become more complex or media rich, and email – with picture and file attachments – is quickly becoming the communications medium of choice, bandwidth and access speeds are becoming a concern for consumers and businesses alike.
- Increased bandwidth requirements will drive the growth in broadband Internet access, in particular DSL. The Yankee Group estimates that the number of DSL lines will grow from 94,000 in 1998 to more than 4.1 million in 2002, representing a 158% annual growth rate.
- NorthPoint is targeting the business data market with its DSL access. The company expects to be in 60 markets by year-end 2000, passing nearly 45% of US homes and 50% of businesses.

Challenges

- Although still very young, the market for broadband Internet services is heating up quickly. NorthPoint competes against cable modem, DSL, ISDN, satellite and regular dial-up access providers. Competitors include Excite@Home, Time Warner's Roadrunner, Covad Communications, Rhythms NetConnections, AOL, EarthLink and Concentric.
- Technology limitations could limit wide-scale DSL deployment. Currently, DSL can only operate within 17,500 feet of a telephone central office.
- NorthPoint's success is dependent on the broad acceptance of DSL as the high-speed Internet access of choice. The planned AOL/Time Warner merger could speed cable broadband penetration, making it the de facto standard, thus limiting DSL's growth.

Bottom Line

NorthPoint is one of the leaders in DSL Internet access, doubling its subscriber base in the fourth quarter of 1999 to 23,500 subscribers. As bandwidth requirements becomes more of an issue, NorthPoint stands to benefit from the strong growth in broadband Internet access expected over the next few years. One of the largest risks for NorthPoint is whether DSL will gain wide-scale acceptance. In the consumer space, it is still too early to tell, particularly in light of the planned AOL/Time Warner merger. However, in the business world, DSL is shaping up to be the broadband platform of choice.

Key Statistics	NPNT
Market Cap (4/20/00):	$1,923m
Free Float:	26.5%
IPO Date:	5/5/99
Offer Price:	$24.00
Price (4/20/00):	$15.00
52 week high:	$48.75
52 week low:	$11.00
Volatility: (avg. daily % ch)	5.1%
Price/Sales:	90.9
Price/Sales-Growth:	4.2

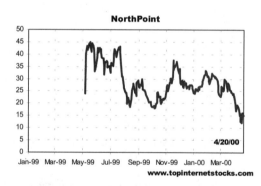

NorthPoint

4/20/00

Jan-99 Mar-99 May-99 Jul-99 Sep-99 Nov-99 Jan-00 Mar-00

www.topinternetstocks.com

Annual Financial Data ($ m)	12/1994	12/1995	12/1996	12/1997	12/1998	12/1999
Revenues	--	--	--	--	0.93	21.14
Operating Profit	--	--	--	-1.63	-25.36	-168.43
Net Income	--	--	--	-1.44	-28.85	-183.70
Subscribers	--	--	--	--	--	23,500
Key Ratios:						
Gross Margin	--	--	--	--	-326.4%	-138.2%
Operating Margin	--	--	--	--	-2724.2%	-796.7%
Net Margin	--	--	--	--	-3098.5%	-869.0%
Marketing as % of Revenues	--	--	--	--	--	--

Open Market, Inc.

http://www.openmarket.com   eBusiness

Address:
1 Wayside Road   Phone: 781.359.3000
Burlington MA 01803   Fax: 781.359.8111
Management:
Chairman: Shikhar Ghosh
President & CEO: Ronald Matros
CFO: Betty Savage

Description

   Open Market was founded in April 1994 to develop Internet-based business applications that could be quickly deployed within organizations. Since then, it has broadened its product offering to include Web-enabled customer relationship management (CRM) and personalized content management software. Open Market's suite of software solutions manage online content, commerce, and customer relationships for Internet-based businesses, and include the Content Server, Transact, Content Centre, Personalization Centre, Marketing Studio, Syndication Centre, Catalog Centre, ShopSite and AuctionNow. Open Market has more than 35,000 customers worldwide including Lycos, AOL, Acer, Ingram Micro and Siemens. Revenues are generated through software licensing (65%) and services (35%). North America accounts for 70% of revenues, and Europe 23%.

Opportunities

- Managing customer relationships is an important strategic imperative where customer acquisition costs are typically six times higher than the cost of retaining existing customers. By focusing on increasing sales to existing customers while efficiently targeting new customers, businesses can drive higher sales while improving margins.
- Open Market has a strong competitive advantage with its "one stop" set of Internet applications that speed deployment, improve efficiencies and reduce total costs for companies conducting business on the Web.
- Open Market is the leader in the Internet commerce software market, with a 20% market share. The company appears to be back on track with strong revenue growth in late 1999.

Challenges

- Open Market competes in the Internet applications and CRM space, a fiercely competitive environment. In addition to similar competitors such as BroadVision and Vignette, it also competes with heavyweights Microsoft, IBM and Oracle.
- In an intensely competitive environment, Open Market has suffered a series of strategic stumbles, which slowed revenue growth through 1998 and early 1999 and cost it valuable market share, down to 20% from over 30% a few years earlier. If the company does not successfully regain focus, it could continue to lose market share and suffer from anemic revenue growth.

Bottom Line

Open Market is back on track again after a difficult period caused by a lack of focus. The company is the market leader in integrated Internet applications for content management, ecommerce and customer relationship management. However, as Open Market knows all too well, the competition is eagerly waiting in the wings for any stumbles in a chance to steal market share. Open Market's recent acquisition of FutureTense helps the company to strengthen its product suite with a more integrated and flexible solution than it could previously offer.

Bottom line? With improved operating momentum, Open Market is set to take the lead again.

Key Statistics	OMKT
Market Cap (4/20/00):	$415.3m
Free Float:	81.9%
IPO Date:	5/23/96
Offer Price:	$18.00
Price (4/20/00):	$9.00
52 week high:	$65.50
52 week low:	$8.75
Volatility: (avg. daily % ch)	4.1%
Price/Sales:	5.0
Price/Sales-Growth:	17.5

OpenMarket

www.topinternetstocks.com

Annual Financial Data ($ m)	12/1994	12/1995	12/1996	12/1997	12/1998	12/1999
Revenues	--	--	22.50	61.26	64.55	83.03
Operating Profit	--	--	-29.12	-59.25	-36.56	-19.72
Net Income	--	--	-26.51	-58.01	-36.97	-19.78
Customers	--	--	--	--	--	--
Key Ratios:						
Gross Margin	--	--	75.6%	81.0%	71.2%	69.2%
Operating Margin	--	--	-129.4%	-96.7%	-56.6%	-23.7%
Net Margin	--	--	-117.8%	-94.7%	-57.3%	-23.8%
Marketing as % of Revenues	--	--	105.8%	59.7%	53.9%	46.2%

Phone.com, Inc.

http://www.phone.com

eBusiness

Address:

800 Chesapeake Dr.   Phone: 650.562.0200
Redwood City, CA 94063   Fax: 650.817.1499

Management:

Chairman & CEO: Alain Rossmann
Executive Vice President: Chuck Parrish
CFO: Alan Black

Description

Phone.com is betting that the next evolution in Internet connectivity will be over wireless phones and other devices. The company was originally founded as Libris, Inc. in December 1994, changed its name to Unwired Planet in April 1996 and changed it again in April 1999 to Phone.com. The company develops software (i.e. browsers and server software) that provide wireless access to the Internet and corporate intranet-based services, including email, news, stock quotes, weather, travel and sports. In late 1999, Phone.com introduced MyPhone, a mobile Internet portal platform that allows network operators to provide customized information services and applications. Customers include AT&T Wireless Services, Bell Atlantic Mobile, Sprint PCS and Deutsche Telecom MobilNet. In the March 2000 quarter, revenues were generated through licensing fees (63%), consulting services (15%), maintenance and support services (22%).

Opportunities

- Digital wireless services has been growing quickly, first in Europe (GSM), and recently in the US (CDMA, TDMA, etc). Dataquest estimates that the number of digital wireless subscribers will grow from 217 million in 1998 to more than 706 million in 2002. Jupiter Communications expects the market for Web-enabled smart phones to grow to more than 80 million in 2003.
- Phone.com has been successful in defining the standard of wireless application protocols (WAP) in partnership with Ericsson, Motorola and Nokia. Phone.com contributed the design and architecture of their wireless Internet technology to help establish WAP as the de facto standard and to guarantee interoperability. This tactic has helped it to establish a strong first-mover position.

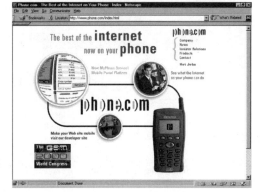

Challenges

- The market for wireless Internet access is still very young, although the competition is heating up quickly. In addition to Microsoft hoping to leverage its Windows CE platform, 3Com's Palm division is developing a wireless platform for mobile phones. Psion PLC has also formed Symbian, a joint venture between Nokia, Ericsson and Motorola to develop the next generation of wireless devices. Privately held AvantGo has also announced plans to develop a browser for the wireless market.
- Revenue concentration risk is a major concern. For the six months ended December 31, 1999, DDI Corp. and AT&T collectively accounted for 36% of total revenues. If Phone.com were to lose one or both of these customers, revenues would be severely impacted.

Bottom Line

Phone.com pioneered the marriage of the cell phone with the Internet. It has also established a strong competitive position by developing the WAP standard in conjunction with Nokia, Ericcson and Motorola in order to guarantee interoperability and help WAP gain wide acceptance. However, because the WAP standard is an open standard, competitors can also use the source code to quickly develop competitive products. But with a customer base of 60 wireless operators worldwide and 2 million subscribers as of March 31, 2000, Phone.com has a significant early lead.

Key Statistics	PHCM
Market Cap (4/20/00):	$4,662m
Free Float:	9.6%
IPO Date:	6/11/99
Offer Price (adj):	$8.00
Price (4/20/00):	$67.69
52 week high:	$208.00
52 week low:	$16.12
Volatility: (avg. daily % ch)	6.9%
Price/Sales:	147.6
Price/Sales-Growth:	30.4

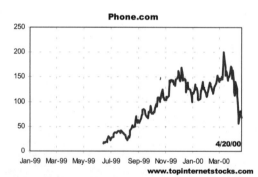

Phone.com

www.topinternetstocks.com

Annual Financial Data ($ m)	6/1995	6/1996	6/1997	6/1998	6/1999	12/1999*
Revenues	--	--	0.29	2.21	13.44	21.33
Operating Profit	-0.10	-2.67	-8.46	-11.61	-106.88	-29.61
Net Income	-0.10	-2.47	-7.99	-10.62	-107.33	-24.94
Subscribers	--	--	--	--	--	700,000
Key Ratios:						
Gross Margin	--	--	-20.9%	47.5%	66.2%	69.5%
Operating Margin	--	--	-2895.5%	-526.3%	-795.1%	-138.8%
Net Margin	--	--	-2736.6%	-481.8%	-798.4%	-116.9%
Marketing as % of Revenues	--	--	1095.2%	227.3%	82.3%	49.4%

* Six months ended December 31, 1999

Portal Software, Inc.

http://www.portal.com   eBusiness

Address:
20883 Stevens Creek Blvd.   Phone: 408.343.4400
Cupertino, CA 95014   Fax: 408.343.4401
Management:
Chairman, President & CEO: John E. Little
CFO: Jack Acosta

Description

Portal Software is the door to customer care and billing over the Internet. The company's beginnings go back as far as 1985 as one of the first online and Internet service providers (ISP). In 1993, taking its experience learned in the online access market, Portal began offering real-time customer management and billing (CM&B) software for providers of Internet-based services. Its flagship product, Infranet, supports creating and managing customer accounts, pricing and provisioning of service offerings, activity tracking, rating and billing. Customers include US West, Microsoft, Juno, Palm Computing and France Telecom. Revenues are derived from software licensing fees (62%) as well as consulting, systems integration, maintenance and training fees.

Opportunities

- The customer management and billing market is being driven by a combination of strong growth in Internet traffic, a renewed focus on customer service, and the trend towards IT outsourcing. Industry estimates place the market for CM&B software at $18 billion in 1998 and growing by over 32% each year.
- Traditional CM&B software has proven too inflexible for Internet-based companies, where business models and services offerings are constantly changing. Portal's IP-centric CM&B software has the flexibility and scalability needed for Internet-based companies.
- Portal's solution provides added value to Internet-based companies through increased revenues (accelerating time to market), reduced costs (minimizing installation, maintenance and servicing costs) and improved customer service (up-to-the minute account information).

Challenges

- Portal competes against traditional billing companies such as Kenan Systems, LHS Group and Saville; against Internet-specific billing companies such as Belle Systems S/A, Solect Technology and TAI Corp., and against internal departments of larger telecomm carriers.
- Portal's sales cycles typically last from three to six months, which could lead to quarterly revenue shortfalls due to timing issues. As a dot-com company, any revenue shortfalls, regardless of the reason, could have a significantly negative impact on the stock price.

Bottom Line

Portal Software is one of the market leaders in IP customer management and billing software solutions for Internet-based businesses. Both revenue and customer growth has been strong for the company, and it has built a strong list of blue-chip customers including Concentric, US West, Qwest, T-Online and Inktomi. Although competitive pressures are always evident in newly emerging markets, Portal has a strong first-mover advantage and a comprehensive set of CM&B solutions, which gives it a significant competitive advantage. The largest near-term risk for the company is its long sales cycles and large average contract sizes, which could result in volatile quarterly revenues, leading to volatile share performance.

Key Statistics	PRSF
Market Cap (4/20/00):	$7,176m
Free Float:	37.1%
IPO Date:	5/6/99
Offer Price (adj):	$7.00
Price (4/20/00):	$45.38
52 week high:	$86.00
52 week low:	$13.88
Volatility: (avg. daily % ch)	6.0%
Price/Sales:	69.7
Price/Sales-Growth:	24.3

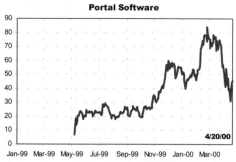

Portal Software

www.topinternetstocks.com

Annual Financial Data ($ m)	1/1995	1/1996	1/1997	1/1998	1/1999	1/2000
Revenues	1.52	1.86	5.05	9.42	26.67	103.00
Operating Profit	-0.20	-0.49	-2.25	-7.39	-17.13	--
Net Income	-0.20	-0.54	-2.27	-7.59	-17.41	-7.60
Customers	--	--	--	--	--	--
Key Ratios:						
Gross Margin	47.9%	85.0%	88.5%	66.8%	62.9%	--
Operating Margin	-13.2%	-26.0%	-44.7%	-78.4%	-64.2%	--
Net Margin	-13.0%	-28.7%	-45.1%	-80.6%	-65.3%	-7.4%
Marketing as % of Revenues	--	2.4%	47.0%	57.7%	52.9%	--

Priceline.com, Inc.

http://www.priceline.com   eTailer

Address:
Five High Ridge Park   Phone: 203.705.3000
Stamford, CT 06905   Fax: 203.595.0160
Management:
Chairman & CEO: Rick Braddock
President & COO: Dan Schulman
CFO: Heidi Miller

Description

Priceline.com takes a unique approach to selling over the Web. It lets its customers "name their price" for anything from airline tickets and hotel rooms, to home mortgages, cars and recently, even groceries. The company's founder Jay Walker, started Priceline in July 1997 with one goal in mind: let the consumer dictate the price for goods and services, not the merchant. With that in mind, the company launched its Web site in April 1998, and quickly captured national attention when it announced that it had received a patent for its "reverse auction" process. As the term implies, the process works by allowing consumers to name the price for a wide variety of goods and services that they would like to buy. Priceline.com then tries to match that price with participating sellers. Initial print and TV advertising using celebrity actor William Shatner (for which he received 125,000 shares in exchange for his efforts) also helped to make Priceline.com a household name.

Priceline has grown quickly since it opened its virtual doors barely two years ago. Now, with over 5 million customers buying everything from airline tickets, to hotel rooms and groceries over its Web site, the company generated an estimated $481 million in sales other services over its Web site in 1999. In early January 2000, the company was selling more than $3 million a day on its site. Its entrance into the online grocery market has also been a success, with Priceline.com selling more than 20 million grocery items during the 5 month period following the November 1999 launch.

Starting in the third quarter of 1999, Priceline began generating licensing revenue by licensing its name-your-price business model. Recent licensees include Alliance Mortgage, WebHouse Club and Perfect YardSale.

Opportunities

- Spending on travel and tourism is growing solidly, and is expected to reach $7.5 trillion by 2010 from an estimated $3.7 trillion in 1999 according to the World Travel and Tourism Council. Roughly 72% of the revenues in this market will be personal travel and tourism. Priceline is the undisputed leader in selling travel services over the Internet as evidenced by its stellar revenue growth – from $35 million in 1998 to over $482 million in 1999.
- As Priceline leverages its existing and future customer base across new revenue channels, its addressable market opportunity increases. The online grocery market, which Priceline entered into in late 1999, is one example. Forrester Research estimates that the online grocery market will grow from an estimated $513 million in 1999 to $16.8 billion by 2004.
- Priceline has patented the reverse auction business model, effectively locking out any potential competition that threatens it. Although the validity of patenting a business model still hasn't been tested in the courtroom, companies have nevertheless been hesitant to enter into this lucrative market.
- The other advantage of patenting the model is the additional revenues that the company can generate through licensing fees. To-date, Priceline has licensed its name-your-price model to Alliance Mortgage, WebHouse Club and Perfect Yardsle.
- One of the benefits of Priceline's reverse auction system is that it can effectively manage its margins and profitability by determining which offer it will match with the customer's bid.

Challenges

- One of Priceline.com's greatest challenges is filling customer orders for airline tickets/bids. At the beginning of 1999, the company had only 18 participating airlines and 90% of bids went unfulfilled. As of the end of 1999, 30 airlines participated in Priceline.com's "reverse auction" and unfulfilled bids fell to 50%. With only half of customers actually able to purchase a ticket over the site, consumers could become disenchanted with Priceline and seek out other alternatives.
- Although Priceline.com dominates the reverse auction business, it faces competition on a number of fronts. On the Web travel front, the company competes against Expedia, Travelocity.com, CheapTickets, traditional travel agencies and airlines, as well as a new airline industry site that is set to launch this summer. On the online grocery front, Priceline competes against WebVan, HomeGrocer and Peapod. With online financial services, it competes against mortgage.com, E-Loan, Quicken Mortgage, and Lending Tree, as well as traditional banks and financial institutions moving online.
- With airline ticket sales accounting for 85% of total revenues in 1999, Priceline.com is significantly dependent on airlines continuing their participation in its service. If airlines are successful at selling excess inventory over their own sites or over the new airline industry site (T2), there may be less incentive to continue the relationship with Priceline.com.

The Bottom Line

Priceline.com has moved ahead at Warp speed since launching its service just two years ago. By early 2000, the company was selling over 80,000 airline tickets per week, up eightfold from the prior year. Customers have grown from less than 200,000 in mid-1998 to over 5 million by March 2000. Recent forays into new revenue channels have also grown at light speed. Since launching its online grocery service in November 1999, the company had sold over 20 million grocery items by April 2000. As the company leverages its model across new revenue channels, its addressable market opportunity will continue to expand. From airline tickets and hotel rooms to home mortgages and groceries, Priceline.com has also recently expanded into gasoline sales and long distance services.

As the company moves into new markets, it will continue to come up against new competitors. Not to mention the fact that existing competitors will continue to attack Priceline.com's leading market position. However, judging by its strong growth metrics, Priceline.com is still leading the way.

Although Priceline.com is dependent on continued relationships with the major airlines, there is little threat posed by the announcement that the major US carriers are banding together to launch an industry-supported online ticket sales platform. With over 700,000 empty seats flown over the US every day, airlines are still dependent on sites like Priceline.com to help sell unfilled seats or excess inventory.

Bottom line? Priceline.com is boldly going where no man has gone before, and in the process exploring new markets for investors.

Key Statistics	PCLN
Market Cap (4/20/00):	$11,547m
Free Float:	13.0%
IPO Date:	3/30/99
Offer Price:	$16.00
Price (4/20/00):	$67.88
52 week high:	$165.00
52 week low:	$45.50
Volatility: (avg. daily % ch)	7.4%
Price/Sales:	23.9
Price/Sales-Growth:	1.9

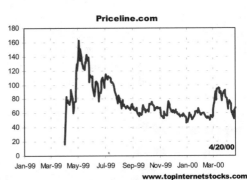

Priceline.com

4/20/00

www.topinternetstocks.com

Annual Financial Data ($ m)	12/1994	12/1995	12/1996	12/1997	12/1998	12/1999
Sales	--	--	--	--	35.24	482.41
Operating Profit	--	--	--	-2.51	-112.79	-1062.21
Net Income	--	--	--	-2.51	-112.24	-1055.09
Customers (m)	--	--	--	--	.70	3.80
Key Ratios:						
Gross Margin	--	--	--	--	-3.7%	12.0%
Operating Margin	--	--	--	--	-320.1%	-220.2%
Net Margin	--	--	--	--	-318.5%	-218.7%
Marketing as % of Sales	--	--	--	--	69.2%	16.5%

Prodigy Communications Corporation

http://www.prodigy.com   eAccess

Address:
44 South Broadway   Phone: 914.448.8000
White Plains, NY 10601   Fax: 914.448.3467
Management:
Chairman & CEO: Samer F. Salameh
President & COO: David C. Trachtenberg
CFO: Allen Craft

Description

Founded in 1984, Prodigy was one of the first online services in the US, providing its own proprietary service back in 1988. For a short time, Prodigy ranked ahead of America Online and second behind industry leader CompuServe. Unfortunately neither IBM nor Sears, which jointly owned the company, were committed to developing Prodigy, and the company's growth stalled. Frustrated with IBM and Sears neglect, Prodigy's management, with the help of other investors, bought the company in an LBO back in 1996. Since then, Prodigy has been hard at work, reducing its cost structure and repositioning itself as a leading ISP, with more than 900 points-of-presence (POPs) in 750 US cities. In a final parting with the past, Prodigy discontinued its old service, Prodigy Classic. Replaced by Prodigy Internet, the new service had over 1.3 million subscribers as of the end of March 2000. Prodigy's major shareholders include Carso Global Telecom and Telmex, which has helped paved the way for Prodigy to begin introducing its services into Mexico in a managed partnership with Telmex and to begin targeting the Hispanic community in the US with bilingual services. In the second quarter of 2000, SBC will let Prodigy manage its consumer and small business Internet service in exchange for a 43% equity stake.

Opportunities

- After an anemic 9% subscriber growth in 1998, Prodigy is bouncing back, with its subscriber base doubling in 1999. This growth has come from a number of recent distribution deals that Prodigy signed in 1999 with Best Buy AST, Acer, Gateway, Toshiba and Sony, among others.

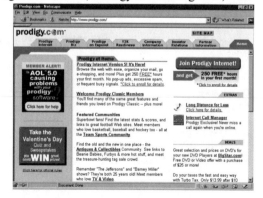

- Prodigy is also expanding into the DSL or broadband market through arrangements with Covad and SBC.

Challenges

- With over 7,500 Internet service providers in the US, competition is fierce, and customer loyalty is low in the consumer ISP market. As a result, providing differentiated services in a commodity business is not an easy task.
- Prodigy does not have a successful track record. It lost the ISP race to CompuServe and AOL in its prior life, and it has only recently begun to show strong subscriber growth.
- Free Internet access is the stealth danger for consumer-oriented ISPs. It started out in Europe and is beginning to make inroads here in the US, particularly in the Hispanic population where household incomes are lower. This is a key demographic group that Prodigy is targeting.

The Bottom Line

Prodigy may have gotten off to a long, slow start in the ISP race, but it is quickly catching up. The company has been aggressively expanding its distribution channels both through specialty retailers and through PC manufacturers, helping the company to accelerate its subscriber growth in the US. However, the real story for Prodigy could be the Mexican and US Hispanic markets. It is here that the company has an edge. In the US, PC and Internet penetration among Hispanic households is far from saturation at only 25% and 17% respectively. In Mexico, Prodigy couldn't wish for a better partner. Telmex effectively controls the local phone market and also controls over half of the Internet dial-up accounts in the country. The bottom line? Strong growth potential, but watch how margins develop. After all, up until recently, the company has not had a stellar track record.

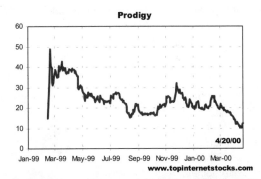

Key Statistics	PRGY
Market Cap (4/20/00):	$799.2m
Free Float:	34.9%
IPO Date:	2/11/99
Offer Price:	$15.00
Price (4/20/00):	$12.38
52 week high:	$35.44
52 week low:	$8.25
Volatility: (avg. daily % ch)	4.7%
Price/Sales:	4.2
Price/Sales-Growth:	10.9

www.topinternetstocks.com

Annual Financial Data ($ m)	12/1994	12/1995	12/1996	12/1997	12/1998	12/1999
Revenues	--	--	98.90	134.20	136.14	189.04
Operating Profit	-1.00	-3.10	-79.00	-119.60	-70.49	-88.25
Net Income	-1.00	-3.10	-90.80	-132.80	-65.08	-80.49
Subscribers (m)	--	--	0.81	0.61	0.67	1.14
Key Ratios:						
Gross Margin	--	--	29.0%	25.3%	31.4%	45.9%
Operating Margin	--	--	-79.9%	-89.1%	-51.8%	-46.7%
Net Margin	--	--	-91.8%	-99.0%	-47.8%	-42.6%
Marketing as % of Revenues	--	--	21.5%	45.1%	30.6%	31.1%

PSINet, Inc.

http://www.psi.net   eAccess

Address:
44483 Knoll Square   Phone: 703.726.4100
Ashburn, VA 20147   Fax: 703.726.4200
Management:
Chairman & CEO: William L. Schrader
President & COO: Harold S. Wills
CFO:

Description

PSINet was founded in 1989 as the first ISP to provide commercial Internet access. Perfomance Systems International, as it was known at the time, expanded into consumer Internet access in 1995, but it quickly changed its mind and sold the consumer assets to MindSpring in 1996, shortly after changing its name to PSINet. Today, it is a leading provider of commercial Internet access, hosting and ecommerce and other IP services to businesses. PSINet also provides network backbone services to other ISPs. In the 24 months ending December 1999, PSINet had acquired over 61 ISPs in Europe, Latin America and Asia, with the result that in 1999, 44% of PSINet's revenues were generated outside the US.

PSINet recently acquired Transaction Network Services in a move that strengthened its position in the booming ecommerce area. TNI handles over 70% of the electronic point-of-sale transactions in the US, more than 20 million transactions a day for nearly 2 million businesses.

Opportunities

- PSINet is operating in the fastest growing segment of the Internet services market – corporate IP and Web hosting solutions. IT research firm, IDC, predicts that the broader business Internet access and value-added IP services will grow 32% compounded annually to nearly $25 billion by 2003.
- By focusing its growth strategy outside the US, PSINet is positioning itself to benefit from an Internet growth rate nearly twice that of the US.
- PSINet is focused primarily on the value-added business market, where customer loyalty and margins are higher, and churn rates are lower.

Challenges

- Although not as intense as on the consumer side, competition is heating up in the business Internet access and IP services market. Concentric, Verio, Globix and others are fighting aggressively to capture market share. In addition, PSINet competes against US telcos such as AT&T, Sprint and Bell Atlantic, and against local telcos in international markets such as Telmex, Telebras and Deutche Telecom.
- PSINet's aggressive acquisition pace could present significant integration risk for the company. If PSINet cannot smoothly integrate the acquisitions into its operations, it could quickly lose recently acquired customers.

The Bottom Line

PSINet is one of the leading providers of corporate Internet access and IP services. With more than 91,000 business customers around the world, PSINet understands where the real growth in Internet services is – outside the US where Internet usage is growing twice as fast as in the US. By focusing on the businesss-oriented, higher margin side of the Internet service providers market and expanding its services to act as a one-stop shop, the company has positioned itself well: helping organizations gain access to the Web, then providing Web hosting, email, and ecommerce solutions. In addition, PSINet's acquisition of Transaction Network Services, the leading ecommerce and electronic point-of-sale transaction processor, will significantly strengthen the company's foothold in the rapidly developing ecommerce market.

Key Statistics	PSIX
Market Cap (4/20/00):	$3,642m
Free Float:	65.1%
IPO Date:	5/2/95
Offer Price (adj):	$6.00
Price (4/20/00):	$23.12
52 week high:	$60.94
52 week low:	$15.50
Volatility: (avg. daily % ch)	4.3%
Price/Sales:	6.6
Price/Sales-Growth:	5.8

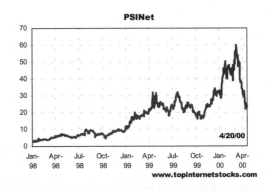

PSINet

www.topinternetstocks.com

Annual Financial Data ($ m)	12/1994	12/1995	12/1996	12/1997	12/1998	12/1999
Revenues	15.21	38.72	84.35	121.90	259.60	554.70
Operating Profit	-4.66	-52.62	-56.08	-49.59	-176.27	-279.40
Net Income	-5.34	-53.16	-55.10	-45.60	-261.87	-416.20
Subscribers	--	--	--	26,400	54,700	91,000
Key Ratios:						
Gross Margin	37.6%	17.0%	23.3%	22.6%	23.2%	28.5%
Operating Margin	-30.6%	-135.9%	-66.5%	-40.7%	-67.9%	-50.4%
Net Margin	-35.1%	-137.3%	-65.3%	-37.4%	-100.9%	-75.0%
Marketing as % of Revenues	23.7%	61.8%	32.1%	21.2%	22.0%	18.7%

PurchasePro.com, Inc.

http://www.purchasepro.com   eBusiness

Address:
3291 North Buffalo Dr.   Phone: 702.316.7000
Las Vegas, NV 89129   Fax: 702.316.7001
Management:
Chairman & CEO: Charles E. Johnson, Jr.
President, COO: Christopher P. Carton
CFO: Richard C. St. Peter

Description

PurchasePro is a pro at connecting buyers and suppliers. The company was founded in October 1996 and began developing its service after studying the purchasing or procurement process of the hospitality industry, launching its e-marketplace in April 1997. PurchasePro's e-marketplace is designed to streamline the procurement cycle, from sourcing and bidding through to order and payment, for buyers and suppliers. The company targets primarily small- to medium-sized businesses (SMEs), which constitute roughly 99% of all businesses in the US.

Revenues are generated through membership fees that companies pay in order to access PurchasePro's e-marketplaces (60%), as well as transaction fees, licensing and advertising fees (40% in aggregate). Customers include Best Western, Carnival Cruise Lines, Caesar's Palace, Mirage Resorts and Marriott International.

Opportunities

- Corporate procurement is an inefficient and fragmented process, costing most organizations 30 to 38% of total revenues. The cost of a corporate purchase transaction can run from $8 to $150 or more because of the manual cost, error and lack of economies of scale (bulk purchasing). Automating the process both internally and externally can lead to a 5 to 25% reduction in operating expenses.

- PurchasePro is targeting primarily small and medium-sized businesses, a market that has been largely ignored, and yet accounts for 99% of all businesses in the US.

- Electronic data interchange (EDI) has been used to a limited extent in automating some of the purchasing process for companies, but its high cost, low flexibility

and lack of an open standard has limited its reach. According to Forrester Research, only 5% of businesses in the US have deployed EDI systems.

Challenges

- Although the eProcurement market is a relatively new market, the barriers to entry are low, making it easy for new competitors to quickly enter the arena. Competitors include Ariba, Commerce One, Oracle and SAP.
- Revenue growth could be volatile because of the long sales cycles needed to close large corporate accounts. This is typically 6-9 months, but has taken as long as 18 months for some contracts. If PurchasePro fails to meet quarterly revenue expectations, share performance could be negatively impacted.

Bottom Line

PurchasePro is one of the newer additions to the budding eProcurement market, but it is quickly growing in size. Its secret? Targeting the 99% of businesses, small and medium-sized companies, that can benefit the most from reducing purchasing costs. As with most e-marketplaces, one of the challenges will be for PurchasePro to sign up enough members that it quickly reaches critical mass: having enough suppliers that corporate purchasers want to use the network and having enough buyers that suppliers can target.

Key Statistics	PPRO
Market Cap (4/20/00):	$997.2m
Free Float:	63.9%
IPO Date:	9/14/99
Offer Price (adj):	$12.00
Price (4/20/00):	$32.00
52 week high:	$175.00
52 week low:	$14.62
Volatility: (avg. daily % ch)	8.9%
Price/Sales:	165.7
Price/Sales-Growth:	63.7

PurchasePro

www.topinternetstocks.com

Annual Financial Data ($ m)	12/1994	12/1995	12/1996	12/1997	12/1998	12/1999
Revenues	--	--	--	0.68	1.67	6.02
Operating Profit	--	--	-0.12	-2.86	-6.48	-72.13
Net Income	--	--	-0.12	-2.99	-6.80	-71.94
Customers	--	--	--	--	--	--
Key Ratios:						
Gross Margin	--	--	--	68.3%	73.3%	86.1%
Operating Margin	--	--	--	-424.2%	-388.2%	-1198.8%
Net Margin	--	--	--	-442.0%	-407.1%	-1195.6%
Marketing as % of Revenues	--	--	--	174.6%	230.0%	166.5%

Quest Software, Inc.

http://www.quest.com   eBusiness

Address:
8001 Irvine Center Dr.   Phone: 949.754.8000
Irvine, CA 92618   Fax: 949.754.8999
Management:
Chairman & CEO: Vincent C. Smith
President: David M. Doyle
CFO: John J. Laskey

Description

Quest helps companies in their search for information across the extended enterprise. The company was founded in 1987 to help organizations improve application performance and database availability in order to facilitate information delivery. Quest offers a suite of software solutions for Internet information management and corporate networks that provides database diagnostics, network monitoring, capacity planning and application problem detection and resolution. Its flagship product, Vista Plus, is a report-based information management system that can search and distribute data over the Internet and corporate networks.

Quest has more than 4,000 customers including Priceline.com, EarthLink, Hewlett Packard and Andersen Consulting. Revenues are generated through software licensing fees (75%) and consulting, maintenance and training services (25%). International revenues account for roughly 21% of total revenues.

Opportunities

- As businesses turn to the Web for business-critical function, low reliability and system downtimes can quickly lead to lost customers and revenues. Quest's software can monitor application components for faults or bottlenecks, reducing downtime as well as being able to quickly capture and analyze information from existing applications over the Web.

- In early 2000, Quest acquired Foglight Software in a move to broaden its solutions offering. Foglight develops the Real-Time Application Performance System (RAPS), a software monitoring system that ensures that mission-critical eBusiness applications are correctly operating.

Challenges

- Competition is strong in the eBusiness solutions market and includes enterprise report management vendors such as Actuate, Computer Associates, Mobius and IBM; hardware and software replication tools vendors such as EMC and Veritas; and database management vendors such as BMC, Compuware, Oracle and Microsoft. In addition, Quest also competes with Oracle in the database management space.
- As with most eBusiness software vendors, Quest is at risk of missing quarterly revenue expectations because of timing issues related to long sales cycles and large order sizes. If Quest does miss revenue expectations (i.e. some contracts do not close before quarter end), share performance could be negatively impacted.

Bottom Line

Although Quest has been around for over a decade as a traditional enterprise software vendor, it has successfully transformed itself into an eBusiness software enabler, and in the process, watched its revenues double on the back of strong demand. The challenge for Quest going forward will be to carefully manage its relationship with Oracle. In addition to being a partner, Oracle is also a competitor in certain areas. As businesses continue to embrace the Web and leverage it throughout their extended enterprises, the demand for Quest's products is expected to continue.

Key Statistics	QSFT
Market Cap (4/20/00):	$4,029m
Free Float:	23.0%
IPO Date:	8/13/99
Offer Price (adj):	$7.00
Price (4/20/00):	$47.25
52 week high:	$98.12
52 week low:	$10.25
Volatility: (avg. daily % ch)	7.11%
Price/Sales:	56.8
Price/Sales-Growth:	54.8

Quest Software

www.topinternetstocks.com

Annual Financial Data ($ m)	12/1994	12/1995	12/1996	12/1997	12/1998	12/1999
Revenues	5.69	9.52	12.86	18.32	34.79	70.87
Operating Profit	0.04	2.34	-0.37	1.45	3.69	4.47
Net Income	0.02	2.36	0.02	0.29	2.35	3.40
Customers	--	--	--	--	--	--
Key Ratios:						
Gross Margin	60.9%	87.0%	81.2%	82.1%	82.9%	89.9%
Operating Margin	0.7%	24.5%	-2.9%	7.9%	10.6%	6.3%
Net Margin	0.3%	24.8%	0.1%	1.6%	6.7%	4.8%
Marketing as % of Revenues	11.8%	22.9%	33.6%	31.9%	34.0%	45.3%

Razorfish, Inc.

http://www.razorfish.com   eServices

Address:
32 Mercer St.   Phone: 212.966.5960
New York, NY 10013   Fax: 212.966.6915

Management:
Chairman: Per I. G. Bystedt
President & CEO: Jeffrey A. Dachis
CFO (interim):   Sue Black

Description

When Jeff Dachis and Craig Kanarick decided to start an interactive Web agency back in January 1995, they opened a dictionary and blindly chose the name of their new company – Razorfish. Since then, Razorfish has gone on to become one of the leading iBuilders, gobbling up scores of companies along the way. In the last two years, Razorfish has acquired twelve Web design and consulting firms, including Spray early in 1999 and I-Cube in November 1999. The company provides creative design, strategic consulting, application development and systems integration to Fortune 1000 clients, including Time Warner, Disney, Sony, and Charles Schwab. Razorfish has been aggressively expanding its core competencies to include wireless Internet solutions through its Mobile Solutions Laboratory.

Opportunities

- As corporate America races to Web-enable their businesses, the demand for iBuilders continues to grow. From an estimated $7.8 billion in 1999, IDC expects the Internet professional services sector to grow more than 57% annually to $78 billion by 2003.
- In a competitive world of "eat or be eaten", Razorfish is high up in the food chain and is well poised to benefit from and survive the wave of consolidations expected in the sector over the next few years.
- Razorfish is positioning itself to be at the forefront of the two major trends in Internet connectivity. Its recent acquisitions of Fuel and Lee Hunt Associates expands the company's expertise into the growing

broadband area. The company is also agressively expanding its wireless technology unit in order to be at the forefront of wireless Internet access.

Challenges

- With barriers to entry nonexistent, virtually anyone can set up shop and call themselves an iBuilder. As a result, competition is fierce. In addition to small one-garage shops and larger pure-play iBuilders, consulting behemoths Andersen Consulting, KPMG, IBM and EDS are also moving into the arena.
- The Internet consulting model is not as scalable as other Internet business models. Revenue growth is largely tied to billable employee growth.
- Razorfish is active on the acquisition path. The company could have difficulties integrating new and existing acquisitions, which could lead to high turnover and lost clients.

The Bottom Line

When it comes to advising, building and integrating Web sites and strategies, Razorfish is one of the top fish in the barrel. The company has been growing quickly through a series of acquisitions, which is vital in an industry where, like Godzilla, size does matter. Having said that, one of the major challenges for Razorfish will be to seamlessly integrate these new and future acquisitions into its school. Razorfish has positioned itself early to take advantage of the wireless Internet trend that is quickly sweeping through the I-world. In addition, the company is also well prepared for the coming broadband revolution.

Key Statistics	RAZF
Market Cap (4/20/00):	$1,765m
Free Float:	49.1%
IPO Date:	4/27/99
Offer Price (adj):	$8.00
Price (4/20/00):	$18.50
52 week high:	$56.94
52 week low:	$12.25
Volatility: (avg. daily % ch)	5.6%
Price/Sales:	10.4
Price/Sales-Growth:	10.1

www.topinternetstocks.com

Annual Financial Data ($ m)	12/1994	12/1995	12/1996	12/1997	12/1998	12/1999
Revenues	2.89	9.51	20.88	42.47	83.86	170.18
Operating Profit	0.79	3.46	2.64	7.99	10.91	28.06
Net Income	0.49	2.11	1.66	4.98	4.08	-14.53
Customers	--	--	--	--	--	--
Key Ratios:						
Gross Margin	52.6%	72.5%	57.7%	54.9%	47.3%	52.4%
Operating Margin	27.4%	36.3%	12.6%	18.8%	13.0%	16.5%
Net Margin	16.8%	22.2%	7.9%	11.7%	4.9%	-8.5%
Marketing as % of Revenues	11.4%	9.6%	9.8%	9.4%	7.5%	7.4%

RealNetworks, Inc.

http://www.real.com   eServices

Address:
1111 Third Avenue, Ste. 2900   Phone: 206.674.2700
Seattle, WA 98101   Fax: 206.674.2699
Management:
Chairman, CEO and Founder: Robert Glaser
COO: Thomas F. Frank
CFO: Paul Bailek

Description

When it comes to Web audio and video, RealNetworks is the face behind the music. The company was founded as Progressive Networks in February 1994 by Robert Glaser, a former Microsoft employee, to develop streaming media software for the Internet. In September 1997, the company changed its name to RealNet-works and went public two months later. So successful has the company's software been, that at the end of 1999 more than 95 million Web users have down-loaded its flagship product, RealPlayer. In addition, more than 1,700 media broad-casters, including ABC, Bloomberg, CNN, and the Wall Street Journal, use RealNetworks technology.

The company's products and services include RealSystem G2 with the RealPlayer for consumers and RealServer for media providers, Real Broadcast Network, a broadcasting service for companies, RealSlideShow for rich power-point presentations, and RealJukebox, which allows users to download and store digital music. RealNetworks generates revenues from three sources: licensing fees (71%), service fees (20%), and advertising (9%).

Opportunities

- The Internet is rapidly developing from a flat, one-dimensional communica-tion medium to a rich environment with audio and video capabilities. Al-ready, there are signs that TV viewership is declining because of the Internet. The coming broadband revolution will accelerate this trend.
- RealNetworks is the de-facto standard in streaming media over the Internet, with an estimated 85% share of the market. The Real.com family of Web sites was the eleventh most visited Web property in December 1999 with 11.9 mil-lion monthly visitors.

Challenges

- Although Microsoft is one of RealNetwork's largest customers, it is also one of the company's main competitors. Microsoft can leverage its monopoly in the operating system and browser market to capture market share from Real-Network. Apple is another competitor with its QuickTime media player, and the company has historically been very strong in the media world. Apple could leverage those ties to increase its market share.

- Digital music delivery, which the company is addressing with its RealJuke-box, is becoming very fragmented with a number of different technologies and players being used. At this point, it is still unclear which technology will emerge as the de facto standard.

The Bottom Line

"What shall we do tonight, watch TV or go on the Internet?" This is a question that is beginning to play out in millions of households. Although still in its early stages, the Internet is already beginning to steal audiences away from TV. RealNetworks, as the underlying technology with an 85% market share, stands to benefit the most from this trend. However, Microsoft is not yet ready to throw in the towel on its MediaPlayer, and it casts a very large shadow over any industry that it targets. Nevertheless, RealNetworks has a dominant lead in an industry that is just beginning to develop. The sound of broadband is the sound of music to RealNetwork's ears.

Key Statistics	RNWK
Market Cap (4/20/00):	$5,818m
Free Float:	25.0%
IPO Date:	11/21/97
Offer Price (adj):	$3.13
Price (4/20/00):	$37.69
52 week high:	$96.00
52 week low:	$25.50
Volatility: (avg. daily % ch)	5.77%
Price/Sales:	44.3
Price/Sales-Growth:	45.4

RealNetworks

www.topinternetstocks.com

Annual Financial Data ($ m)	12/1994	12/1995	12/1996	12/1997	12/1998	12/1999
Revenues	--	1.81	14.01	32.72	66.38	131.24
Operating Profit	-0.55	-1.60	-4.02	-13.16	-24.09	-3.04
Net Income	-0.55	-1.50	-3.79	-11.17	-19.95	6.93
Registered Users (m)	--	--	--	--	--	95.0
Key Ratios:						
Gross Margin	--	96.6%	84.4%	80.2%	80.9%	82.9%
Operating Margin	--	-88.0%	-28.7%	-40.2%	-36.3%	-2.3%
Net Margin	--	-82.8%	-27.0%	-34.1%	-30.1%	5.3%
Marketing as % of Revenues	--	67.2%	53.8%	61.5%	50.4%	40.7%

Redback Networks, Inc.

http://www.redback.com   eBusiness

Address:
1195 Borregas Ave.   Phone: 408.571.5000
Sunnyvale CA 94089   Fax: 408.541.0325
Management:
Chairman: Pierre R. Lamond
President & CEO: Dennis L. Barsema
CFO: Craig M. Gentner

Description

Redback Networks was founded in August 1996 to provide advanced networking systems that enable carriers, cable operators and service providers to rapidly deploy broadband access and services. The company's Subscriber Management Systems™ (SMSs) are intelligent networking devices that connect and manage large number of subscribers using any of the major broadband access technologies such as Digital Subscriber Line (DSL), cable and wireless. To deliver integrated transport solutions for metropolitan optical networks, Redback's SmartEdge™ multi-service platforms leverage powerful advances in application-specific integrated circuit (ASIC), IP and optical technology. Customers include UUNET, EarthLink, Sprint, GTE and Bell Atlantic.

Opportunities

- In the race for more bandwidth, broadband promises to be the Internet access of choice for millions of Americans. IDC estimates that by 2003, 9 million US homes will have high-speed cable access, up from 1.3 million in 1999. DSL access is expected to grow from 200,000 lines in 1999 to more than 12 million in 2003.
- Redback has an early market leadership over many of its competitors and can count four of the five local phone companies (RBOCs) as customers.
- Its products allow service providers to deploy high-speed services more quickly and at lower cost than currently possible. The SMS 10000 supports up to 100,000 simultaneous subscribers, 150 times the amount available through most routers.

Challenges

- Broadband Internet access has been slow to get off the ground primarily on the DSL access side, and the majority of Redback's customers are RBOCs or other carriers that offer DSL access. In addition, the pending AOL/Time Warner merger could rapidly speed cable access as the de facto standard for broadband connectivity. As of year end 1999, Redback had few customers in this area.
- Redback competes with several other companies that offer or are set to offer similar services including such heavyweights as Cisco, Alcatel, Lucent and Nortel. These larger competitors have the advantage of a larger customer base and the ability to offer a broader range of services to customers.
- Revenues are concentrated among a few customers. In the December 1999 quarter, two customers accounted for 29% of revenues. If Redback were to lose key customers, revenue growth could be curtailed.

Bottom Line

Redback is set to profit from the growing demand for more bandwidth. The company can already count as its customers four of the five local telephone companies as well as a number of other carriers. However, going forward, the company faces stiff competition from such industry heavyweights as Cisco, Nortel and Lucent as they extend their solutions into the systems management area. Nevertheless, Redback has a first mover advantage, enabling it to gain market leadership in the coming broadband revolution. If it can maintain and extend that lead, it has a chance of becoming the next Cisco of the Information Age.

Key Statistics	RBAK
Market Cap (4/20/00):	$5,561m
Free Float:	19.1%
IPO Date:	5/18/99
Offer Price (adj):	$5.75
Price (4/20/00):	$63.00
52 week high:	$198.50
52 week low:	$16.25
Volatility: (avg. daily % ch)	6.2%
Price/Sales:	86.5
Price/Sales-Growth:	14.5

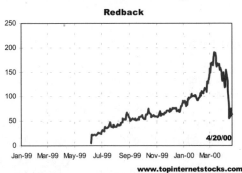

Redback

www.topinternetstocks.com

Annual Financial Data ($ m)	12/1994	12/1995	12/1996	12/1997	12/1998	12/1999
Revenues	--	--	--	0.05	9.21	64.27
Operating Profit	--	--	-0.14	-4.55	-9.88	-9.76
Net Income	--	--	-0.14	-4.41	-9.88	-7.92
Customers	--	--	--	--	--	--
Key Ratios:						
Gross Margin	--	--	--	39.6%	60.9%	71.0%
Operating Margin	--	--	--	-9472.9%	-107.3%	-15.2%
Net Margin	--	--	--	-9189.6%	-107.3%	-12.3%
Marketing as % of Revenues	--	--	--	--	--	--

Retek, Inc.

http://www.retek.com   eBusiness

Address:
801 Nicollet Mall   Phone: 612.630.5700
Minneapolis MN 55402   Fax: 612.630.5710
Management:
Chairman & CEO: John Buchanan
President: Gordon Masson
CFO: Gregory Effertz

Description

Retek provides Web-based supply chain (inventory) management software for the retailing industry. Retek, Inc. was spun-off from HNC Software but had its roots in Retek Logistics, a warehouse management software provider, which was founded in 1985. The company's suite of software solutions allow retailers to mange the entire demand and supply chain process, from product design and manufacturing through to inventory management. Retek also operates the retail.com network, a B2B ecommerce platform for the retail industry.

Major customers include AnnTaylor, Brooks Brothers, Rite Aid, Disney Stores and Hallmark. Licensing and maintenance revenues account for 78% of revenues, with consulting and professional services accounting for the remaining 22%.

Oportunities

- The Internet is providing businesses not only with a new distribution channel to reach customers, but also a cost-effective, scalable and rapidly deployable way to manage the inventory process.
- Retek's software helps retailers identify sales trends at the cash register (point-of-sale) and tie that in with the production and inventory process, through real-time Web-based access. This helps retailers tailor the production process, reducing production of low demand products that could lead to inventory build up and later mark downs, and increasing production of high demand items.

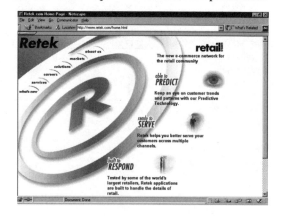

Challenges

- Retek competes on several fronts: in the supply chain software market, the company competes against SAP, IBM and JDA Software. In the B2B marketplace (retail.com), Retek competes against Ariba, Commerce One, FreeMarkets and others.
- 25% of Retek's revenues are generated through a partnership with Oracle (Oracle Retail), and Oracle has the right to terminate that relationship at any time. If this were to occur, it could lead to substantial revenue shortfalls for the company.
- The company has changed its revenue recognition method, accounting for the sales of software contracts over several quarters rather than at the initial signing. Although providing greater transparency, revenue growth is expected be moderate in 2000 under the new accounting change.

Bottom Line

Retek has a long history of developing inventory management and predictive software through its parent, HNS Software. Now it has taken that experience to the Web and has quickly carved out a strong niche for itself as a Web-centric supply chain solutions provider and a B2B ecommerce hub (through retail.com) for the retail industry. Retek's decision to change its method of accounting for software contracts will provide greater transparency to future revenue growth but would slow revenue growth through 2000. Bottom line: Retek has a strong leadership position, which it can leverage for its retail.com marketplace.

Key Statistics	RETK
Market Cap (4/20/00):	$912.6m
Free Float:	12.1%
IPO Date:	11/18/99
Offer Price:	$15.00
Price (4/20/00):	$19.62
52 week high:	$122.81
52 week low:	$15.50
Volatility: (avg. daily % ch)	13.9%
Price/Sales:	13.2
Price/Sales-Growth:	51.4

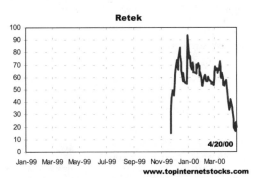

Retek

www.topinternetstocks.com

Annual Financial Data ($ m)	12/1994	12/1995	12/1996	12/1997	12/1998	12/1999
Revenues	1.91	3.84	13.43	30.92	55.03	69.16
Operating Profit	-0.33	-0.54	1.42	6.62	8.09	-7.10
Net Income	-0.32	-0.24	2.23	3.48	3.88	-5.37
Customers	--	--	--	--	--	--
Key Ratios:						
Gross Margin	12.9%	18.2%	71.1%	88.2%	74.8%	66.8%
Operating Margin	-17.2%	-14.0%	10.6%	21.4%	14.7%	-10.3%
Net Margin	-16.8%	-6.4%	16.6%	11.2%	7.0%	-7.8%
Marketing as % of Revenues	--	--	14.1%	26.7%	25.6%	28.4%

Rhythms NetConnections

http://www.rhythms.com   eAccess

Address:
6933 South Revere Parkway   Phone: 303.476.4200
Englewood, CO 80112   Fax: 303.476.4201
Management:
Chairman & CEO: Catherine M. Hapka
President & COO: Steve Stringer
CFO: Scott C. Chandler

Description

Rhythms dances to the music of broadband. The company was founded in February 1997 to provide high-speed Internet access through digital subscriber lines (DSL) ranging from 128 Kbps to 7.1 Mbps rates. It first began offering commercial service in April 1998 and has since grown its base of installed DSL lines to 12,500 in early 2000. The company offers DSL service in 38 metropolitan areas through 1,225 central offices. In addition to offering DSL access, the company also provides networking solutions for large businesses. Rhythms has struck a number of strategic relationships in a bid to extend its distribution network. In 1999, it partnered with Microsoft to offer a DSL version of Microsoft's MSN, entered into a strategic relationship with MCI WorldCom where MCI would commit to sell at least 100,000 DSL lines, and signed a deal with Qwest Communications whereby Qwest would resell Rhythms DSL service to its customers.

Opportunities

- As Web sites become more complex or media rich, and email is increasingly being sent with pictures or other file attachments, bandwidth is becoming a real concern. This demand for increased bandwidth will drive the growth of broadband access.
- The Yankee group estimates that the number of DSL lines will grow from 94,000 in 1998 to more than 4.1 million in 2002, a 158% annual growth rate.
- By year-end 2000, Rhythms expects to bring its total metropolitan area coverage to 70 markets with 2,000 central offices. This would represent a reach of 50% of businesses and 45% of homes in the US.

Challenges

- Rhythms competes in the broadband Internet access market both against cable Internet access providers including Excite@Home and Time Warner, against DSL providers including Covad, NorthPoint, DSL.net, and against local telecommunication companies that are deploying their own DSL lines.
- Technology limitations could limit wide DSL deployment. Currently, DSL can only operate within 17,500 feet (or about 3 miles) of a telephone central office. Any further, and the signal degrades to an unusable level.
- Rhythms success is dependent on the widescale acceptance of DSL broadband access. The planned AOL/Time Warner merger could speed cable broadband penetration, making it the de facto standard, thus limiting DSL growth.

Bottom Line

Rhythms dances to the broadband beat. In doing so, it has become the third largest provider of DSL access and stands to benefit from the expected rapid growth in high-speed Internet access. Rhythms has also forged some strong distribution agreements with Microsoft, MCI WorldCom and Qwest Communications. However, one of the greatest risks for Rhythms is whether DSL will gain widescale acceptance. In the consumer world, the jury is still out on that, particularly in light of the AOL/Time Warner merger. However, in the business world, DSL is shaping up to be the broadband platform of choice.

Key Statistics	RTHM
Market Cap (4/20/00):	$1,608m
Free Float:	18.0%
IPO Date:	4/7/99
Offer Price:	$21.00
Price (4/20/00):	$20.81
52 week high:	$88.50
52 week low:	$18.06
Volatility: (avg. daily % ch)	6.2%
Price/Sales:	145.0
Price/Sales-Growth:	7.3

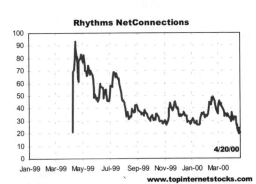

Rhythms NetConnections

www.topinternetstocks.com

Annual Financial Data ($ m)	12/1994	12/1995	12/1996	12/1997	12/1998	12/1999
Revenues	--	--	--	--	0.53	11.09
Operating Profit	--	--	--	-2.54	-28.40	-189.17
Net Income	--	--	--	-2.42	-36.33	-218.88
Customers	--	--	--	--	--	--
Key Ratios:						
Gross Margin	--	--	--	--	-789.2%	-514.7%
Operating Margin	--	--	--	--	-5379.0%	-1705.9%
Net Margin	--	--	--	--	-6881.4%	-1973.8%
Marketing as % of Revenues	--	--	--	--	715.2%	--

RSA Security Inc.

http://www.rsasecurity.com   eSecurity

Address:
20 Crosby Dr.   Phone: 781.301.5000
Bedford, MA 01730   Fax: 781.301.5170
Management:
Chairman: Charles R. Stuckey, Jr.
President & CEO: Arthur W. Coviello, Jr.
CFO: John F. Kennedy

Description

RSA Security, formerly known as Security Dynamics, wants to be the most trusted name in eSecurity. The company was founded in 1984, acquired RSA Data Security in July 1996 and changed its name to RSA Security in 1999. RSA focuses on four areas of Internet and network security: user identification and authentication; access control and privilege management; data privacy, integrity and authentication; and security administration and audit. RSA's security solutions are divided into three major product areas: ACE/Server and SecurID, a two-factor authentication service; Keon, public key infrastructure (PKI) and digital certificates; and BSAFE Encryption, a set of platform-independent security tools. RSA has more than 6,000 customers including the majority of Fortune 500 companies. International sales account for 30% of total revenues.

Opportunities

- Security is becoming a concern as consumers turn to the Web for online shopping and as businesses rely on the Web for mission-critical functions. This "mainstreaming" of the Internet will drive the growth in security solutions. IDC estimates that the Internet security market will expand to $7.4 billon in 2002, from an estimated $3.1 billion in 1998.
- Corporate IT budgets in 1999 were focused on solving Y2K concerns, which slowed the spending on Internet security solutions. This is expected to reverse in 2000 as businesses accelerate their IT spending on security solutions.
- An increase in security attacks, including the widescale hacker attacks on many of the major Web sites in February 2000, should help to drive IT security spending.

Challenges

- Competition in the eSecurity market is strong, and RSA competes on several fronts including in network hardware security, PKI and digital certificates, smart card technology and against application software companies. Competitors include VeriSign, Network Associates and Secure Computing. RSA also competes indirectly against firewall and other security vendors including Check Point, Axent, and Microsoft.
- RSA has been attempting to refocus its strategy and rebrand itself (through a name change) after a difficult 1998. If it is unable to recapture revenue momentum in 2000, shares could fall back to mid-1999 levels.

Bottom Line

RSA is betting on 2000 being the year of Internet security. As one of the leading Internet security companies, it also suffered from pre-Y2K spending shifts. Now it stands to benefit from post-Y2K spending shifts, as IT budgets again flow into the eSecurity sector. Although it faces increasing competition from several fronts, the company has a strong market advantage and looks to be positioning itself well with its newest suite of Keon products, which target the growing PKI and digital ID space. Digital signatures are increasingly being accepted as legally binding, a factor that will help to spur rapid growth in this area.

Key Statistics	RSAS
Market Cap (4/20/00):	$2,023m
Free Float:	77.0%
IPO Date:	12/14/94
Offer Price (adj):	$4.00
Price (4/20/00):	$50.88
52 week high:	$93.06
52 week low:	$15.88
Volatility: (avg. daily % ch)	3.9%
Price/Sales:	9.3
Price/Sales-Growth:	34.0

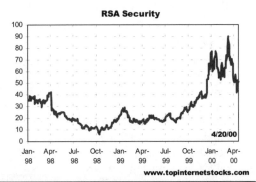

RSA Security

4/20/00

www.topinternetstocks.com

Annual Financial Data ($ m)	12/1994	12/1995	12/1996	12/1997	12/1998	12/1999
Revenues	24.13	50.81	86.42	140.63	171.33	218.13
Operating Profit	2.44	9.30	8.77	19.95	8.31	6.77
Net Income	1.25	7.73	13.69	17.05	29.42	183.76
Customers	--	--	--	--	--	--
Key Ratios:						
Gross Margin	79.6%	82.3%	78.7%	79.6%	76.2%	79.3%
Operating Margin	10.1%	18.3%	10.2%	14.2%	4.8%	3.1%
Net Margin	5.2%	15.2%	15.8%	12.1%	17.2%	84.2%
Marketing as % of Revenues	37.3%	28.5%	28.7%	29.8%	39.0%	41.2%

S1 Corporation

http://www.s1.com   eBusiness

Address:
3390 Peachtree Rd. Ste. 1700   Phone: 404.812.6200
Atlanta, GA 30326   Fax: 404.812.6727
Management:
Chairman: Michel Akkermans
CEO: James S. Mahan
CFO: Robert Stockwell

Description

S1 traces its history back to Security First Network Bank, which launched the first Internet bank in 1995. After selling the online bank to Royal Bank of Canada in 1998, S1 focused on providing online banking and financial software and services to financial institutions. The company has continued to expand its financial software business, buying rivals, FICS Group and Edify in 1999. S1's suite of financial software solutions allows financial institutions to offer online bill paying, fund transfers, online account statements, cash management, financial reporting and other services over the Internet. Its products are divided into three families: the S1 Consumer Suite, S1 Business Suite and S1 Corporate Suite. The company also offers account aggregation services through its wholly-owned VerticalOne subsidiary. Revenues are generated through software licensing (21%), professional services (61%), data centers (10%) and third-party sales (9%).

Opportunities

- The number of households banking online in the US is expected to jump from 6.6 million in 1998 to more than 32 million in 2003 according to IT research firm, IDC. Fueling this growth is the forecasted 15,800 banks that will be offering online banking services in 2003, up from around 1,200 in 1998.
- The growth in online banking will in turn drive the growth in online banking applications. In 2000, IDC estimates that Internet banking applications will account for a third of the total US banking applications market.
- S1 has been seeing strong growth on several fronts and is quickly growing its customer base. The partnership with Zurich Financial is expected to significantly strengthen S1's position in Europe.

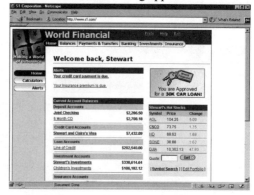

Challenges

- Competition is strong in the online financial applications market. S1 competes against such companies as Digital Insight, BROKAT Infosystems AG, Corillian and Sybase (Financial Fusion). In addition, it also competes against in-house IT teams at the major banks.
- Integration risk is an issue for S1 as it attempts to smoothly integrate the global operations of a number of recent acquisitions.
- The bulk of S1's revenues are generated through professional services, which include consulting, integration and training. As long as professional services are the main revenue generator for the company, revenue growth will be tied to employee growth, limiting scalability.

Bottom Line

S1 is riding the online banking wave. The company has successfully repositioned itself as a leading provider of software and expertise to other banks that are moving online. This strategy has paid off for the company, with the result that both revenue and customer growth has been accelerating. The company has also formed a number of key strategic relationships with Hewlett Packard, Intuit, Andersen Consulting. and others. The relationship with Anderson Consulting helps S1 to mitigate the challenge associated with the limited scalability in the professional services area. S1 is also expanding its data center or ASP model, with the goal of it accounting for 50% of the revenue mix within three years. S1 is on the way to be the eBanking enabler, already powering many of the major online banks including E*Trade's Telebanc, NetBank, Wingspan and CitiFinancial to name a few.

Key Statistics	SONE
Market Cap (4/20/00):	$2,293m
Free Float:	67.9%
IPO Date:	5/23/96
Offer Price (adj):	$10.00
Price (4/20/00):	$44.94
52 week high:	$142.25
52 week low:	$25.12
Volatility: (avg. daily % ch)	4.6%
Price/Sales:	24.7
Price/Sales-Growth:	8.7

S1

www.topinternetstocks.com

Annual Financial Data ($ m)	12/1994	12/1995	12/1996	12/1997	12/1998	12/1999*
Revenues	--	--	1.27	10.83	24.18	92.89
Operating Profit	--	-0.05	-19.50	-28.78	-29.14	-127.32*
Net Income	--	-1.48	-22.06	-27.99	-30.81	-125.09
Customers	--	--	--	--	--	--
Key Ratios:						
Gross Margin	--	--	-183.9%	-28.3%	24.5%	42.7%
Operating Margin	--	--	-1538.7%	-265.8%	-120.5%	-137.1%
Net Margin	--	--	-1741.0%	-258.5%	-127.4%	-134.7%
Marketing as % of Revenues	--	--	170.0%	39.8%	19.5%	13.1%

* includes roughly $110 million intangible non-cash charges and one-time charges tied to acquisitions in 1999

Sapient Corporation

http://www.sapient.com   eServices

Address:
1 Memorial Drive   Phone: 617.621.0200
Cambridge, MA 02412   Fax: 617.621.1300
Management:
Co-Chairman & Co-CEO: Jerry A. Greenberg
Co-Chairman & Co-CEO: J. Stuart Moore
Co-COO: Sheeroy D. Desai
Co-COO: Desmond P. Varady

Description

Founded in 1991 by Co-CEOs, Jerry Greenberg and Stuart Moore, Sapient started out as an IT consulting firm focusing on designing and implementing client/server applications. It began expanding into Internet-based applications in 1994 and continued that course with a series of targeted acquisitions following its IPO in April 1996. Today, Sapient is one of the leading firms in the iBuilders sector, providing end-to-end solutions to Global 1000 companies.

Sapient's approach follows a similar path as many of its successful peers: providing end-to-end Internet solutions by combining several core services including strategic consulting, marketing and brand development; creative design; technology development and systems integration; and program management.

The company delivers its service through five industry business groups including financial services, retail and distribution, media, entertainment and communications, manufacturing, energy services and government or public sector. Customers include E*Trade, Banc Boston, Nordstrom and United Parcel Service. Sapient's five largest clients account for approximately 26% of revenues.

Opportunities

- As corporate America rushes to leverage the Internet within its existing business strategies, the market for Web integration firms is expected to skyrocket from an estimated $7 billion in 1998 to $78 billion in 2003, according to IT research firm, IDC.
- In contrast to Web design shops that recently transformed into integrated solutions providers, Sapient, as an IT-consulting-shop-turned-Web-integrator, has a stronger track record in complex systems integration.
- Even with its fixed price, fixed time frame approach, Sapient has been able to efficiently manage its resources, posting some of the highest operating margins in its peer group.

Challenges

- Barriers to entry are low-to-nonexistent in the integrated solutions provider, or iBuilders, market, leading to a fiercely competitive industry. Hundreds of companies compete in a "me-too" environment, all promoting virtually the same core competencies. In addition to the smaller players, giant consulting firms such as Andersen Consulting, PricewaterhouseCoopers and McKinsey are also entering the fray, making differentiation difficult.
- The Web integration market is a high-growth industry. However, it is not as scalable as other Internet businesses. Revenue growth is tied largely to billable employee growth.

Bottom Line

Sapient knows how to build complex Web solutions. As one of the leading firms in the iBuilders sector, Sapient has built a solid reputation in a "me-too" market crowded with hundreds of other firms who also deliver integrated Web solutions. It also helps to be operating in an industry where the demand for quality iBuilders is likely to outpace the supply over the next few years. If Sapient is to continue its stellar growth, it will need to become more aggressive on the acquisition front, adding employees and customers in order to boost revenues. This will be the company's main challenge: effectively managing future acquisitions without losing key personnel and clients. In the Internet world, like Godzilla, size does matter.

Key Statistics	SAPE
Market Cap (4/20/00):	$3,851m
Free Float:	42.0%
IPO Date:	4/4/96
Offer Price (adj):	$5.25
Price (4/20/00):	$66.25
52 week high:	$151.19
52 week low:	$23.88
Volatility: (avg. daily % ch)	3.5%
Price/Sales:	13.9
Price/Sales-Growth:	20.5

Sapient

www.topinternetstocks.com

Annual Financial Data ($ m)	12/1994	12/1995	12/1996	12/1997	12/1998	12/1999
Revenues	11.80	24.48	49.80	92.03	164.87	276.84
Operating Profit	2.46	4.90	9.54	18.20	15.10	44.74
Net Income	1.59	2.91	6.70	12.55	9.36	30.30
Customers	--	--	--	--	--	--
Key Ratios:						
Gross Margin	62.4%	52.1%	53.1%	51.5%	51.1%	51.4%
Operating Margin	20.8%	20.0%	19.2%	19.8%	9.2%	16.2%
Net Margin	13.5%	11.9%	13.5%	13.6%	5.7%	10.9%
Marketing as % of Revenues	2.3%	4.6%	4.9%	6.6%	6.8%	7.7%

Scient Corporation

http://www.scient.com   eServices

Address:
One Front St. 28th Fl.   Phone: 415.733.8200
San Francisco, CA 94111   Fax: 415.733.8299
Management:
Chairman and Founder: Eric Greenberg
President and CEO: Robert M. Howe
CFO: William H. Kurtz

Description

Scient is one of the leading companies in the developing Internet professional services, or iBuilders, sector. Like many of its counterparts, the company is relatively new on the Internet scene, having been launched in November 1997 by its founder, Eric Greenberg. However, being a "newbie" is not a detraction, where everything runs on Internet time. Barely eighteen months after being incorporated, the company went public in May 1999.

Scient focuses on building eBusiness systems for technology, financial services and ecommerce companies. The company provides strategic consulting, creative design, application development and systems integration for over 47 clients, including AIG, Chase Manhattan, First Union and PlanetRX.

Opportunities

- The Internet professional services market is expected to blossom from an estimated $7.8 billion in 1998 to over $78 billion by 2003. Leading the 57% annual growth, is corporate America's rush to embrace the Internet within its business and throughout its value chain, from suppliers and business partners to its customers.
- Demand for higher quality iBuilders is likely to outpace the supply over the next few years, leading to strong revenue growth for the market leaders.
- Like most consulting companies, the key assets are its employees. Scient has the edge within its space, generating some of the highest revenues per employee in the industry.

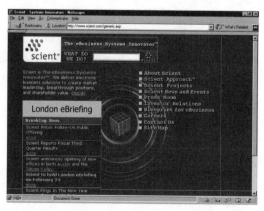

Challenges

- Barriers to entry are virtually nonexistent, and practically anyone can hang out their cybershingle and call themselves an iBuilder, leading to intense competition. iBuilders currently number in the hundreds, if not thousands, and range from small one and two man shops to the giant consulting firms like McKinsey & Co., Andersen Consulting and PricewaterhouseCoopers as well as IBM, EDS and Sapient.
- Although a high-growth industry, the Internet consulting market is not as scalable as other Internet business models. Revenue growth is tied to employee growth.
- Scient has no long-term client contracts, and revenues are concentrated among a handful of clients. The top three clients account for roughly 28% of revenues. The loss of key clients could severely impact revenue growth.

The Bottom Line

Scient sees itself as the eBusiness Systems Innovator™, and judging by the list of blue-chip clients and stellar revenue growth – 581% yoy in the December 1999 quarter, it has achieved that status. Heading forward, the challenge will be twofold: managing the growth internally while minimizing turnover and staving off competition both from hungry young competitors like Razorfish and from heavy-weight consultants like IBM and Anderson Consulting, who are quickly becoming Web savvy.

Key Statistics	SCNT
Market Cap (4/20/00):	$3,050m
Free Float:	33.0%
IPO Date:	5/15/99
Offer Price (adj):	$10.00
Price (4/20/00):	$43.19
52 week high:	$133.75
52 week low:	$13.88
Volatility: (avg. daily % ch)	5.3%
Price/Sales:	30.7
Price/Sales-Growth:	4.0

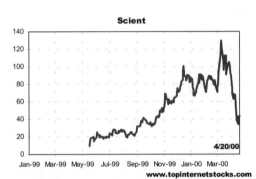

Scient

www.topinternetstocks.com

Annual Financial Data ($ m)	3/1995	3/1996	3/1997	3/1998	3/1999	12/1999*
Revenues	--	--	--	0.18	20.68	89.89
Operating Profit	--	--	--	-1.22	-12.35	-20.67
Net Income	--	--	--	-1.16	-11.70	-18.25
Customers	--	--	--	--	--	47
Key Ratios:						
Gross Margin	--	--	--	43.0%	48.5%	53.2%
Operating Margin	--	--	--	-678.8%	-59.7%	-23.0%
Net Margin	--	--	--	-647.5%	-56.6%	-20.3%
Marketing as % of Revenues	--	--	--	--	--	--

* Nine months ended December 31, 1999

Silknet Software, Inc.

http://www.silknet.com   eBusiness

Address:
50 Phillippe Cote St.   Phone: 603.625.0070
Manchester, NH 03101   Fax: 603.625.0428
Management:
Chairman & CEO: James C. Wood
COO: Nigel K. Donovan
CFO: Patrick J. Scannell, Jr.

Description

Silknet believes customer service is the key to success on the Internet. The company was founded in March 1995 with the idea of making the Web a self-service tool for businesses. Silknet's software integrates all customer interactions, whether in person, via the telephone or email or over the Web, so that companies have an up-to-the-second customer profile on each individual customer. Its suite of software applications (eBusiness System, eSales, eCommerce and eService) provide personalized marketing, sales, ecommerce and customer support services through a single Web interface.

Silknet has signed up a number of strong customers including Microsoft, 3Com, Compaq and KPMG. Revenues are generated through licensing fees (70%) and service revenues (30%).

Opportunities

• The strong growth in Internet usage and the increasing familiarity of the Web as a daily part of many consumers' lives is fueling the trend towards Web-based customer service. This is evident by the number of people that are by-passing annoying, automated phone help, and turning to the Web for answers to common questions. Gartner Group estimates that by 2001, businesses will receive 25% of all customer contacts and inquiries over email or the Web.

• Companies can dramatically improve customer satisfaction and improve sales through personalized Web sites that seamlessly tie in marketing, sales and customer support. According to Forrester Research, only 13% of Web sites attempt to deliver any type of personalization.

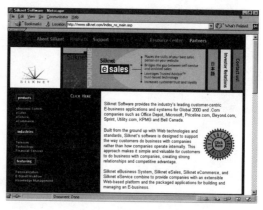

Challenges

- Competition is intense in the customer service, or customer relationship management (CRM), space. In addition to Net startups such as Kana and eGain, Silknet competes against more established companies such as BroadVision, Siebel Systems, Clarify and Oracle.
- Revenue concentration risk is a key challenge. Because of the large size of the typical order and the early stage of its development, Silknet had at least one customer that accounted for more than 24% of total revenues in the past eight quarters. If Silknet were to lose key customers or fail to close large orders in a quarter, revenue growth could fluctuate significantly.

Bottom Line

Silknet is one of the emerging leaders in Web-centric customer relationship management software, offering one of the most comprehensive suite of applications in the sector. By focusing on the customer-service side of the equation, Silknet has positioned itself to take advantage of the renewed focus on the value of customer relationships. Other companies are also beginning to target this area though, including Kana, BroadVision and Oracle. But judging by the blue-chip list of customers and partners (Cisco, Microsoft, E*Trade and CMGI), Silknet has the edge.

Note: Silknet was acquired by Kana Communications on April 19, 2000.

Key Statistics	SILK
Market Cap (12/31/00):	$2,720m
Free Float:	43.9%
IPO Date:	5/5/99
Offer Price:	$15.00
Price (12/31/00):	$165.75
52 week high:	$167.50
52 week low:	$23.19
Volatility: (avg. daily % ch)	6.4%
Price/Sales:	121.4
Price/Sales-Growth:	75.0

Silknet

www.topinternetstocks.com

Annual Financial Data ($ m)	6/1995	6/1996	6/1997	6/1998	6/1999	12/1999*
Revenues	--	0.27	0.19	3.65	13.92	14.05
Operating Profit	-0.06	-0.46	-2.69	-6.14	-10.01	-8.69
Net Income	-0.06	-0.47	-2.75	-6.00	-9.37	-7.31
Customers	--	--	--	--	--	--
Key Ratios:						
Gross Margin	--	47.0%	75.8%	62.0%	73.3%	73.2%
Operating Margin	--	-172.2%	-1387.6%	-168.3%	-71.9%	-61.8%
Net Margin	--	-174.8%	-1418.6%	-164.6%	-67.4%	-52.0%
Marketing as % of Revenues	--	12.4%	457.7%	131.7%	77.7%	59.7%

* Six months ended December 31, 1999

SportsLine.com, Inc.

http://www.cbs.sportsline.com   eContent

Address:
6340 NW Fifth Way   Phone: 954.351.2120
Fort Lauderdale, FL 33309   Fax: 954.351.9175
Management:
Chairman, President & CEO: Michael Levy
CFO: Kenneth W. Sanders

Description

SportsLine.com was founded in 1994 with the goal of being the number one source of information for sports on the Internet. The company officially launched its flagship Website in June 1995 and renamed it CBS SportsLine.com in March 1997 after CBS took a 12% equity stake in the company. SportsLine.com produces the official Web sites for Major League Baseball, the PGA Tour and a number of celebrity Web sites. The company's Web site has more than one million pages of content on dozens of different sports, including the usual American fare of football, baseball, basketball and golf. SportsLine.com is also attempting to expand its international appeal by offering content on soccer, cricket, cycling and rugby on its subsidiary Sports.com. In addition to offering sports content on its own sites, SportsLine.com has agreements with America Online, Excite@Home and other horizontal portals to be the primary sports content provider on their sites.

Opportunities

- Internet advertising has grown quickly in the last few years and has already eclipsed outdoor advertising in revenues. From an estimated $2.9 billion in 1999, more than $12.5 billion in ad revenues will be generated over the Internet by 2003.
- Roughly 20% of all television advertising is targeted towards sports, and some of the highest ad dollars are commanded by sporting events like the SuperBowl and Olympic events. If Internet advertising categories mimic television, there is tremendous opportunity for growth in sports-related advertising.
- SportsLine.com is one of the most visited sports-oriented portals on the Web, with 3.8 million people visiting its sites each month.

Challenges

- SportsLine.com competes aggressively for viewers and ad dollars in the hyper-competitive eContent space. In addition to its arch-rival, ESPN.com, SportsLine.com also competes against Yahoo!, AOL, Time Warner (CNNSi.com), FoxSports.com and others.
- As SportsLine.com expands its international presence, it has made some strategic stumbles, including promoting soccernet before realizing that outside of the US, soccer is not used for the game commonly called football, fussball or fútbol in 98% of the world. Going global means not thinking American, but locally, a tough challenge for many US companies.
- By selling its ecommerce operations to MVP.com in late 1999, SportsLine divested a potentially lucrative incremental revenue stream in order to focus on being an advertising-driven company. This puts the company more at risk to any downturn in the Internet advertising market.

The Bottom Line

GOOOOAAAL! SportsLine.com is betting on millions of loyal sports fans following dozens of different sports visiting its site for the latest news, scores and inside scoops. Although it is trailing behind AOL's Sports Channel and ESPN.com, the company has been building its audience reach, both in the US and abroad. By divesting its ecommerce business to MVP.com, SportsLine.com has limited its upside revenue potential, albeit with the trade-off of higher margins and a stable ad revenue stream of $20 million a year for 10 years. What sets SportsLine.com apart is its strong partnership with CBS that it can leverage in order to drive viewers to its site.

Key Statistics	SPLN
Market Cap (4/20/00):	$573.8m
Free Float:	56.0%
IPO Date:	11/13/97
Offer Price:	$12.50
Price (4/20/00):	$22.12
52 week high:	$83.25
52 week low:	$11.12
Volatility: (avg. daily % ch)	5.1%
Price/Sales:	9.5
Price/Sales-Growth:	9.8

Sportsline.com

www.topinternetstocks.com

Annual Financial Data ($ m)	12/1994	12/1995	12/1996	12/1997	12/1998	12/1999
Revenues	--	0.10	3.06	12.01	30.55	60.28
Operating Profit	-0.44	-6.18	-16.37	-34.97	-39.84	-57.71
Net Income	0.40	-6.11	-16.10	-34.18	-35.51	-17.10
Unique Visitors (m)	--	--	--	--	--	3.86
Key Ratios:						
Gross Margin	--	-718.0%	-38.4%	13.2%	43.6%	43.5%
Operating Margin	--	-6182.0%	-535.4%	-291.1%	-130.4%	-95.7%
Net Margin	--	-6108.0%	-526.6%	-284.5%	-116.2%	-28.4%
Marketing as % of Revenues	--	1456.0%	232.7%	116.7%	67.0%	60.5%

Spyglass, Inc.

http://www.spyglass.com   eBusiness

Address:
1240 E. Diehl Rd.   Phone: 630.505.1010
Naperville, IL 60563   Fax: 630.505.4944
Management:
Chairman & CEO: Douglas Colbeth
President & COO: Martin J. Leamy
CFO: Gary L. Vilchick

Description

Spyglass has its eye on Internet appliances. The company was one of the original Internet companies, developing the Mosaic browser along with Marc Andreesen (who went on to head up Netscape) at the University of Illinois in the early 1990's. In 1993, it released the popular Mosiac browser, defining the Web as we know it today. The company quickly became a success – until Microsoft and Netscape began giving away their browsers. Spyglass' fall from grace was swift, with the stock falling from a high of $60 to $4 in barely two years.

Today, the new and improved Spyglass is targeting the information appliance market, developing mini-browsers and software that can be used in a host of different items, from TV set top boxes to smart phones and printers. Revenues are generated through software licensing (40%) and consulting services (60%). Customers include Motorola, NEC, Nokia, Sony and Toshiba.

Opportunities

- The Internet has quickly become mainstream with over 184 million people accessing the Web in 1999. By 2003, Pegasus Research estimates that the number of Internet users will climb to 430 million people worldwide.
- This growth in Internet usage will drive the demand for both PC and non-PC Internet devices. International Data Corporation estimates that the annual number of information appliance shipments will increase from 14 million units in 1999 to 56 million units in 2002, with the installed base of information appliances growing from 26 million in 1999 to 151 million by 2002.

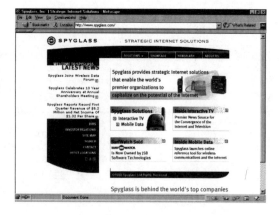

Challenges

- Spyglass is up against strong competition in several different areas. In the non-PC browser market, it competes against JavaSoft, Liberate Technologies, Microsoft and Phone.com. In the non-PC Web server market, it competes against 3Soft, emWare, Integrated Systems and Wind River. In the professional services area, it competes against a wide number of competitors including BSquare, IBM, Phone.com and Sun Microsystems.
- The majority of Spyglass' revenues is on the professional services or consulting side, an area that is not as scalable as on the Internet technology side. In consulting, revenue growth is largely tied to employee growth. In addition, Spyglass' services business has been characterized by low gross margins, falling to 45% in 1999 from 61% in 1998.

Bottom Line

Spyglass sees its future in non-PC Web-enabled devices. This is an area that is expected to grow very quickly. In fact, IDC estimates that the number of non-PC devices will actually surpass the number of personal computers sold within a few years. Spyglass has a good chance of being at the forefront of that growth. However, the road will not be easy, and the company has fallen from grace before. In addition, the competition is much more intense today than it was back in the mid-1990s.

Key Statistics	SPYG
Market Cap (4/20/00):	$694.0m
Free Float:	90.7%
IPO Date:	6/28/95
Offer Price (adj):	$4.25
Price (4/20/00):	$40.62
52 week high:	$95.25
52 week low:	$9.69
Volatility: (avg. daily % ch)	5.0%
Price/Sales:	21.7
Price/Sales-Growth:	52.5

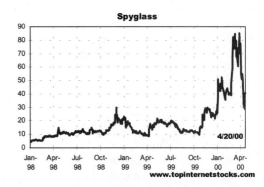

Spyglass

www.topinternetstocks.com

Annual Financial Data ($ m)	9/1994	9/1995	9/1996	9/1997	9/1998	9/1999
Revenues	4.67	12.14	22.31	21.30	21.17	29.61
Operating Profit	0.77	3.03	3.67	-15.68	-11.28	-3.28
Net Income	1.38	2.18	3.46	-14.15	-10.03	-1.90
Customers	--	--	--	--	--	--
Key Ratios:						
Gross Margin	76.7%	85.5%	90.9%	85.8%	73.7%	65.8%
Operating Margin	16.5%	24.9%	16.4%	-73.6%	-53.3%	-11.1%
Net Margin	29.7%	17.9%	15.5%	-66.5%	-47.4%	-6.4%
Marketing as % of Revenues	22.9%	27.2%	26.7%	39.0%	43.0%	27.8%

StarMedia Network, Inc.

http://www.starmedia.com   eContent

Address:
29 West 36th Street, 5th Fl.   Phone: 212.548.9600
New York, NY 10018   Fax: 212.631.9100
Management:
Chairman, Founder and CEO: Fernando Espuelas
President and Cofounder: Jack Chen
CFO: Steven J. Heller

Description

Viva el Internet! StarMedia is hoping to be the destination of choice for 15 million Latin American, US Hispanic and Iberian Web surfers. The company was founded in March 1996 by co-founders Fernando Espuelas and Jack Chen. Since launching its Web site in December 1996, StarMedia has grown quickly, thanks in large part to more than $90 million in capital supplied by VC heavyweights, Flatiron Partners, Chase Capital Partners and others.

The company offers Spanish and Portuguese content centered around 21 interest-specific channels including local and regional news, entertainment, business, sports and classified ads. Once the visitor chooses a home country, the content is tailored to provide a local flavor, taking into account regional dialects and cultural differences. In addition, StarMedia also provides free email, chat rooms and has recently expanded into providing free Internet access in partnership with CMGI in Latin America. In a bid to expand into the ecommerce arena, StarMedia partnered with SkyBox Services to solve the difficulties commonly associated with buying products from US eTailers and having them shipped south of the border. StarMedia collects a percentage of revenues from products sold over its site. StarMedia is also aggressively expanding into the wireless Internet arena.

Since going public in May 1999, StarMedia has been busy on the acquisition front, buying nine smaller portals, Web search engines and other Internet properties in the region. Growth for the Latin American portal site has been extremely strong. In the March 2000 quarter, the number of page views increased 1492% yoy to 2.1 billion, active email accounts grew 670% yoy to 3.3 million, and revenues climbed 531% to $10.1 million. Major advertising partners include Fox, Citibank, Ford and MTV.

Opportunities

- Latin America is the newest and fastest growing region in terms of Internet users, growing at more than 40% compounded annually. From an estimated 6.2 million users in 1999, Pegasus Research estimates that more than 20.8 million Latin Americans will be surfing the Web in 2003.
- StarMedia is the first and largest portal/community/hub in Latin America. Being the first in the region, the company has significant lead time over new entrants in the Spanish and Portuguese portal race. First-mover advantage is a strong competitive advantage in the Internet world. This translates to higher advertising rates which stand at an average $53 (per CPM) or one and a half the average rate for the Internet industry.
- Although StarMedia is a Latin American portal, its advertising revenue flow is less dependant on economic conditions, due to the nature of the typical Internet user in the region. Latin American Internet users represent the top 20% of the population which typically control 65% of the wealth. In fact, StarMedia has stated that during the financial crisis in Brazil, the company sold the same if not more advertising, reflecting its ability to weather economic downturns in Latin America. In addition, over 95% of StarMedia's revenues are in US dollars, making the company's revenue stream less susceptible to currency fluctuations.

Challenges

- Internet penetration is very low in Latin America and will likely remain low in the foreseeable future. In contrast to the US where 31% of the population is currently surfing the Web, only 4% of Latin Americans are likely to be on the Net in 2003. Holding up the growth are a number of factors including low per capita GDP, low PC ownership, few phone lines and poor infrastructure.
- StarMedia may have first-mover advantage, but that is no guarantee that it will retain the lead. Competition is just heating up and promises to be intense. In addition to heavyweights like AOL and Yahoo!, StarMedia is facing competition from other regional players including UniversOnline, Telefonica/Ole, El Sitio, Yupi and others.
- As a result of fierce competition in the Latin American portal space, advertising rates are expected to fall significantly to the industry norm in a process called reversion to the mean. This means that intensifying competition could drive average CPM rates from $53 down to levels below $40.
- In the "not all revenues are created equal" category, StarMedia deserves mention. Barter revenues accounted for roughly 14% of total revenues for the company in the March 2000 quarter. Barter revenues, also called reciprocal ad arrangements, are booked as revenues but do not actually translate into cash. Rather, as the name implies, it is an "I'll advertise with your firm if you advertise with mine" arrangement.

The Bottom Line

StarMedia is the undisputed leader in the Latin American portal race and looks to be able to maintain that lead at least over the next few years. However, it won't be an easy task as the competitive playing field becomes more intense. Now that StarMedia is branching out into providing Internet access throughout the region, the company will compete head-to-head with already well-entrenched players including Telmex in Mexico and UOL and Telephonica in Brazil. However, StarMedia does have the advantage of entering the region with strong partners in the form of Ericsson and CMGI.

Growth has been strong for the company on several different metrics. Page views grew 1492%, email accounts jumped 670%, and revenues were up over 530% in the March 2000 quarter. Although a number of US companies are beginning to enter the region, StarMedia does have the edge. What counts in Latin America is local content for the local Internet user. This has been an overlooked fact for many US Web portals offering content that is often US-centric although translated into Spanish.

Bottom line? StarMedia is an excellent Internet play on an emerging growth story. However, there are a lot of players chasing the small pot of Web surfers in the region. Keep an eye on how well StarMedia maintains its lead.

Key Statistics	STRM
Market Cap (4/20/00):	$1,349m
Free Float:	51.0%
IPO Date:	5/26/99
Offer Price:	$15.00
Price (4/20/00):	$20.75
52 week high:	$70.00
52 week low:	$17.50
Volatility: (avg. daily % ch)	6.0%
Price/Sales:	67.1
Price/Sales-Growth:	27.0

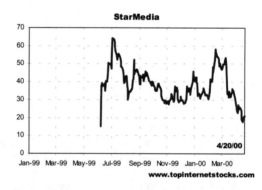

StarMedia

www.topinternetstocks.com

Annual Financial Data ($ m)	12/1994	12/1995	12/1996	12/1997	12/1998	12/1999
Revenues	--	--	--	0.47	5.76	20.09
Operating Profit	--	--	-0.13	-3.56	-46.64	-96.33
Net Income	--	--	-0.13	-3.53	-45.97	-90.67
Email Accounts (m)	--	--	--	--	0.29	2.50
Key Ratios:						
Gross Margin	--	--	--	-161.2%	-23.3%	-65.2%
Operating Margin	--	--	--	-754.0%	-810.0%	-479.5%
Net Margin	--	--	--	-746.8%	-798.4%	-451.4%
Marketing as % of Revenues	--	--	--	447.0%	508.5%	265.8%

TD Waterhouse Group, Inc.

http://www.waterhouse.com   eFinancials

Address:
100 Wall Street   Phone: 212.806.3500
New York, NY 10005   Fax: 212.361.6656
Management:
Chairman: A. Charles Baillie
CEO: Stephen D. McDonald
CFO: B. Kevin Sterns

Description

TD Waterhouse, the online discount broker with Canadian roots, traces its US history back to 1979 when it started out as a subsidiary of Toronto-Dominion Bank. The firm began offering online trading in 1992 and Internet-based trading in 1996. TD Waterhouse, which also offers a broad range of brokerage, mutual fund and other consumer financial products, went public in June 1999.

TD Waterhouse is the third largest online discount broker, with 3.3 million customer accounts, 2.2 million of which are active and 1.3 million which traded online in 1999. Total customer assets reached $150 billion in January 1999. Roughly 70% of customer trades are conducted online. The company has been expanding internationally with operations in Australia, the UK, Hong Kong and India. TD Waterhouse is planning to expand operations into Japan and Europe in 2000. In November 1999, the company teamed up with Charles Schwab and Ameritrade to build an online investment bank set to launch in early 2000.

Opportunities

- Online trading has exploded onto the investment management scene with nearly 8 million investors now trading online. By 2003, more than 25 million US investors are expected to be trading over the Internet.
- TD Waterhouse, with its network of more than 200 branches, is the second largest online broker next to Charles Schwab. It expects to aggressively increase the number of customer accounts by 1 million in 2000.
- With a "click and mortar" strategy, TD Waterhouse has a network of brokers that can still conduct customer trades in case of online system outages.

Challenges

- The online brokerage industry is one of the most competitive areas on the Internet, with more than 160 brokerage firms offering online trading. In addition to the hundreds of discount brokers competing online, traditional full-service firms are also moving online with discounted trading. Competitors include Charles Schwab, E*Trade, Ameritrade and Datek Securities.
- TD Waterhouse is spending $100 million in advertising in the hopes of adding 1 million new accounts in 2000. This aggressive marketing campaign could set off another round of marketing wars with the end result that marketing costs go up without significant growth in customer accounts.

Bottom Line

TD Waterhouse is the third largest online discount broker with more than 1.3 million online accounts and the second largest discount broker with 3.3 million. Customer account growth is expected to continue its strong growth trend. However, as the industry becomes more competitive, margins are likely to trend lower, due to a combination of higher marketing costs and lower trading fees. At least for the leaders, online customer growth is expected to be strong enough to offset declining margins. In this environment, only the strong will likely survive – one of which is TD Waterhouse.

Key Statistics	TWE
Market Cap (4/20/00):	$7,528m
Free Float:	10.0%
IPO Date:	6/23/99
Offer Price:	$24.00
Price (4/20/00):	$20.00
52 week high:	$27.25
52 week low:	$11.44
Volatility: (avg. daily % ch)	3.2%
Price/Sales:	6.7
Price/Sales-Growth:	11.2

TD Waterhouse

www.topinternetstocks.com

Annual Financial Data ($ m)	10/1994	10/1995	10/1996	10/1997	10/1998	10/1999
Net Revenues	218.46	257.25	370.79	446.63	614.46	960.10
Operating Profit	49.68	64.59	67.67	78.62	103.48	182.50
Net Income	28.26	37.24	26.30	36.21	48.71	97.30
Active Accounts (m)	.41	.50	.71	.96	1.61	1.90
Key Ratios:						
Gross Margin	--	--	--	--	--	--
Operating Margin	22.7%	25.1%	18.2%	17.6%	16.8%	19.0%
Net Margin	12.9%	14.5%	7.1%	8.1%	7.9%	10.1%
Marketing as % of Revenues	3.6%	5.1%	3.9%	4.1%	5.4%	6.5%

24/7 Media, Inc.

http://www.247media.com　　　　　　　　　　　　　　eServices

Address:
1250 Broadway 27th Fl.　　　　Phone:　212.231.7100
New York, NY 10001　　　　　　Fax:　　212.760.1774
Management:
Chairman:　　　　　　　　　　　R. Theodore Ammon
President & CEO:　　　　　　　　David J. Moore
CFO:　　　　　　　　　　　　　　C. Andrew Johns

Description

When it comes to online advertising, 24/7 is always there for its clients. It is one of the leading companies in the Internet advertising and direct marketing space, born out of the merger and acquisition in January 1998 of three different companies, Petry Interactive, Advercomm and Interactive Imaginations. 24/7 serves and tracks ads on a network of sites that reach 58% of online users in the US. Its network of properties include the 24/7 Network, a collection of over 400 large sites, ContentZone, a collection of 2,500 smaller sites and 24/7 Europe. In addition, 24/7 also develops email-based direct marketing services for companies targeting its managed database of more than 20 million opt-in email addresses. Major Web sites in 24/7's network include AT&T WorldNet, EarthLink, Maquest.com, and Goto.com.

Opportunities

- The rapid acceptance of the Internet as a new media for news, content and information has fueled the growth in Internet advertising. From virtually no revenues in 1995, Web advertising has already surpassed outdoor advertising in total revenues. Pegasus Research estimates that the online advertising market will grow from an estimated $2.9 billion in 1999 to more than $12.5 billion by 2003.

- 24/7 acquired email marketing company, Sift, and opt-in email database company, ConsumerNet, in a move to strengthen its direct marketing products under the 24/7 Mail division. By year end 1999, 24/7 Mail had over 20 million opt-in email addresses under its management.

Challenges

• Competition in the online advertising and marketing space is intense, and includes industry leader, DoubleClick, and CMGI's Engage Technologies (includes AdSmart and Flycast). In addition, 24/7 also competes for advertising dollars against such large eContent companies as Yahoo!, AOL, Microsoft's MSN and AltaVista.

• Revenue concentration risk is a concern for 24/7. Its top ten advertisers and ad agencies account for roughly 33% of total revenues, and the top ten Web sites on which it serves ads account for 40% of total ad revenues. If 24/7 were to lose either major advertisers or Web properties, revenue growth could slow.

Bottom Line

24/7 Media is one of the leading Internet advertising and marketing companies in the rapidly growing Internet advertising market. Although it trails industry leader, DoubleClick, in several key metrics, 24/7 looks on track to narrow the spread between itself and the number one online ad company. However, not to be forgotten is CMGI and its set of advertising properties including Engage Technologies, AdSmart and Flycast. Bottom line? 24/7 has been enjoying strong growth throughout its business, and relative to its competitors, 24/7 Media's valuation is more compelling.

Key Statistics	TFSM
Market Cap (4/20/00):	$491.8m
Free Float:	73.2%
IPO Date:	8/14/98
Offer Price:	$14.00
Price (4/20/00):	$18.94
52 week high:	$65.25
52 week low:	$15.00
Volatility: (avg. daily % ch)	5.4%
Price/Sales:	5.5
Price/Sales-Growth:	1.6

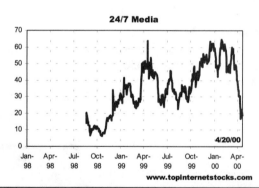

24/7 Media

www.topinternetstocks.com

Annual Financial Data ($ m)	12/1994	12/1995	12/1996	12/1997	12/1998	12/1999
Revenues	--	0.15	1.54	3.15	20.87	90.01
Operating Profit	-0.04	-1.17	-6.76	-5.21	-25.73	-43.07
Net Income	-0.04	-1.17	-6.80	-5.31	-25.16	-39.06
Customers	--	--	--	--	--	--
Key Ratios:						
Gross Margin	--	-30.3%	-3.3%	47.4%	22.6%	26.7%
Operating Margin	--	-768.4%	-438.5%	-165.5%	-123.3%	-47.8%
Net Margin	--	-768.4%	-440.7%	-168.6%	-120.6%	-43.4%
Marketing as % of Revenues	--	75.7%	145.3%	53.1%	39.5%	26.0%

uBid, Inc.

http://www.ubid.com

eTailer

Address:

8550 W. Bryn Mawr Rd., Ste. 200
Chicago, IL 60631

Phone: 773.272.5000
Fax: 773.272.4000

Management:

Chairman, President & CEO: Gregory K. Jones
CFO: Thomas E. Werner

Description

uBid is ready to take your bid for excess and close-out merchandise. The company was founded in April 1997 as an online auction site for Creative Computers' excess and refurbished inventory. Realizing that it could unlock greater value for shareholders, Creative Computers spun-off uBid in an IPO in December 1998. Since its first auction in December 1997, uBid has auctioned over 1.3 million items and has registered over 1.03 million users. uBid operates auctions in five categories including computer products, consumer electronics, housewares, sporting goods and jewelry. Computer products and consumer electronics are responsible for over 90% of total sales. Revenues are generated either through purchasing merchandise from manufacturers and reselling to consumers or through a consignment fee. In the first nine months of 1999, consignment revenues accounted for less than 11% of sales.

Opportunities

- In October 1999, uBid partnered with Go/Infoseek to provide a co-branded auction site. This potentially extends uBid's reach to the 22 million people visiting the Go Network of sites.
- uBid has been extending its model towards the B2B auction marketplace, which holds seven to eight times greater revenue potential than in the B2C space. In July 1999, uBid entered into an agreement with Cahners to auction industrial equipment products. The company launched its first B2B marketplace in the fourth quarter of 1999 targeted towards pre-owned construction equipment (www.ironmall.com).

Challenges

- uBid competes in the computer and consumer electronics auction markets with a number of other auction sites including manufacturer's own sites. In addition to Egghead.com and Cyberian Outpost which merged in late 1999, uBid could face competition from Amazon.com and eBay as these companies expand into the business-to-person auction space from person-to-person auctions.
- uBid buys inventory first from the manufacturer before selling it to the consumer. As such, uBid carries the full risk of not being able to sell the merchandise and having to sell it below cost (inventory and price risk).
- Success in the online auction place is dependant upon reaching critical mass. If uBid cannot attract enough manufacturers to offer a large selection, consumers may go elsewhere. Conversely, if there are few consumers buying, manufacturers may sell their excess inventory on other distribution channels.

Bottom Line

uBid, I bid, we all bid. At least, that is what the company is hoping. After a difficult early 1999, uBid is repositioning itself with new product categories and a push into the lucrative B2B auction space. Competition is intense in the online auction space, but the greatest challenge facing uBid is lessening its inventory and price risk, which will limit profitability. At year end 1999, uBid was one of the most attractively valued eTailers, and as it continues to extend its model into the B2B marketplace, the stock could see significant upside potential.

Key Statistics	UBID
Market Cap (4/20/00):	$173.7m
Free Float:	86.8%
IPO Date:	12/4/98
Offer Price:	$15.00
Price (4/20/00):	$14.94
52 week high:	$76.00
52 week low:	$12.50
Volatility: (avg. daily % ch)	5.6%
Price/Sales:	0.8
Price/Sales-Growth:	0.3

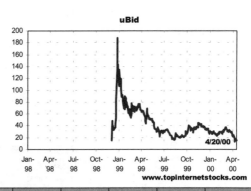

www.topinternetstocks.com

Annual Financial Data ($ m)	12/1994	12/1995	12/1996	12/1997	12/1998	12/1999
Sales	--	--	--	0.01	48.23	204.93
Operating Profit	--	--	--	-0.29	-10.00	-26.70
Net Income	--	--	--	-0.31	-10.17	-25.50
Customers (m)	--	--	--	--	0.23	1.03
Key Ratios:						
Gross Margin	--	--	--	11.1%	8.2%	9.3%
Operating Margin	--	--	--	-3188.9%	-20.7%	-13.0%
Net Margin	--	--	--	-3477.8%	-21.1%	-12.4%
Marketing as % of Sales	--	--	--	111.1%	5.9%	10.8%

USinternetworking, Inc.

http://www.usi.net   eServices

Address:
One USi Plaza   Phone: 800.839.4874
Annapolis, MD 21401   Fax: 410.573.1906
Management:
Chairman & CEO: Christopher R. McCleary
COO: Andrew A. Stern
CFO: Chuck Teubner

Description

USinternetworking was founded in January 1998 to provide software applications that midsized and Fortune 1000 companies could rent over the Internet from USi's servers. Rather than spending upwards of $1 million to purchase, install and maintain enterprise-level software, middle market companies can lease the software over the Internet from USi for $20,000 to $75,000 per month, with the average contract size at $38,000 per month. USi rents software as part of its IMAP services in the following areas: ecommerce platforms from BroadVision and Microsoft Site Server, customer relationship management software from Siebel, accounting and human resources software from Lawson and PeopleSoft, data warehousing from Sagent, corporate messaging from Microsoft Exchange, and procurement solutions from Ariba. In the first quarter of 2000, revenues were generated through its IMAP services (78%) and IT professional services (22%). USi had 147 client contracts at the end of the first quarter 2000, including from Hershey, HP Shoping.com, Knoll Pharmaceutical, Liberty Financial and Samsung.

Opportunities

- The Web hosting and applications services market is being driven by the trend towards outsourcing as companies are faced with a shortage of in-house IT expertise. In addition, corporations are finding that it is more cost-effective to outsource functions where they do not have the expertise, allowing them to focus on their core competencies.

- The market for application service providers (ASP) is a new market that is expected to grow rapidly. Forrester research estimates that the ASP market will expand to $21 billion in 2001 from less than $1 billion in 1997.

- USi has a market leadership position in the ASP market, with a solid suite of software solutions from some of the leading software companies including BroadVision, Microsoft, Siebel and Ariba.

Challenges

- USi competes aggressively on several fronts that include non-facilities application hosting companies such as Corio and Interliant, and Web hosting businesses such as Concentric and Exodus. In addition, USi also competes with in-house solutions where customers buy the software from vendors such as BroadVision, Microsoft, Siebel and PeopleSoft, and implement internally.
- The ASP market is still very young, and it is not yet proven whether the concept of rented or leased applications will be widely accepted by corporate America.

Bottom Line

USinternetworking has a strong first-mover advantage in the software-for-rent market. It also has solid partners (BroadVision, Microsoft, Ariba, PeopleSoft) in terms of the software that it packages as part of the IMAP solutions. Herein though is one of the challenges for USi. If it loses one of those partners then it would lose the right to provide that software to new customers. If USi can successfully manage those relationships while continuing to manage its growth, it will be a strong player in a potentially rapidly growing market.

Key Statistics	USIX
Market Cap (4/20/00):	$2,030m
Free Float:	47.0%
IPO Date:	4/9/99
Offer Price (adj):	$9.33
Price (4/20/00):	$21.44
52 week high:	$71.62
52 week low:	$6.37
Volatility: (avg. daily % ch)	7.5%
Price/Sales:	58.2
Price/Sales-Growth:	7.6

USinternetworking

www.topinternetstocks.com

Annual Financial Data ($ m)	12/1994	12/1995	12/1996	12/1997	12/1998	12/1999
Revenues	--	--	--	--	4.12	35.51
Operating Profit	--	--	--	--	-30.14	-101.13
Net Income	--	--	--	--	-32.45	-103.32
Customers	--	--	--	--	7	109
Key Ratios:						
Gross Margin	--	--	--	--	-36.1%	-12.1%
Operating Margin	--	--	--	--	-731.1%	-284.8%
Net Margin	--	--	--	--	-787.2%	-290.9%
Marketing as % of Revenues	--	--	--	--	--	103.0%

USWeb/CKS (marchFIRST)

http://usweb.com   eServices

Address:
410 Townsend St.   Phone: 415.369.6700
San Francisco, CA 94107   Fax: 415.284.7090
Management:
Chairman: Mark Kvamme
CEO: Robert Shaw
COO: Bob Clarkson
CFO: Carolyn Aver

Description

USWeb has been at the forefront of transforming businesses for the digital economy. The company was founded in December 1995 as a Web design company but grew quickly through a whirlwind of acquisitions – 19 by the time it went public in December 1997. Continuing its acquisition spree, USWeb merged with marketing services company, CKS Group in 1998. Through September 1999, the company had completed 46 acquisitions. USWeb provides strategy consulting, branding, creative design, technology development, and systems implementation and integration. In addition, USWeb also provides marketing services including corporate identity and product branding, advertising, direct marketing and media placement services. Customers include Apple, NBCi and Williams Sonoma.

Opportunities

- The iBuilders market is growing quickly as businesses rush to develop comprehensive eBusiness strategies, but lack the capabilities in-house. According to IDC, the Internet professional services market is expected to grow tenfold by 2003 to an estimated $78 billion.
- USWeb has a strong market leadership position, with over 50 offices around the world and 4,000 employees.
- The planned Whittman-Hart merger would extend USWeb's expertise into the traditional IT systems market enabling it to provide complete end-to-end integration.

Challenges

- With barriers to entry virtually non-existent, competition in the iBuilders space is intense. Hundreds of companies ranging from small garage shops to Big Five consultancies all promise the same core competencies in a "me too" environment. Differentiation in the space is difficult.
- USWeb has been growing rapidly by acquiring or "buying" revenues. In the last three years, the company has acquired 46 companies and is set to merge with consulting firm Whittman-Hart in early 2000. Growing quickly through acquisitions can backfire if the company is unable to quickly and smoothly integrate the various acquisitions. The Whittman-Hart merger in particular, could pose significant integration challenges, which could lead to high employee turnover and loss of clients.

Bottom Line

USWeb delivers time-to-value for clients and intends to do the same for investors. The company has a strong market leadership position in the iBuilders space through its rapid acquisition pace, ranking as the top Internet consultant. Although competition is fierce within the marketplace that USWeb operates, the greatest challenge going forward is likely to come from itself. The planned merger with Whitmann-Hart will double USWeb's employee base to nearly 8,000 employees, presenting substantial integration risk. If USWeb can successfully integrate Whittman into its fold, the new company will be a powerhouse with few if any equals.

Key Statistics	MRCH
Market Cap (4/20/00):	$3,494m
Free Float:	72.0%
IPO Date:	12/5/97
Offer Price:	$6.50
Price (4/20/00):	$24.12
52 week high:	$81.12
52 week low:	$19.75
Volatility: (avg. daily % ch)	4.3%
Price/Sales:	6.8
Price/Sales-Growth:	5.5

marchFIRST (USWeb/CKS)

www.topinternetstocks.com

Annual Financial Data ($ m)	12/1994	12/1995	12/1996	12/1997	12/1998	12/1999
Revenues	28.99	43.66	66.39	114.30	228.60	510.95
Operating Profit	4.99	6.58	-2.60	-43.06	-184.84	-198.66
Net Income	4.92	5.81	-3.36	-50.67	-188.28	-175.02
Customers	--	--	--	--	--	--
Key Ratios:						
Gross Margin	36.4%	33.9%	37.8%	32.5%	25.9%	29.4%
Operating Margin	17.2%	15.1%	-3.9%	-37.7%	-80.9%	-38.9%
Net Margin	17.0%	13.3%	-5.1%	-44.3%	-82.4%	-34.3%
Marketing as % of Revenues	2.1%	2.1%	22.5%	20.4%	12.0%	9.2%

Verio, Inc.

http://www.verio.com   eAccess

Address:
8005 S. Chester St. Ste. 200   Phone: 303.645.1900
Englewood, CO 80112   Fax: 303.792.5644
Management:
Chairman: Steven C. Halstedt
President & CEO: Justin L. Jaschke
CFO: Peter B. Fritzinger

Description

Since March 1996, when Verio was founded to provide Internet access services and solutions to small and medium-sized businesses, the company has grown quickly through a series of acquisitions and strategic investments – 53 by mid-1999. In addition to providing dial-up and high speed access for businesses, the company offers value-added virtual private networks, Web hosting and ecommerce solutions to more than 300,000 businesses. These value-added, higher margin services account for more than 53% of revenues. Verio has customers in more than 170 countries, though international revenues account for less than 10% of total revenues. Verio's key assets are its shared Web hosting platforms, its Tier One IP backbone for carrying Internet traffic, its diverse and global distribution channels and its 300,000 business customers.

The company went public in May 1998. Since then, the company has raised over $1.5 billion in capital through equity and debt which it used to make acquisitions and continue its infrastructure investments, including a 650,000 square foot data center. This capital was also used to finance further acquisitions, including Hiway Technologies, from which it acquired 180,000 hosted Web sites and digitalNation in July 1999, thus strengthening its position in the dedicated server area.

In March 1999, Verio signed a three-year agreement with AOL to market and provide business Web hosting and ecommerce capabilities for the ISP Goliath. The deal cost Verio $18.5 million total. In addition, AOL would also receive a share of revenues if exceeding a predetermined amount.

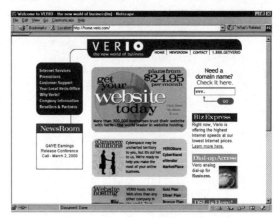

Opportunities

- Verio is a leading IP services company with over 340,000 Web hosting accounts. This is the fastest growing area of the Internet services market according to Dataquest, estimated to grow at more than 85% compounded annually to $6 billion in revenues by 2003.
- By shifting more of its business on cost efficient national services, like the Tier One backbone, accounting, billing, and customer care, Verio has been seeing significant margin improvements. The company's gross margin also improved due to the shift in revenue mix toward more profitable Web hosting services. In 1999, gross margins expanded nearly to 69.3% from 55.2% in the previous year as enhanced services increased to 53% of revenues from 37%.
- Central to Verio's strategy is to form strategic partnerships to market and distribute its value-added services. Such deals include Verio's three-year co-branding deal with AOL, private label agreements with major telcommunication companies including NTT in Japan, Swisscom, Infostrada, Qwest, RBOCS and roughly 5,000 other third-party resellers. This allows Verio to leverage is services across many different distribution channels, lowering account acquisition costs for the company.
- Verio's focus for growth going forward is expected to be on expanding its product set, extending its distribution channels, and increasing its presence in international markets, particularly in Europe. The company already has a sizeable presence on the Continent, hosting over 50,000 Web sites for European businesses. Its recent deal with AOL to extend its Web hosting, domain name registration and ecommerce services in the UK with AOL's free Netscape Online service should help it to aggressively grow its European customer base.

Challenges

- Competition is beginning to pick up steam in the Web hosting and business IP services market, with Concentric, PSINet, Globix and others fighting aggressively to capture market share. Verio, as the leader in Web hosting, is facing competition on all sides as the major telecommunication companies also begin to compete in this highly profitable area.
- Pursuing a strategy of growth through acquisitions could present a challenge in smoothly integrating new acquisitions. If Verio is unable to smoothly integrate the operations of these new companies into Verio's own operations, customer disruptions could result.
- Verio relies significantly on third-party distribution channels and other resellers to market and distribute its IP and Web hosting services. If Verio loses these distribution channels and marketing partners, it could have a significant impact on revenue growth.
- As with most Internet companies, Verio is incurring significant losses and could continue to operate at a loss for several years as it continues to grow through acquisitions and invest in infrastructure build up. Much of these past acquisitions and infrastructure developments have been financed through debt, which could place additional strains on Verio's financial future.

The Bottom Line

When it comes to Web hosting, Verio is at the top of the pack, with more than 340,000 Web hosting accounts, three times that of its nearest competitor. Verio has also tightened its marketing and distribution partnership with AOL by extending its relationship to the UK through Netscape Online's free Internet access. This should help Verio aggressively grow its Web hosting and other value-added businesses in Europe where growth rates are higher than in the US.

However, as the competitive landscape heats up, future growth will not come easy. In addition to competitors like Concentric, Exodus, and PSINet, large telecommunication companies are also nipping at Verio's heels in the hopes of cashing in on the lucrative Web hosting and IP services market.

The key to Verio's growth going forward is its ability to form strong marketing relationships and distribution channels with major partners and to pursue growth on the acquisition front. So far, it is off to a good start through its relationships with AOL in the US and Europe.

Bottom line thoughts? Good company, strong market opportunity and proven ability to execute its strategy.

Key Statistics	VRIO
Market Cap (4/20/00):	$2,175m
Free Float:	67.9%
IPO Date:	5/12/98
Offer Price (adj):	$11.50
Price (4/20/00):	$27.62
52 week high:	$84.94
52 week low:	$22.56
Volatility: (avg. daily % ch)	4.2%
Price/Sales:	8.4
Price/Sales-Growth:	7.4

Verio

www.topinternetstocks.com

Annual Financial Data ($ m)	12/1994	12/1995	12/1996	12/1997	12/1998	12/1999
Revenues	--	--	2.37	35.69	120.65	258.39
Operating Profit	--	--	-6.28	-40.29	-91.02	-118.03
Net Income	--	--	-5.12	-46.07	-121.96	-187.94
Hosted Web Sites	--	--	--	--	180,000	340,000
Key Ratios:						
Gross Margin	--	--	58.8%	55.2%	45.0%	69.3%
Operating Margin	--	--	-265.5%	-112.9%	-75.4%	-45.7%
Net Margin	--	--	-216.6%	-129.1%	-101.1%	-72.7%
Marketing as % of Revenues	--	--	--	30.0%	27.0%	23.5%

VeriSign, Inc.

http://www.verisign.com   eSecurity

Address:
1350 Charleston Rd.   Phone: 650.961.7500
Mountain View, CA 94043   Fax: 650.961.7300
Management:
Chairman: D. James Bidzos
President & CEO: Stratton Sclavos
CFO: Dana Evan

Description

VeriSign builds trust on the Internet. The company was founded in 1995 and quickly became the leader in digital certificates and Public Key Infrastructure (PKI) on the Internet, helping consumers and businesses conduct secure communications and transactions over the Web and on private networks. International revenues are growing rapidly and accounted for an estimated 26% of total revenues in 1999. In December 1999, VeriSign acquired Signio in order to enter the online payments market, and Thawte Consulting, a leading international vendor of digital certificates. Key customers include Bank of America, Federal Reserve Bank of NY, VISA, Softbank, AT&T, Kodak and Barclays PLC. In March 2000, VeriSign and Network Solutions announced an intent to merge in order to provide a more comprehensive suite of products and services for corporations looking to move onto the Web.

Opportunities

- As more consumers and businesses are rushing onto the Web, security is becoming a real concern. The growth in ecommerce transactions and communications will drive the growth in security solutions. IDC estimates that the Internet security market will grow to $7.4 billion in 2002 from an estimated $3.1 billion in 1998. Giga Information Group estimates that the issuance of digital certificates will grow tenfold by 2002 to 247 million certificates.

- Corporate spending on security solutions was delayed in 1999, with most IT budgets dedicated to solving Y2K issues. In 2000, IT spending on security issues is expected to accelerate, leading to strong revenue growth for the market leaders.

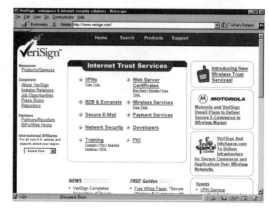

- The acquisition of Thawte, the largest digital certificates vendor outside the US, will accelerate VeriSign's international growth. Thawte has a distributed agent network in over 22 countries. In addition, both companies are the only two vendors commercially distributing 128-bit Web site certificates.

Challenges

- VeriSign competes with a number of other players in the digital certificates and PKI markets. These competitors include Entrust, Baltimore Technologies, CyberTrust, RSA Security, IBM and Microsoft.
- The adoption of digital certificates could be slowed by the lack of standards and different technologies used. Different certificate providers do not always support certificates from other vendors.

Bottom Line

VeriSign is the leader in digital certificates and PKI technology. The explosive growth in ecommerce transactions and digital communications is expected to fuel strong growth in the Internet security area. Although the lack of standards and the inability of competing vendor's certificates to be used by each other is a potential stumbling block to wide-scale adoption, VeriSign's Digital ID is quickly emerging as the industry standard. It has been adopted by the US Department of Defense, the State of California and a number of other government agencies. It is also used by all of the top 50 Web sites and Fortune 500 companies with a Web presence. That is a strong endorsement.

Key Statistics	VRSN
Market Cap (4/20/00):	$12,297m
Free Float:	76.1%
IPO Date:	1/30/98
Offer Price (adj):	$3.50
Price (4/20/00):	$118.50
52 week high:	$258.50
52 week low:	$22.88
Volatility: (avg. daily % ch)	5.0%
Price/Sales:	145.0
Price/Sales-Growth:	123.2

VeriSign

www.topinternetstocks.com

Annual Financial Data ($ m)	12/1994	12/1995	12/1996	12/1997	12/1998	12/1999
Revenues	--	--	1.36	13.36	38.93	84.78
Operating Profit	--	--	-11.06	-18.50	-19.59	-3.31
Net Income	--	--	-10.29	-18.59	-16.19	3.96
Website Certificates	--	--	--	--	97,000	215,000
Key Ratios:						
Gross Margin	--	--	-105.8%	27.5%	50.0%	62.4%
Operating Margin	--	--	-815.6%	-138.5%	-50.3%	-3.9%
Net Margin	--	--	-758.7%	-139.2%	-41.6%	4.7%
Marketing as % of Revenues	--	--	360.3%	88.5%	58.9%	40.3%

Verity, Inc.

http://www.verity.com   eBusiness

Address:
894 Ross Dr.   Phone: 408.541.1500
Sunnyvale, CA 94089   Fax: 408.541.1600
Management:
Chairman & CEO: Gary J. Sbona
President: Anthony J. Bettencourt
CFO: James Ticehurst

Description

Verity was founded in 1988 to create search applications for US intelligence agencies like the CIA and the NSA. Initially known as a search-and-retrieval applications provider, the company is now "a leading provider of knowledge retrieval solutions" for companies. In plainspeak, Verity provides software that can search and view information over the Internet and enterprises, across multiple databases and locations and in different file formats. Its integrated suite of software indexes and classifies data for search and retrieval, enabling it to be organized and navigated before being disseminated or published.

Verity has over 1,000 corporations using its products, including Adobe Systems, AT&T, CNET, The Wall Street Journal, the Financial Times, Fujitsu, Sybase and Tandem. Software licensing revenues account for 72% of total revenues, with services (maintenance, consulting and training) accounting for the rest.

Opportunities

- With the explosive growth in the Web comes the growth in the volume of information that is available on the Web. Forrester Research estimates that 1.5 million new pages are being added to the Web every day.
- As corporations bring more of their business functions online, there is a growing need to be able to quickly search for data and publish it on the Internet or over Intranets. Popular search engines such as Yahoo! and WebCrawler can quickly find Web sites, but they cannot find precise data nor publish it on-the-fly.
- Verity's integrated technology can quickly find, organize, and publish specific data on the Web or another platform. The company has a market

leadership position in the retrieval and publishing arena, with solid technology and a blue-chip customer base.

Challenges

- The knowledge retrieval space, where Verity is positioned, is fiercely competitive. A number of companies offer search and retrieval services including Dataware, PC Docs, Inktomi, Oracle and Microsoft. Verity can continue to maintain its lead only as long as it has a superior technology.
- Verity's sales are typified by large contracts to a few clients. Because of the long sales cycles, there is a risk that Verity can fail to close some contracts in a particular quarter, leading to timing-related revenue shortfalls.

Bottom Line

Verity knows how to find and retrieve data quickly, publish it on corporate portals, and provide technology for customer care or ecommerce applications. It has a blue-chip list of clients including Ernst & Young, Xerox and Home Depot. Although the company has had a troublesome track record in its twelve-year history, new management has helped Verity to sharpen its focus, resulting in improved business momentum. The major risk for the shares however, is that Verity could miss some quarterly revenue targets because of timing issues, resulting in volatile price swings. Nevertheless, Verity has a strong market-leadership position in its favor.

Key Statistics	VRTY
Market Cap (4/20/00):	$832.5m
Free Float:	86.9%
IPO Date:	10/6/95
Offer Price (adj):	$6.00
Price (4/20/00):	$26.62
52 week high:	$63.75
52 week low:	$14.44
Volatility:	4.5%
(avg. daily % ch)	
Price/Sales:	11.5
Price/Sales-Growth:	30.7

Verity

www.topinternetstocks.com

Annual Financial Data ($ m)	5/1995	5/1996	5/1997	5/1998	5/1999	2/2000*
Revenues	15.89	30.72	42.67	38.86	64.43	65.70
Operating Profit	-5.58	-1.39	-19.48	-17.66	11.65	15.36
Net Income	-5.84	-0.31	-17.93	-16.51	12.13	18.83
Customers	--	--	--	--	--	--
Key Ratios:						
Gross Margin	77.7%	84.2%	84.6%	80.4%	90.9%	90.1%
Operating Margin	-35.1%	-4.5%	-45.7%	-45.5%	18.1%	23.4%
Net Margin	-36.7%	-1.0%	-42.0%	-42.5%	18.8%	28.7%
Marketing as % of Revenues	58.4%	48.5%	50.4%	58.6%	41.7%	41.7%

* Nine months ended February 29, 2000

VerticalNet, Inc.

http://www.verticalnet.com   eBusiness

Address:
2 Walnut Grove Dr., Suite 150   Phone: 215.328.6100
Horsham, PA 19044   Fax: 215.443.3336
Management:
Chairman: Douglas A. Alexander
President & CEO: Mark L. Walsh
CFO: Gene S. Godick

Description

   VerticalNet is standing tall in the B2B sector. Founded originally as Water
Online to provide an online information database and community to the industrial
water industry back in July 1995, the company changed its name to VerticalNet in
1996 and began adding other industries to its collection of sites. In February 1999,
the company completed its IPO, rising 184% on its first day.

   VerticalNet operates over 55 industry-specific Web sites designed as B2B
trading communities. These branded sites are grouped into ten sectors including
advanced technologies, communications, environmental, food and packaging,
food service/hospitality, healthcare, manufacturing and metals, science, and services. Revenues are generated from advertising fees, storefront hosting, and ecommerce transactions. The majority of VerticalNet's revenues are generated from
advertising, with barter revenues accounting for roughly 23% of revenues in 1999.

Opportunities

- According to Veronis, Suhler & Associates, the B2B advertising market is a
  $78 billion industry that is expected to grow to $104 billion by 2003. Although still in its embryotic stage, VerticalNet is one of the leading players in
  the online B2B advertising market, with a significant first-mover advantage.

- VerticalNet's strategy is to
  build its user base through
  compelling content and
  community services then to
  leverage that user base to
  generate ecommerce revenues.

- The company is also ex-
  panding into foreign markets, entering Japan with
  Softbank, and Europe with
  British Telecommunica-
  tions.

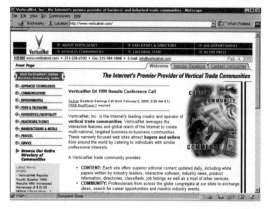

Challenges

- Although VerticalNet hopes to develop vertical B2B trading exchanges, the company's model is still one of a series of cyber-trade journals, providing content and generating revenue through advertising fees. E-commerce revenues accounted for less than an estimated 8% of total revenue in 1999.
- Competition in the B2B vertical trading exchanges is young, but quickly intensifying. Verticals also compete with horizontal trading exchanges such as Commerce One and Ariba.
- VerticalNet's rapid acquisition pace could pose a challenge in smoothly integrating the various companies. In a fast evolving climate, such a stumble could turn out to be fall.

Bottom Line

VerticalNet's formula for success is straightforward: (Content + Community + Commerce) x Strategic Relationships = VerticalNet. The company has an early advantage in developing vertical industrial communities. However, first-mover advantage is no guarantee of future success, and in the coming battle between verticals and horizontals, it is still too early to predict the winners. Customers appreciate the depth of verticals, but like the selection (of buyers and suppliers) of horizontals. For now though, with B2B ecommerce soon to be measured in the trillions of dollars, there is enough growth for both.

Key Statistics	VERT
Market Cap (4/20/00):	$3,055m
Free Float:	42.0%
IPO Date:	2/11/99
Offer Price (adj):	$4.00
Price (4/20/00):	$41.62
52 week high:	$148.38
52 week low:	$13.56
Volatility: (avg. daily % ch)	6.7%
Price/Sales:	147.2
Price/Sales-Growth:	26.2

VerticalNet

www.topinternetstocks.com

Annual Financial Data ($ m)	12/1994	12/1995	12/1996	12/1997	12/1998	12/1999
Revenues	--	0.02	0.29	0.79	3.14	20.76
Operating Profit	--	-0.21	-0.70	-4.66	-13.23	-33.40
Net Income	--	-0.21	-0.71	-4.78	-13.59	-53.48
Storefront Customers	--	--	--	--	735	1,795
Key Ratios:						
Gross Margin	--	-50.0%	24.9%	-33.3%	-3.3%	58.5%
Operating Margin	--	-1312.5%	-246.7%	-588.9%	-421.9%	-160.9%
Net Margin	--	-1318.8%	-248.8%	-603.4%	-433.7%	-257.6%
Marketing as % of Revenues	--	918.8%	94.0%	290.5%	251.8%	127.0%

Vignette Corporation

http://www.vignette.com   eBusiness

Address:
901 S. Mo Pac Expy., Bldg. 3   Phone: 512.306.4300
Austin TX 78746   Fax: 512.306.4500
Management:
President & CEO: Greg Peters
CFO: Joel Katz

Description

Vignette is one of the leaders in Internet relationship management (IRM) solutions, and is expanding . Founded in December 1995, the company's flagship StoryServer software is a platform for building online business applications, delivering customization, content management, decision support and enterprise/database integration. Other products include Syndication Server which manages content on affiliate or partner sites, and Multi-Channel Server, to manage customer touch points (customer communications). Vignette has over 500 customers including PricewaterhouseCoopers, RR Donnely & Sons, US West and ZDNet. Revenues are generated from software licenses and from consulting, maintenance and support services. Software licensing accounts for roughly 52% of revenues.

Opportunities

- According to Forrester Research, the average conversion rate for first-time visitors to an ecommerce site is only 2.7%, roughly the same rate as for unsolicited direct mailings. Businesses can significantly increase that rate by developing targeted (i.e. personalized) sites that attract first-time visitors and build customer loyalty. Vignette's solutions help companies improve their conversion rates, build customer loyalty and reduce site development times by up to two-thirds.

- Revenues were up sixfold in the December 1999 quarter. Customer growth has also been solid, with Vignette adding 125 new customers in the fourth quarter of 1999. Vignette is also strong overseas, where Internet usage is beginning to expand. International revenues accounted for approximately 16% of total revenues in 1999.

Challenges

- Vignette competes on three fronts: with in-house development efforts by potential customers; other eBusiness solutions providers such as BroadVision; and specialized firms such as Interwoven.
- Service or consulting revenues are responsible for roughly half of Vignette's total revenues. However, service revenues are not a scalable business model to the same extent that software licensing is. If Vignette cannot improve its revenue mix, then revenue growth will become largely a function of employee growth.

Bottom Line

With Vignette, the race is on. The company is one of the fastest growing eBusiness solutions provider in an industry that is expected to top $8.7 billion by 2003. Recent acquisitions, including Engine 5 and Data Sage, also help the company to expand its product offering to include a more comprehensive package of eBusiness solutions. Although competition is all around Vignette, the greater challenge will be to improve its revenue mix to a more scalable model while improving margins in its services area. If Vignette can execute in these two areas while continuing to grow aggressively, it can remain one of the top eBusiness companies.

Key Statistics	VIGN
Market Cap (4/20/00):	$10,071m
Free Float:	83.0%
IPO Date:	2/19/99
Offer Price (adj):	$3.17
Price (4/20/00):	$52.75
52 week high:	$100.62
52 week low:	$7.00
Volatility: (avg. daily % ch)	5.7%
Price/Sales:	112.9
Price/Sales-Growth:	25.1

Vignette

www.topinternetstocks.com

Annual Financial Data ($ m)	12/1994	12/1995	12/1996	12/1997	12/1998	12/1999
Revenues	--	--	--	3.02	16.21	89.19
Operating Profit	--	--	-3.69	-7.64	-26.37	-46.20
Net Income	--	--	-3.63	-7.47	-26.20	-42.48
Customers	--	--	--	--	--	518
Key Ratios:						
Gross Margin	--	--	--	51.2%	36.4%	58.7%
Operating Margin	--	--	--	-252.7%	-162.7%	-51.8%
Net Margin	--	--	--	-247.2%	-161.7%	-47.6%
Marketing as % of Revenues	--	--	--	164.2%	98.0%	55.6%

Vitria Technology, Inc.

http://www.vitria.com   eBusiness

Address:
945 Stewart Dr.   Phone: 408.212.2700
Sunnyvale, CA 94086   Fax: 408.212.2720
Management:
President & CEO: JoMei Chang
CFO: Paul Auvil

Description

Vitria is the eBusiness platform company. The company was founded in October 1994 by former Tibco Software co-founders JoMei Chang and Dale Skeen to develop and market end-to-end eBusiness software solutions. It's BusinessWare suite of software applications address four key requirements for companies: automating internal and external work flow, ensuring open communications between customer and partners, integrating various IT systems and analyzing business processes in real-time.

Vitria has a strong list of blue-chip customers including 3Com, Deutsche Bank, Bell South, FedEx and Sprint. Revenues are generated through software licensing (69%) and maintenance, consulting and training services (27%). Vitra also receives a government grant (4%) reimbursing the company for certain research and development expenses.

Opportunities

- Businesses are increasingly turning to the Internet to link and integrate disparate IT systems because of its common standard, flexibility and rapid deployment. Industry estimates indicate that businesses are budgeting 40% of their IT spending to integrate disparate IT systems through the extended enterprise.
- Because Vitria uses Internet technology, its suite of software solutions is more scalable than that provided by traditional enterprise application integrator (EAI) vendors. In addition, Vitria's software can be deployed faster and at a lower cost than traditional EAI solutions.

Challenges

- Vitria competes on several fronts. On one front, Vitria competes against enterprise application integrators such as Active Software, CrossWorlds, Neon and Tibco. On another front, it competes against Web-centric eBusiness or B2B solutions providers such as WebMethods.
- Revenue concentration risk is a key issue. In the first nine months of 1999, sales to Vitria's ten largest clients accounted for 58% of revenues, and Sprint accounted for 11%. If Vitria were to lose key customers, revenue growth could slow substantially.

Bottom Line

Vitria is the ebusiness enabler, providing a comprehensive end-to-end set of solutions for companies looking to the Web to transform their organizations. Vitria's software is scalable, flexible and quick to deploy, helping businesses create a strong competitive advantage. However, other companies also promise end-to-end solutions, adding to the competitive pressure. Vitria at least, has a solid strategy for growth: partner with major systems integrators, including Andersen Consulting, Deloitte Consulting and Sapient, to leverage as distribution channels.

Key Statistics	VITR
Market Cap (4/20/00):	$5,408m
Free Float:	28.9%
IPO Date:	9/17/99
Offer Price (adj):	$4.00
Price (4/20/00):	$42.75
52 week high:	$106.00
52 week low:	$7.62
Volatility: (avg. daily % ch)	9.8%
Price/Sales:	171.5
Price/Sales-Growth:	54.7

Vitria

www.topinternetstocks.com

Annual Financial Data ($ m)	12/1994	12/1995	12/1996	12/1997	12/1998	12/1999
Revenues	0.07	0.38	2.03	3.64	7.63	31.54
Operating Profit	-0.09	-0.25	0.24	-0.66	-9.88	-15.44
Net Income	-0.09	-0.24	0.24	-0.58	-9.57	-14.11
Customers	--	--	--	--	--	100
Key Ratios:						
Gross Margin	100.0%	96.0%	42.4%	55.7%	61.9%	75.5%
Operating Margin	-126.9%	-66.8%	11.6%	-18.0%	-129.5%	-49.0%
Net Margin	-126.9%	-63.0%	12.0%	-16.0%	-125.5%	-44.7%
Marketing as % of Revenues	--	--	3.9%	31.4%	86.2%	63.4%

Wit Capital Group, Inc.

http://www.witcapital.com   eFinancial

Address:
826 Broadway, 6th Fl.   Phone: 212.253.4000
New York, NY 10003   Fax: 212.253.4428
Management:
Chairman & co-CEO: Robert H. Lessin
President & co-CEO: Ronald Readmond
CFO: M. Bernard Siegel

Description

Wit Capital is the first online investment banking firm, providing public underwriting, private equity, strategic advisory services and institutional research. Wit allows individual investors to participate in IPOs over the Internet on a first-come, first-served basis. The company was born out of founder Andrew Klein's experience raising money over the Internet in 1996 for his microbrewery, Spring Street Brewery. Fresh with the experience of the world's first Internet IPO, Andrew Klein decided to launch Wit Capital in September 1997 as a platform to distribute IPOs to individual investors. The company initially got off to a slow start, until it hired former vice-chairman of Salomon Smith Barney, Bob Lessin, and former vice-chairman of Charles Schwab, Ron Readmond, to be co-CEOs. In June 1999, on the eve of its IPO, Goldman Sachs took a 22% equity stake in Wit Capital.

As the company has grown, it has also expanded its services, offering investment banking services, research, strategic advisor services and online brokerge and trading services. In January 2000, Wit Capital acquired Soundview Technology Group in a move to extend its reach into the institutional investor market.

In the first quarter of 2000, Wit Capital's revenues were generated through investment banking activities (57%), brokerage (34%), asset management fees (7%), and interest and investment income (2%).

Opportunities

- Online investing has been taking the US by storm. From less than 2 million online brokerage accounts in 1996, 8 million investors were trading online in 1999, with that number expected to grow to more than 25 million by 2003.
- Originally off to a slow start, Wit's underwriting business has been quickly picking up steam. In the first nine months of 1999, the company participated in 94 public offerings compared to 28 in the same period in 1998.
- Wit's recent acquisition of Soundview Technology helps extend the firm's footprint into the institutional investor area. This could help Wit Capital to capture more underwriting business and better share allocation, as it better guarantees Wit's ability to place IPOs and other issuances.

Challenges

- Wit Capital's greatest challenge is its exposure to any slowdown in equity market performance. Because the company earns roughly 70% of revenues from Internet-related investment banking activities, any stockmarket correction could significantly reduce the number of equity offerings.
- Although Wit may have pioneered online investment banking, it is facing tough competition from a host of new firms including E*Offering and W.R. Hambrecht, as well as the old boy network of Morgan Stanley, Goldman Sachs, Merrill Lynch and DLJ.

Bottom Line

Wit Capital hopes to outwit the competition. Although that could prove a challenge, given the tough competition in the form of traditional titans like Morgan Stanley, Merrill Lynch and Goldman Sachs as well as online newcomer, E*Offering, Wit Capital is well-positioned to do so. It has built a solid management and research team to support its underwriting efforts, and it can operate from a lower cost structure than its larger counterparts, offering IPO-aspirants lower commission fees. Wit Capital's Soundview acquisition also helps expand its distribution channel into the institutional investor market, thus better guaranteeing IPO placement. In the world of online investment banking, Wit Capital is at the forefront.

Key Statistics	WITC
Market Cap (4/20/00):	$1953.0m
Free Float:	10.5%
IPO Date:	6/4/99
Offer Price:	$9.00
Price (4/20/00):	$10.88
52 week high:	$38.00
52 week low:	$9.00
Volatility: (avg. daily % ch)	5.7%
Price/Sales:	19.6
Price/Sales-Growth:	0.9

Wit Capital

www.topinternetstocks.com

Annual Financial Data ($ m)	12/1994	12/1995	12/1996	12/1997	12/1998	12/1999
Net Revenues	--	--	0.04	0.25	2.04	48.62
Operating Profit	--	--	-1.76	-2.97	-8.79	-20.34
Net Income	--	--	-1.77	-2.99	-8.79	20.90
Active Accounts	--	--	--	--	--	62,800
Key Ratios:						
Gross Margin	--	--	--	--	--	--
Operating Margin	--	--	-4287.8%	-1207.3%	-431.5%	-41.8%
Net Margin	--	--	-4326.8%	-1216.7%	-431.5%	43.0%
Marketing as % of Revenues	--	--	795.1%	204.5%	59.2%	5.3%

Yahoo! Inc.

http://www.yahoo.com   eContent

Address:
3420 Central Expressway   Phone: 408.731.3300
Santa Clara, CA 95051   Fax: 408.731.3301
Management:
Chairman & CEO: Timothy Koogle
President & COO: Jeffrey Mallett
SVP, CFO: Gary Valenzuela

Description

   Do you Yahoo!? At least Yahoo!'s founders, David Filo and Jerry Yang, do. From their humble beginnings in April 1994, when they started their guide as a way to keep track of their personal interests on the Internet, Yahoo! has grown to be one of the most recognized brands on the Web, and one of the leading portals, or hubs on the World Wide Web, with over 650 million page views per day, 145 million different visitors a month and 3,565 advertisers on its properties of sites. Although the company does not officially acknowledge it, the name Yahoo! allegedly stands for "Yet Another Hierarchical Officious Oracle".

   Incorporated in March 1995, Yahoo! is one of the first navigational directories for the Web. But Yahoo! is more than just a directory. The company has a simple concept: to be the only place that anyone has to go to get connected to anything or anybody. An ambitious mission to say the least, yet one that Yahoo! is close to achieving. Through a series of acquisitions, Yahoo! has grown to be one of the leading horizontal portals offering everything from news, email, online calendars, chat rooms and community sites, to online stores, auctions, bill payments and career services.

   Major acquisitions include online store hosting services Viaweb in June 1998, direct marketing company Yoyodyne in October 1998, home page builder and community site, GeoCities in May 1999 and Internet broadcaster, Broadcast.com in July 1999. The majority of Yahoo!'s revenues come from banner and sponsorship advertising.

   The company has been positioning itelf as the global Internet brand, with the result being that Yahoo! operates in 22 different international markets and in 13 different languages. International visitors were 40 million in December 1999, or one-third of its total visitor base.

Opportunities

- Yahoo! is one of the leading horizontal portals with brand recognition and reach that few Internet companies can hope to match. That is good news in the portal wars. Although Internet advertising is expect to grow from an estimated $2.9 billion in 1999 to $12.5 billion in 2003 according to estimates by Pegasus Research, only the largest digital media sites will receive the lion's portion of ad revenues. The Internet Advertising Bureau estimates that the top 10 online media properties receive 75% of all advertising dollars.
- In contrast to most other Internet companies, Yahoo! is already earning profits and enjoys high margins. Gross margins are around 86%, and operating margins are between the company's target of 30%-36%. Because of the scalable nature of Yahoo!'s business, Yahoo! could see operating margins approach 40% within the next few years. This translates to solid earnings in the years ahead.
- One of the trends that is emerging is high-speed or broadband Internet access. Yahoo! is well-positioned to benefit from this trend. The company's acquisition of Internet audio and video broadcaster, Broadcast.com gives Yahoo! the rich media content and platform that it needs as broadband penetration into US households accelerates and consumers expect rich, interactive content.
- Now that Yahoo! has virtually conquered the US, it has set its sites on international markets including Europe, Asia and Latin America. The company has over 22 regional sites translated into 13 different languages. In many of these markets there is little or no competition, giving Yahoo! significant first-mover advantage in regions where Internet users are growing twice as fast as in the US. International revenues accounted for 14% of total revenues in the first quarter of 2000.

Challenges

- In addition to fierce competition from the other horizontal portals like AOL, MSN, and Lycos, Yahoo! is also facing competition from vertical or niche portals like SportsLine, CBS MarketWatch and iVillage. This means that not only is Yahoo! facing frontal assaults from the major portals in a bid to win visitors, but it is also in danger of being chipped away at its base by smaller, nimbler competitors.
- Barriers to entry are virtually nonexistent in the portal space. Once Yahoo! develops a new service, its competitors can usually have the same or similar service up and running virtually overnight, making differentiation difficult. In the portal space, where one portal can look virtually the same as the next, differentiation is all that separates success from failure.
- Yahoo! has not been able to generate significant ecommerce dollars, and it may be difficult to generate in the future. Many online retailers have also been disappointed with the lack of revenues coming from placement agreements with the portals. If this disappointment were to continue, eTailers could pull or not renew their contracts with the portal companies. Yahoo! Auctions also faces stiff competition from established eTailers eBay and Amazon.com.

The Bottom Line

Yahoo! is the king of portals and is a name synonymous with the Internet. It has proven that in a marketplace where there are no barriers to entry and competitors can copy your look and feel virtually overnight, that branding does make a difference. Yahoo! has also been aggressively setting the standard by adding new services while improving others, forcing the other portals to play a constant game of follow-the-leader.

However, that does not give Yahoo! the chance to sit back and relax. With everyone gunning for Yahoo!, the company needs to continue to raise the bar, not giving the competition a chance to catch up. Increased personalization, more in-depth content and new services including online banking and enhanced shopping services are just a few of the areas that Yahoo! is targeting.

With Internet usage growing at twice the rate outside the US as inside, international penetration is one area that Yahoo! has smartly targeted. It already has a presence in 22 international markets, and one-third of its traffic is from outside the borders of the US. Having a significant early lead in many international markets, Yahoo! could potentially see half of its traffic coming from outside the US within a few years.

Key Statistics	YHOO
Market Cap (4/20/00):	$66,550m
Free Float:	40.0%
IPO Date:	4/12/96
Offer Price (adj):	$1.08
Price (4/20/00):	$122.50
52 week high:	$250.06
52 week low:	$55.00
Volatility: (avg. daily % ch)	4.3%
Price/Sales:	113.6
Price/Sales-Growth:	81.1

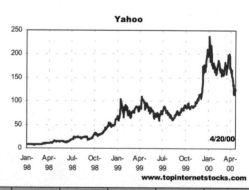

www.topinternetstocks.com

Annual Financial Data ($ m)	12/1994	12/1995	12/1996	12/1997	12/1998	12/1999
Revenues	--	1.62	23.79	84.11	245.10	588.61
Operating Profit	--	-1.09	-16.94	-48.91	-13.72	66.73
Net Income	--	-1.02	-12.43	-43.38	-12.67	61.13
Unique Visitors (m)	--	--	--	--	27.38	42.36
Key Ratios:						
Gross Margin	--	87.0%	69.4%	76.4%	78.7%	82.7%
Operating Margin	--	-67.2%	-71.2%	-58.2%	-5.6%	11.3%
Net Margin	--	-62.7%	-52.2%	-51.6%	-5.2%	10.4%
Marketing as % of Revenues	--	45.6%	78.3%	69.5%	50.9%	35.5%

ZDNet Group

http://www.zdnet.com   eContent

Address:
28 East 28th Street   Phone: 212.503.3500
New York, NY 10016   Fax: 212.503.4599
Management:
Chairman: Eric Hippeau
President & CEO: Daniel L. Rosenweig
CFO: Massimo De Nadai

Description

ZDNet is in a neck-to-neck race with CNET to be the leading technology-focused portal and community site on the Web, with more than 9.6 million Web surfers visiting its property of sites each month. ZDNet, launched in 1994, is the Internet division of Ziff-Davis, the leading global technology media and marketing company founded in 1927. Shares in the online division were floated as a tracking stock in March 1999. ZDNet has a network of 60 sites providing technology news, software downloads, product listings and reviews, bulletin boards, chat rooms and more. ZDNet also offers online access to Ziff-Davis' library of magazines including *Inter@ctive Week*, *PC Computing*, *PC Week*, and *PC Magazine*.

Ziff Davis and ZDNet plan to eliminate the tracking stock through a reorganization and divestiture of Ziff Davis' publishing assets by the second half of 2000.

Opportunities

- IT research firm, International Data Corporation (IDC) estimates that the worldwide market for IT products and services will grow from approximately $750 billion in 1997 to more than $1.1 trillion by 2002. This growth will be accompanied by an expanding base of consumers and IT professionals interested in IT-focused news.
- Internet advertising, although a new medium, has already surpassed outdoor advertising in revenues. By 2003, Pegasus Research estimates that Internet advertising will grow to more than $12.5 billion from $2.9 billion in 1999.
- ZDNet has one of the strongest tech followings on the Web with 9.6 million monthly visitors.

Challenges

- Competition is intense in the online portal space. In addition to competing for IT-related traffic and ad dollars against other technology-focused sites like CNET, EarthWeb, Internet.com and IDG, ZDNet also competes against horizontal portals such as Yahoo!, AOL and Lycos for advertising dollars.
- There are a number of uncertainties associated with the planned restructuring of Ziff-Davis and ZDNet. ZDNet's parent company, Ziff-Davis, has been plagued by poor revenue growth and high debt levels over the past year. It is uncertain how much debt the planned ZDNet, Inc. will carry after the asset sales and reorganization. In addition, Computer Shopper will be the one offline publishing asset that will be transferred to the new company. Computer Shopper would represent a significant share of total revenues, and Computer Shopper has been experiencing declining revenues.

The Bottom Line

ZDNet is one of the strongest technology-focused brands in the online content space. It has more than 9.6 million monthly visitors browsing, reading news, chatting, and downloading software on its collection of 60 different sites. The one concern for ZDNet is its tracking stock status and its dependence on Ziff Davis. However, this is set to change in summer 2000, when Ziff Davis sells most of its poorly performing traditional publishing assets and merges with ZDNet. This transaction will create a new entity, ZDNet, Inc., and eliminate the tracking stock. For investors looking to profit from the strong interest in online technology content, ZDNet is one of the star players in this field.

Key Statistics	ZDZ
Market Cap (4/20/00):	$943.0m
Free Float:	13.0%
IPO Date:	3/31/99
Offer Price:	$19.00
Price (4/20/00):	$12.56
52 week high:	$43.38
52 week low:	$11.62
Volatility: (avg. daily % ch)	5.0%
Price/Sales:	9.1
Price/Sales-Growth:	10.6

ZDNet

www.topinternetstocks.com

Annual Financial Data ($ m)	12/1994	12/1995	12/1996	12/1997	12/1998	12/1999
Revenues	--	--	16.22	32.22	56.14	104.18
Operating Profit	--	--	-17.41	-22.48	-7.51	4.78
Net Income	--	--	-16.93	-21.24	-7.88	1.94
Unique Visitors (m)	--	--	--	--	--	9.61
Key Ratios:						
Gross Margin	--	--	8.3%	26.9%	53.3%	63.9%
Operating Margin	--	--	-107.4%	-69.8%	-13.4%	4.6%
Net Margin	--	--	-104.4%	-65.9%	-14.0%	1.9%
Marketing as % of Revenues	--	--	--	--	--	--

5

Glossary

Absolute Daily Percentage Change – A measure of volatility for stock returns. The average absolute change in percent for stock prices. For example, if a stock, such as AOL, has an average absolute daily percentage change of 3.3%, the share price will move up or down 3.3% each day on average. See also *Standard Deviation*.

ARPANET – The Advanced Research Projects Agency Network was the beginning of the Internet. Established in 1969, it was developed by the US Department of Defense as a communications network to link computers together in case of a nuclear attack. The first two universities linked together were UCLA and the Stanford Research Institute.

Backbone – The high-speed network connecting the Internet together. Similar to the human body, the backbone is the central nervous system of the Internet from which all other connections branch out.

Bandwidth – The amount of data that can be sent over a communications network, usually measured in bytes per second.

Banner – A rectangular graphic, usually 468 x 60 pixels, which is used as an advertising element on a Web page.

Boolean Logic – A method for searching the Web for information. It refers to a form of logic named after the English mathematician George Boole and is used to conduct database queries using AND, OR, NOT and other operators.

Browser – A software program that is used to view Web pages. The main Web browsers are Netscape Navigator and Microsoft Internet Explorer.

Burn Rate (BR) – Cash divided by operating expenses plus non cash charges (depreciation and amortization) in the most recent quarter. This is a measure of how long a company can survive before it runs out of cash.

Bytes per second (Bps) – A measure of how fast different devices communicate. Technically, a byte is 8 bits and refers to one character of information.

Cable Modem – A modem used for Internet access over coaxial cable lines. This is a competing high-speed or broadband technology to DSL.

Cache – A way to store information or data so that it can be quickly retrieved at a later point.

Cash Ratio (CR) – Cash divided by current liabilities. This is a measure of liquidity, often called the liquidity ratio.

Certificate Authority (CA) – A company that issues and manages digital certificates, guaranteeing that the identification of the person holding the certificate is authentic.

Churn Rate – Monthly cancellation rate of subscribers as a percentage of total subscribers. This is a metric used for Internet service providers as an indication of how successful they are at retaining customers.

Clickthrough Rate – The amount in percent that a person clicks on a banner ad on a Web page and is taken to the advertiser's Web site.

Code Division Multiple Access (CDMA) – A digital cellular technology used to transmit wireless voice and data by sending it as code over various frequencies. It is a competing technology to GSM and TDMA.

Cookie – A text file (*cookie.txt*) on a PC that records Web site data such as passwords, sites visited and other personal information. Cookies are used by Web sites to customize Web pages or advertising campaigns for a particular Web site visitor.

Cost per Thousand (CPM) – The most common pricing structure for Internet advertising. It refers to the number of times that a particular advertisement is displayed or presumably seen by Web surfers. Average banner advertising rates are around $34 per thousand impressions.

Digital Certificate – A digital ID similar to a driver's license that verifies a user's identity. Digital certificates are issued and managed by a certificate authority (CA).

Digital Subscriber Line (DSL) –Technology used to send data at high speeds over standard copper telephone lines. There are two types of DSL: ADSL and SDSL. Asymmetric digital subscriber line (ADSL) has higher data transmission speeds on incoming or downstream data than on outgoing or upstream data. Symmetric digital subscriber line (SDSL) has the same upstream and downstream transmission rates.

Firewall – A gateway that protects private networks from unauthorized access. Firewalls are typically hardware/software combinations that are used to protect corporate intranets using packet filters and proxy functions.

Flash Crowds – This refers to a published event (i.e. Victoria Secret's Superbowl promotion) that receives an overwhelming amount of interest leading to network congestion. The term dates back to a 1973 Larry Niven science fiction story in which the development of teleportation causes thousands of people to suddenly teleport in to a location where anything interesting is occurring.

Free Float (FF) – The number of shares available for trading by the public. This is an important measure of liquidity for shares in Internet and other high technology companies. In general, a company with a small free float will have more volatile share price movements than companies with a larger free float. It is calculated by taking the number of shares outstanding and subtracting the number of shares owned by insiders and Rule 144 shares.

Global System for Mobile Communications (GSM) – The leading cellular technology used in over 100 countries throughout Europe, Asia and parts of North America. It is a narrowband variation of TDMA.

Gross Margin (GM) – Gross profit divided by total revenues expressed as a percentage. This is a measure of how successful a company is at managing its cost of goods sold.

Growth at Any Price (GAAP) – This is one of the strategies that Internet companies pursue in order to quickly capture market share. Not to be confused with GAAP – Generally Accepted Accounting Principles. See also GARP.

Growth at a Reasonable Price (GARP) – This is one of the strategies that Internet companies pursue as they scale back marketing and other operating expenses in a move towards profitability.

Hits – The number of times a file or graphic is accessed by a server. Sometimes used as a measure of Web site traffic, it is an inaccurate metric as a visitor looking at one page can generate 10-20 hits depending on the number of graphics on that Web page.

Host – The main computer or server connected to a network. On the Internet, it is the computer with the unique domain name or IP address.

Hypertext Markup Language (HTML) – The language of the Web using codes or tags to create documents for viewing on the World Wide Web.

Hyperlinks –The underlined elements on a Web page that link to another page or site. Users can select the link by clicking on it, and they will be taken to the other location. Hyperlinks are based on the hypercards used by Apple Macintosh computers in the late 1980's.

Internet – A public network of computers that is the successor to ARPANET. The term Internet was first used to refer to the global communications network in the early 1970's.

Internet Protocol (IP) – Defines how data or packets are sent over the Internet by identifying the address of a particular packet.

Kilobyte (Kb) – 1,024 bytes. Because computers use binary rather than decimal systems, a kilobyte is 2 to the 10th power. See also megabyte.

Market Capitalization (MV) – Total shares outstanding multiplied by the current price. Also referred to as market value.

Market Value (MV) – Total shares outstanding multiplied by the current price. Also referred to as market capitalization.

Megabyte (MB) – 1,048,576 bytes. Because computers use binary rather than decimal systems, a megabyte is 2 to the 20th power.

Operating Margin (OM) – Operating profit divided by total revenues expressed as a percentage. This indicates how successful a company is at managing its expenses in order to generate profits.

Point of Presence (POP) – The local presence for Internet access providers. It generally refers to the local telephone number that subscribers can dial for Internet access.

Portal – A term used to refer to Web sites such as Yahoo! that offer a broad range of services including news, sports, search engines, email, communities, chat rooms, etc. Horizontal portal refers to those sites that offer a broad array of news and information, while vertical portals are those sites that focus on niche areas such as sports (SportsLine.com), technology (ZDNet) and finance (MarketWatch.com).

Price/Earnings (P/E) – Stock price divided by earnings per share. For Internet companies, price/earnings is currently not a meaningful valuation metric as the majority of Internet companies are still in the hypergrowth phase of their lifecycle and are not yet generating profits.

Price/Sales (P/S) – Price divided by trailing four quarter sales. This is one of the core ratios for valuing Internet and other high growth companies. In contrast to P/E ratios where earnings can be managed, Price/sales is a more absolute figure.

Price/Sales-to-Growth (PSG) – Price/sales divided by trailing four quarter revenue growth. Price/sales-to-growth allows valuation comparisons between companies with varying growth rates.

Protocol – A common language or communication rules used by networked computers in order to determine how data will be transferred and when the transmission will end. There are several different types of protocols including ftp, http, PPP and TCP/IP.

Public Access Points (PAP) – The entrance to the Internet.

Return on Equity (ROE) – Net income available to common shareholders divided by common equity for the period. It is expressed as a percentage. ROE is an indication of how effectively shareholder investments are being utilized to generate profits.

Router – The hardware that sends data packets to the proper destination by looking at the addresses and sending the data through the best route.

Spider – A Web program or robot that roams through the Web finding documents and hyperlinks in order to catalog the Web for search engines. These programs are also known as bots and webcrawlers.

Standard Deviation (SD) – A measure of volatility for stock returns. Standard deviation measures the risk or dispersion of stock returns from an expected value. See also *Absolute Daily Percentage Change*.

Time Division Multiple Access (TDMA) – A digital cellular technology used to transmit wireless voice and data by dividing a frequency or channel into time slots in order to increase the amount of data that can be carried. It is a competing technology to GSM and CDMA.

Trailing Four Quarter (T4Q) – Trailing four quarters or the last 12 months.

Transmission Control Protocol/Internet Protocol (TCP/IP) – A suite of protocols used to address, move and verify delivery of data packets over the Internet. TCP/IP works on any type of operating system including Windows, NT, Unix and Mac OS.

Uniform Resource Locator (URL) – The global addresses of the Internet. The first part of the address (http://) refers to the protocol to use, and the second part is the domain location (www.topinternetstocks.com).

Volatility (SD, AB%CH) – A measure of risk. Volatility can be measured by either standard deviation or absolute daily percentage change. See also *Standard Deviation* and *Absolute Daily Percentage Change*.

Web Site – The location or URL on the World Wide Web.

World Wide Web (WWW) – The graphical portion of the Internet, combining hypertext documents, graphics, audio and video files. The World Wide Web was developed by Tim Berners-Lee at CERN in Switzerland in 1991.

Index

About the Author

Greg Kyle, one of the world's most influential Internet experts, is president and founder of Pegasus Research International, the leading independent Internet research firm. His Pegasus Internet Index (INTDEX™), a market capitalization-weighted index of 50 stocks segmented into seven distinct groups, is rated by *CBS Marketwatch* as one of the most comprehensive Internet indices for Internet investors. *Barron's*, which says that "Pegasus gives the lowdown on Net business," rated Pegasus as one of the most comprehensive websites for tracking Internet-related stocks and trends. Prior to founding Pegasus, Kyle was head of the North American equity research team at Union Bank of Switzerland in Zurich. He is the publisher of *Internet Stock Watch*, a weekly analysis and commentary on the leading Internet companies and trends, and is senior editor of *Inside New Media*.